C-3717 CAREER EXAMINATION SERIES

This is your
PASSBOOK for...

Fire Protection Inspector

Test Preparation Study Guide
Questions & Answers

NATIONAL LEARNING CORPORATION®

COPYRIGHT NOTICE

This book is SOLELY intended for, is sold ONLY to, and its use is RESTRICTED to individual, bona fide applicants or candidates who qualify by virtue of having seriously filed applications for appropriate license, certificate, professional and/or promotional advancement, higher school matriculation, scholarship, or other legitimate requirements of education and/or governmental authorities.

This book is NOT intended for use, class instruction, tutoring, training, duplication, copying, reprinting, excerption, or adaptation, etc., by:

1) Other publishers
2) Proprietors and/or Instructors of "Coaching" and/or Preparatory Courses
3) Personnel and/or Training Divisions of commercial, industrial, and governmental organizations
4) Schools, colleges, or universities and/or their departments and staffs, including teachers and other personnel
5) Testing Agencies or Bureaus
6) Study groups which seek by the purchase of a single volume to copy and/or duplicate and/or adapt this material for use by the group as a whole without having purchased individual volumes for each of the members of the group
7) Et al.

Such persons would be in violation of appropriate Federal and State statutes.

PROVISION OF LICENSING AGREEMENTS – Recognized educational, commercial, industrial, and governmental institutions and organizations, and others legitimately engaged in educational pursuits, including training, testing, and measurement activities, may address request for a licensing agreement to the copyright owners, who will determine whether, and under what conditions, including fees and charges, the materials in this book may be used them. In other words, a licensing facility exists for the legitimate use of the material in this book on other than an individual basis. However, it is asseverated and affirmed here that the material in this book CANNOT be used without the receipt of the express permission of such a licensing agreement from the Publishers. Inquiries re licensing should be addressed to the company, attention rights and permissions department.

All rights reserved, including the right of reproduction in whole or in part, in any form or by any means, electronic or mechanical, including photocopying, recording, or by any information storage and retrieval system, without permission in writing from the Publisher.

Copyright © 2024 by
National Learning Corporation

212 Michael Drive, Syosset, NY 11791
(516) 921-8888 • www.passbooks.com
E-mail: info@passbooks.com

PUBLISHED IN THE UNITED STATES OF AMERICA

PASSBOOK® SERIES

THE *PASSBOOK® SERIES* has been created to prepare applicants and candidates for the ultimate academic battlefield – the examination room.

At some time in our lives, each and every one of us may be required to take an examination – for validation, matriculation, admission, qualification, registration, certification, or licensure.

Based on the assumption that every applicant or candidate has met the basic formal educational standards, has taken the required number of courses, and read the necessary texts, the *PASSBOOK® SERIES* furnishes the one special preparation which may assure passing with confidence, instead of failing with insecurity. Examination questions – together with answers – are furnished as the basic vehicle for study so that the mysteries of the examination and its compounding difficulties may be eliminated or diminished by a sure method.

This book is meant to help you pass your examination provided that you qualify and are serious in your objective.

The entire field is reviewed through the huge store of content information which is succinctly presented through a provocative and challenging approach – the question-and-answer method.

A climate of success is established by furnishing the correct answers at the end of each test.

You soon learn to recognize types of questions, forms of questions, and patterns of questioning. You may even begin to anticipate expected outcomes.

You perceive that many questions are repeated or adapted so that you can gain acute insights, which may enable you to score many sure points.

You learn how to confront new questions, or types of questions, and to attack them confidently and work out the correct answers.

You note objectives and emphases, and recognize pitfalls and dangers, so that you may make positive educational adjustments.

Moreover, you are kept fully informed in relation to new concepts, methods, practices, and directions in the field.

You discover that you are actually taking the examination all the time: you are preparing for the examination by "taking" an examination, not by reading extraneous and/or supererogatory textbooks.

In short, this PASSBOOK®, used directedly, should be an important factor in helping you to pass your test.

FIRE PROTECTION INSPECTOR

JOB DESCRIPTION

Under supervision, performs work in the conduct of inspections to detect violations of laws, rules and regulations which are intended to reduce or eliminate fire hazards or assist in extinguishing fires; performs related work.

EXAMPLES OF TYPICAL TASKS

Witnesses hydrostatic tests of standpipe systems; inspects installation of range hood suppression systems; issues necessary violations for repair if the fire suppression systems are defective; checks owner's or representative's Certificate of Fitness for proper type and expiration date; researches applicable codes, such as building code, fire code and health code; receives complaints from the public and governmental agencies with regard to possible fire hazards; refers complaints to appropriate agency when non-Fire Department related; checks for presence of fire extinguisher and that it meets Fire Department Code Requirements; inspects air valves and emergency fuel shut-offs on tank trucks; inspects tank compartments and lids on tank trucks; fills out appropriate forms as required; performs related work as required.

TEST

The written test will be of the multiple-choice type and is designed to measure the ability to understand and apply instructions and written material, knowledge of fire extinguishing techniques, standpipe and sprinkler systems, field inspections regarding violations constituting hazardous conditions, laws, rules and regulations intended to reduce or eliminate fire hazards; general ability to read, understand and apply laws, rules and regulations relating to fire protection and prevention; aptitude for inspectional work; legal procedures, and other related areas including; written comprehension, written expression, problem sensitivity, deductive reasoning, inductive reasoning, information ordering, spatial orientation, and visualization.

HOW TO TAKE A TEST

I. YOU MUST PASS AN EXAMINATION

A. WHAT EVERY CANDIDATE SHOULD KNOW

Examination applicants often ask us for help in preparing for the written test. What can I study in advance? What kinds of questions will be asked? How will the test be given? How will the papers be graded?

As an applicant for a civil service examination, you may be wondering about some of these things. Our purpose here is to suggest effective methods of advance study and to describe civil service examinations.

Your chances for success on this examination can be increased if you know how to prepare. Those "pre-examination jitters" can be reduced if you know what to expect. You can even experience an adventure in good citizenship if you know why civil service exams are given.

B. WHY ARE CIVIL SERVICE EXAMINATIONS GIVEN?

Civil service examinations are important to you in two ways. As a citizen, you want public jobs filled by employees who know how to do their work. As a job seeker, you want a fair chance to compete for that job on an equal footing with other candidates. The best-known means of accomplishing this two-fold goal is the competitive examination.

Exams are widely publicized throughout the nation. They may be administered for jobs in federal, state, city, municipal, town or village governments or agencies.

Any citizen may apply, with some limitations, such as the age or residence of applicants. Your experience and education may be reviewed to see whether you meet the requirements for the particular examination. When these requirements exist, they are reasonable and applied consistently to all applicants. Thus, a competitive examination may cause you some uneasiness now, but it is your privilege and safeguard.

C. HOW ARE CIVIL SERVICE EXAMS DEVELOPED?

Examinations are carefully written by trained technicians who are specialists in the field known as "psychological measurement," in consultation with recognized authorities in the field of work that the test will cover. These experts recommend the subject matter areas or skills to be tested; only those knowledges or skills important to your success on the job are included. The most reliable books and source materials available are used as references. Together, the experts and technicians judge the difficulty level of the questions.

Test technicians know how to phrase questions so that the problem is clearly stated. Their ethics do not permit "trick" or "catch" questions. Questions may have been tried out on sample groups, or subjected to statistical analysis, to determine their usefulness.

Written tests are often used in combination with performance tests, ratings of training and experience, and oral interviews. All of these measures combine to form the best-known means of finding the right person for the right job.

II. HOW TO PASS THE WRITTEN TEST

A. NATURE OF THE EXAMINATION

To prepare intelligently for civil service examinations, you should know how they differ from school examinations you have taken. In school you were assigned certain definite pages to read or subjects to cover. The examination questions were quite detailed and usually emphasized memory. Civil service exams, on the other hand, try to discover your present ability to perform the duties of a position, plus your potentiality to learn these duties. In other words, a civil service exam attempts to predict how successful you will be. Questions cover such a broad area that they cannot be as minute and detailed as school exam questions.

In the public service similar kinds of work, or positions, are grouped together in one "class." This process is known as *position-classification*. All the positions in a class are paid according to the salary range for that class. One class title covers all of these positions, and they are all tested by the same examination.

B. FOUR BASIC STEPS

1) Study the announcement

How, then, can you know what subjects to study? Our best answer is: "Learn as much as possible about the class of positions for which you've applied." The exam will test the knowledge, skills and abilities needed to do the work.

Your most valuable source of information about the position you want is the official exam announcement. This announcement lists the training and experience qualifications. Check these standards and apply only if you come reasonably close to meeting them.

The brief description of the position in the examination announcement offers some clues to the subjects which will be tested. Think about the job itself. Review the duties in your mind. Can you perform them, or are there some in which you are rusty? Fill in the blank spots in your preparation.

Many jurisdictions preview the written test in the exam announcement by including a section called "Knowledge and Abilities Required," "Scope of the Examination," or some similar heading. Here you will find out specifically what fields will be tested.

2) Review your own background

Once you learn in general what the position is all about, and what you need to know to do the work, ask yourself which subjects you already know fairly well and which need improvement. You may wonder whether to concentrate on improving your strong areas or on building some background in your fields of weakness. When the announcement has specified "some knowledge" or "considerable knowledge," or has used adjectives like "beginning principles of..." or "advanced ... methods," you can get a clue as to the number and difficulty of questions to be asked in any given field. More questions, and hence broader coverage, would be included for those subjects which are more important in the work. Now weigh your strengths and weaknesses against the job requirements and prepare accordingly.

3) Determine the level of the position

Another way to tell how intensively you should prepare is to understand the level of the job for which you are applying. Is it the entering level? In other words, is this the position in which beginners in a field of work are hired? Or is it an intermediate or advanced level? Sometimes this is indicated by such words as "Junior" or "Senior" in the class title. Other jurisdictions use Roman numerals to designate the level – Clerk I, Clerk II, for example. The word "Supervisor" sometimes appears in the title. If the level is not indicated by the title, check the description of duties. Will you be working under very close supervision, or will you have responsibility for independent decisions in this work?

4) Choose appropriate study materials

Now that you know the subjects to be examined and the relative amount of each subject to be covered, you can choose suitable study materials. For beginning level jobs, or even advanced ones, if you have a pronounced weakness in some aspect of your training, read a modern, standard textbook in that field. Be sure it is up to date and has general coverage. Such books are normally available at your library, and the librarian will be glad to help you locate one. For entry-level positions, questions of appropriate difficulty are chosen – neither highly advanced questions, nor those too simple. Such questions require careful thought but not advanced training.

If the position for which you are applying is technical or advanced, you will read more advanced, specialized material. If you are already familiar with the basic principles of your field, elementary textbooks would waste your time. Concentrate on advanced textbooks and technical periodicals. Think through the concepts and review difficult problems in your field.

These are all general sources. You can get more ideas on your own initiative, following these leads. For example, training manuals and publications of the government agency which employs workers in your field can be useful, particularly for technical and professional positions. A letter or visit to the government department involved may result in more specific study suggestions, and certainly will provide you with a more definite idea of the exact nature of the position you are seeking.

III. KINDS OF TESTS

Tests are used for purposes other than measuring knowledge and ability to perform specified duties. For some positions, it is equally important to test ability to make adjustments to new situations or to profit from training. In others, basic mental abilities not dependent on information are essential. Questions which test these things may not appear as pertinent to the duties of the position as those which test for knowledge and information. Yet they are often highly important parts of a fair examination. For very general questions, it is almost impossible to help you direct your study efforts. What we can do is to point out some of the more common of these general abilities needed in public service positions and describe some typical questions.

1) General information

Broad, general information has been found useful for predicting job success in some kinds of work. This is tested in a variety of ways, from vocabulary lists to questions about current events. Basic background in some field of work, such as sociology or economics, may be sampled in a group of questions. Often these are principles which have become familiar to most persons through exposure rather than through formal training. It is difficult to advise you how to study for these questions; being alert to the world around you is our best suggestion.

2) Verbal ability

An example of an ability needed in many positions is verbal or language ability. Verbal ability is, in brief, the ability to use and understand words. Vocabulary and grammar tests are typical measures of this ability. Reading comprehension or paragraph interpretation questions are common in many kinds of civil service tests. You are given a paragraph of written material and asked to find its central meaning.

3) Numerical ability

Number skills can be tested by the familiar arithmetic problem, by checking paired lists of numbers to see which are alike and which are different, or by interpreting charts and graphs. In the latter test, a graph may be printed in the test booklet which you are asked to use as the basis for answering questions.

4) Observation

A popular test for law-enforcement positions is the observation test. A picture is shown to you for several minutes, then taken away. Questions about the picture test your ability to observe both details and larger elements.

5) Following directions

In many positions in the public service, the employee must be able to carry out written instructions dependably and accurately. You may be given a chart with several columns, each column listing a variety of information. The questions require you to carry out directions involving the information given in the chart.

6) Skills and aptitudes

Performance tests effectively measure some manual skills and aptitudes. When the skill is one in which you are trained, such as typing or shorthand, you can practice. These tests are often very much like those given in business school or high school courses. For many of the other skills and aptitudes, however, no short-time preparation can be made. Skills and abilities natural to you or that you have developed throughout your lifetime are being tested.

Many of the general questions just described provide all the data needed to answer the questions and ask you to use your reasoning ability to find the answers. Your best preparation for these tests, as well as for tests of facts and ideas, is to be at your physical and mental best. You, no doubt, have your own methods of getting into an exam-taking mood and keeping "in shape." The next section lists some ideas on this subject.

IV. KINDS OF QUESTIONS

Only rarely is the "essay" question, which you answer in narrative form, used in civil service tests. Civil service tests are usually of the short-answer type. Full instructions for answering these questions will be given to you at the examination. But in case this is your first experience with short-answer questions and separate answer sheets, here is what you need to know:

1) Multiple-choice Questions

Most popular of the short-answer questions is the "multiple choice" or "best answer" question. It can be used, for example, to test for factual knowledge, ability to solve problems or judgment in meeting situations found at work.

A multiple-choice question is normally one of three types—
- It can begin with an incomplete statement followed by several possible endings. You are to find the one ending which *best* completes the statement, although some of the others may not be entirely wrong.
- It can also be a complete statement in the form of a question which is answered by choosing one of the statements listed.

- It can be in the form of a problem – again you select the best answer.

Here is an example of a multiple-choice question with a discussion which should give you some clues as to the method for choosing the right answer:

When an employee has a complaint about his assignment, the action which will *best* help him overcome his difficulty is to
- A. discuss his difficulty with his coworkers
- B. take the problem to the head of the organization
- C. take the problem to the person who gave him the assignment
- D. say nothing to anyone about his complaint

In answering this question, you should study each of the choices to find which is best. Consider choice "A" – Certainly an employee may discuss his complaint with fellow employees, but no change or improvement can result, and the complaint remains unresolved. Choice "B" is a poor choice since the head of the organization probably does not know what assignment you have been given, and taking your problem to him is known as "going over the head" of the supervisor. The supervisor, or person who made the assignment, is the person who can clarify it or correct any injustice. Choice "C" is, therefore, correct. To say nothing, as in choice "D," is unwise. Supervisors have and interest in knowing the problems employees are facing, and the employee is seeking a solution to his problem.

2) True/False Questions

The "true/false" or "right/wrong" form of question is sometimes used. Here a complete statement is given. Your job is to decide whether the statement is right or wrong.

SAMPLE: A roaming cell-phone call to a nearby city costs less than a non-roaming call to a distant city.

This statement is wrong, or false, since roaming calls are more expensive.

This is not a complete list of all possible question forms, although most of the others are variations of these common types. You will always get complete directions for answering questions. Be sure you understand *how* to mark your answers – ask questions until you do.

V. RECORDING YOUR ANSWERS

Computer terminals are used more and more today for many different kinds of exams.
For an examination with very few applicants, you may be told to record your answers in the test booklet itself. Separate answer sheets are much more common. If this separate answer sheet is to be scored by machine – and this is often the case – it is highly important that you mark your answers correctly in order to get credit.
An electronic scoring machine is often used in civil service offices because of the speed with which papers can be scored. Machine-scored answer sheets must be marked with a pencil, which will be given to you. This pencil has a high graphite content which responds to the electronic scoring machine. As a matter of fact, stray dots may register as answers, so do not let your pencil rest on the answer sheet while you are pondering the correct answer. Also, if your pencil lead breaks or is otherwise defective, ask for another.

Since the answer sheet will be dropped in a slot in the scoring machine, be careful not to bend the corners or get the paper crumpled.

The answer sheet normally has five vertical columns of numbers, with 30 numbers to a column. These numbers correspond to the question numbers in your test booklet. After each number, going across the page are four or five pairs of dotted lines. These short dotted lines have small letters or numbers above them. The first two pairs may also have a "T" or "F" above the letters. This indicates that the first two pairs only are to be used if the questions are of the true-false type. If the questions are multiple choice, disregard the "T" and "F" and pay attention only to the small letters or numbers.

Answer your questions in the manner of the sample that follows:

32. The largest city in the United States is
    A. Washington, D.C.
    B. New York City
    C. Chicago
    D. Detroit
    E. San Francisco

1) Choose the answer you think is best. (New York City is the largest, so "B" is correct.)
2) Find the row of dotted lines numbered the same as the question you are answering. (Find row number 32)
3) Find the pair of dotted lines corresponding to the answer. (Find the pair of lines under the mark "B.")
4) Make a solid black mark between the dotted lines.

VI. BEFORE THE TEST

Common sense will help you find procedures to follow to get ready for an examination. Too many of us, however, overlook these sensible measures. Indeed, nervousness and fatigue have been found to be the most serious reasons why applicants fail to do their best on civil service tests. Here is a list of reminders:

- Begin your preparation early – Don't wait until the last minute to go scurrying around for books and materials or to find out what the position is all about.
- Prepare continuously – An hour a night for a week is better than an all-night cram session. This has been definitely established. What is more, a night a week for a month will return better dividends than crowding your study into a shorter period of time.
- Locate the place of the exam – You have been sent a notice telling you when and where to report for the examination. If the location is in a different town or otherwise unfamiliar to you, it would be well to inquire the best route and learn something about the building.
- Relax the night before the test – Allow your mind to rest. Do not study at all that night. Plan some mild recreation or diversion; then go to bed early and get a good night's sleep.
- Get up early enough to make a leisurely trip to the place for the test – This way unforeseen events, traffic snarls, unfamiliar buildings, etc. will not upset you.
- Dress comfortably – A written test is not a fashion show. You will be known by number and not by name, so wear something comfortable.

- Leave excess paraphernalia at home – Shopping bags and odd bundles will get in your way. You need bring only the items mentioned in the official notice you received; usually everything you need is provided. Do not bring reference books to the exam. They will only confuse those last minutes and be taken away from you when in the test room.
- Arrive somewhat ahead of time – If because of transportation schedules you must get there very early, bring a newspaper or magazine to take your mind off yourself while waiting.
- Locate the examination room – When you have found the proper room, you will be directed to the seat or part of the room where you will sit. Sometimes you are given a sheet of instructions to read while you are waiting. Do not fill out any forms until you are told to do so; just read them and be prepared.
- Relax and prepare to listen to the instructions
- If you have any physical problem that may keep you from doing your best, be sure to tell the test administrator. If you are sick or in poor health, you really cannot do your best on the exam. You can come back and take the test some other time.

VII. AT THE TEST

The day of the test is here and you have the test booklet in your hand. The temptation to get going is very strong. Caution! There is more to success than knowing the right answers. You must know how to identify your papers and understand variations in the type of short-answer question used in this particular examination. Follow these suggestions for maximum results from your efforts:

1) Cooperate with the monitor

The test administrator has a duty to create a situation in which you can be as much at ease as possible. He will give instructions, tell you when to begin, check to see that you are marking your answer sheet correctly, and so on. He is not there to guard you, although he will see that your competitors do not take unfair advantage. He wants to help you do your best.

2) Listen to all instructions

Don't jump the gun! Wait until you understand all directions. In most civil service tests you get more time than you need to answer the questions. So don't be in a hurry. Read each word of instructions until you clearly understand the meaning. Study the examples, listen to all announcements and follow directions. Ask questions if you do not understand what to do.

3) Identify your papers

Civil service exams are usually identified by number only. You will be assigned a number; you must not put your name on your test papers. Be sure to copy your number correctly. Since more than one exam may be given, copy your exact examination title.

4) Plan your time

Unless you are told that a test is a "speed" or "rate of work" test, speed itself is usually not important. Time enough to answer all the questions will be provided, but this does not mean that you have all day. An overall time limit has been set. Divide the total time (in minutes) by the number of questions to determine the approximate time you have for each question.

5) Do not linger over difficult questions

If you come across a difficult question, mark it with a paper clip (useful to have along) and come back to it when you have been through the booklet. One caution if you do this – be sure to skip a number on your answer sheet as well. Check often to be sure that you have not lost your place and that you are marking in the row numbered the same as the question you are answering.

6) Read the questions

Be sure you know what the question asks! Many capable people are unsuccessful because they failed to *read* the questions correctly.

7) Answer all questions

Unless you have been instructed that a penalty will be deducted for incorrect answers, it is better to guess than to omit a question.

8) Speed tests

It is often better NOT to guess on speed tests. It has been found that on timed tests people are tempted to spend the last few seconds before time is called in marking answers at random – without even reading them – in the hope of picking up a few extra points. To discourage this practice, the instructions may warn you that your score will be "corrected" for guessing. That is, a penalty will be applied. The incorrect answers will be deducted from the correct ones, or some other penalty formula will be used.

9) Review your answers

If you finish before time is called, go back to the questions you guessed or omitted to give them further thought. Review other answers if you have time.

10) Return your test materials

If you are ready to leave before others have finished or time is called, take ALL your materials to the monitor and leave quietly. Never take any test material with you. The monitor can discover whose papers are not complete, and taking a test booklet may be grounds for disqualification.

VIII. EXAMINATION TECHNIQUES

1) Read the general instructions carefully. These are usually printed on the first page of the exam booklet. As a rule, these instructions refer to the timing of the examination; the fact that you should not start work until the signal and must stop work at a signal, etc. If there are any *special* instructions, such as a choice of questions to be answered, make sure that you note this instruction carefully.

2) When you are ready to start work on the examination, that is as soon as the signal has been given, read the instructions to each question booklet, underline any key words or phrases, such as *least, best, outline, describe* and the like. In this way you will tend to answer as requested rather than discover on reviewing your paper that you *listed without describing*, that you selected the *worst* choice rather than the *best* choice, etc.

3) If the examination is of the objective or multiple-choice type – that is, each question will also give a series of possible answers: A, B, C or D, and you are called upon to select the best answer and write the letter next to that answer on your answer paper – it is advisable to start answering each question in turn. There may be anywhere from 50 to 100 such questions in the three or four hours allotted and you can see how much time would be taken if you read through all the questions before beginning to answer any. Furthermore, if you come across a question or group of questions which you know would be difficult to answer, it would undoubtedly affect your handling of all the other questions.

4) If the examination is of the essay type and contains but a few questions, it is a moot point as to whether you should read all the questions before starting to answer any one. Of course, if you are given a choice – say five out of seven and the like – then it is essential to read all the questions so you can eliminate the two that are most difficult. If, however, you are asked to answer all the questions, there may be danger in trying to answer the easiest one first because you may find that you will spend too much time on it. The best technique is to answer the first question, then proceed to the second, etc.

5) Time your answers. Before the exam begins, write down the time it started, then add the time allowed for the examination and write down the time it must be completed, then divide the time available somewhat as follows:
    - If 3-1/2 hours are allowed, that would be 210 minutes. If you have 80 objective-type questions, that would be an average of 2-1/2 minutes per question. Allow yourself no more than 2 minutes per question, or a total of 160 minutes, which will permit about 50 minutes to review.
    - If for the time allotment of 210 minutes there are 7 essay questions to answer, that would average about 30 minutes a question. Give yourself only 25 minutes per question so that you have about 35 minutes to review.

6) The most important instruction is to *read each question* and make sure you know what is wanted. The second most important instruction is to *time yourself properly* so that you answer every question. The third most important instruction is to *answer every question*. Guess if you have to but include something for each question. Remember that you will receive no credit for a blank and will probably receive some credit if you write something in answer to an essay question. If you guess a letter – say "B" for a multiple-choice question – you may have guessed right. If you leave a blank as an answer to a multiple-choice question, the examiners may respect your feelings but it will not add a point to your score. Some exams may penalize you for wrong answers, so in such cases *only*, you may not want to guess unless you have some basis for your answer.

7) Suggestions
    a. Objective-type questions
        1. Examine the question booklet for proper sequence of pages and questions
        2. Read all instructions carefully
        3. Skip any question which seems too difficult; return to it after all other questions have been answered
        4. Apportion your time properly; do not spend too much time on any single question or group of questions

5. Note and underline key words – *all, most, fewest, least, best, worst, same, opposite*, etc.
6. Pay particular attention to negatives
7. Note unusual option, e.g., unduly long, short, complex, different or similar in content to the body of the question
8. Observe the use of "hedging" words – *probably, may, most likely*, etc.
9. Make sure that your answer is put next to the same number as the question
10. Do not second-guess unless you have good reason to believe the second answer is definitely more correct
11. Cross out original answer if you decide another answer is more accurate; do not erase until you are ready to hand your paper in
12. Answer all questions; guess unless instructed otherwise
13. Leave time for review

   b. Essay questions
     1. Read each question carefully
     2. Determine exactly what is wanted. Underline key words or phrases.
     3. Decide on outline or paragraph answer
     4. Include many different points and elements unless asked to develop any one or two points or elements
     5. Show impartiality by giving pros and cons unless directed to select one side only
     6. Make and write down any assumptions you find necessary to answer the questions
     7. Watch your English, grammar, punctuation and choice of words
     8. Time your answers; don't crowd material

8) Answering the essay question

Most essay questions can be answered by framing the specific response around several key words or ideas. Here are a few such key words or ideas:

M's: manpower, materials, methods, money, management
P's: purpose, program, policy, plan, procedure, practice, problems, pitfalls, personnel, public relations

   a. Six basic steps in handling problems:
     1. Preliminary plan and background development
     2. Collect information, data and facts
     3. Analyze and interpret information, data and facts
     4. Analyze and develop solutions as well as make recommendations
     5. Prepare report and sell recommendations
     6. Install recommendations and follow up effectiveness

   b. Pitfalls to avoid
     1. *Taking things for granted* – A statement of the situation does not necessarily imply that each of the elements is necessarily true; for example, a complaint may be invalid and biased so that all that can be taken for granted is that a complaint has been registered

2. *Considering only one side of a situation* – Wherever possible, indicate several alternatives and then point out the reasons you selected the best one
3. *Failing to indicate follow up* – Whenever your answer indicates action on your part, make certain that you will take proper follow-up action to see how successful your recommendations, procedures or actions turn out to be
4. *Taking too long in answering any single question* – Remember to time your answers properly

IX. AFTER THE TEST

Scoring procedures differ in detail among civil service jurisdictions although the general principles are the same. Whether the papers are hand-scored or graded by machine we have described, they are nearly always graded by number. That is, the person who marks the paper knows only the number – never the name – of the applicant. Not until all the papers have been graded will they be matched with names. If other tests, such as training and experience or oral interview ratings have been given, scores will be combined. Different parts of the examination usually have different weights. For example, the written test might count 60 percent of the final grade, and a rating of training and experience 40 percent. In many jurisdictions, veterans will have a certain number of points added to their grades.

After the final grade has been determined, the names are placed in grade order and an eligible list is established. There are various methods for resolving ties between those who get the same final grade – probably the most common is to place first the name of the person whose application was received first. Job offers are made from the eligible list in the order the names appear on it. You will be notified of your grade and your rank as soon as all these computations have been made. This will be done as rapidly as possible.

People who are found to meet the requirements in the announcement are called "eligibles." Their names are put on a list of eligible candidates. An eligible's chances of getting a job depend on how high he stands on this list and how fast agencies are filling jobs from the list.

When a job is to be filled from a list of eligibles, the agency asks for the names of people on the list of eligibles for that job. When the civil service commission receives this request, it sends to the agency the names of the three people highest on this list. Or, if the job to be filled has specialized requirements, the office sends the agency the names of the top three persons who meet these requirements from the general list.

The appointing officer makes a choice from among the three people whose names were sent to him. If the selected person accepts the appointment, the names of the others are put back on the list to be considered for future openings.

That is the rule in hiring from all kinds of eligible lists, whether they are for typist, carpenter, chemist, or something else. For every vacancy, the appointing officer has his choice of any one of the top three eligibles on the list. This explains why the person whose name is on top of the list sometimes does not get an appointment when some of the persons lower on the list do. If the appointing officer chooses the second or third eligible, the No. 1 eligible does not get a job at once, but stays on the list until he is appointed or the list is terminated.

X. HOW TO PASS THE INTERVIEW TEST

The examination for which you applied requires an oral interview test. You have already taken the written test and you are now being called for the interview test – the final part of the formal examination.

You may think that it is not possible to prepare for an interview test and that there are no procedures to follow during an interview. Our purpose is to point out some things you can do in advance that will help you and some good rules to follow and pitfalls to avoid while you are being interviewed.

What is an interview supposed to test?

The written examination is designed to test the technical knowledge and competence of the candidate; the oral is designed to evaluate intangible qualities, not readily measured otherwise, and to establish a list showing the relative fitness of each candidate – as measured against his competitors – for the position sought. Scoring is not on the basis of "right" and "wrong," but on a sliding scale of values ranging from "not passable" to "outstanding." As a matter of fact, it is possible to achieve a relatively low score without a single "incorrect" answer because of evident weakness in the qualities being measured.

Occasionally, an examination may consist entirely of an oral test – either an individual or a group oral. In such cases, information is sought concerning the technical knowledges and abilities of the candidate, since there has been no written examination for this purpose. More commonly, however, an oral test is used to supplement a written examination.

Who conducts interviews?

The composition of oral boards varies among different jurisdictions. In nearly all, a representative of the personnel department serves as chairman. One of the members of the board may be a representative of the department in which the candidate would work. In some cases, "outside experts" are used, and, frequently, a businessman or some other representative of the general public is asked to serve. Labor and management or other special groups may be represented. The aim is to secure the services of experts in the appropriate field.

However the board is composed, it is a good idea (and not at all improper or unethical) to ascertain in advance of the interview who the members are and what groups they represent. When you are introduced to them, you will have some idea of their backgrounds and interests, and at least you will not stutter and stammer over their names.

What should be done before the interview?

While knowledge about the board members is useful and takes some of the surprise element out of the interview, there is other preparation which is more substantive. It *is* possible to prepare for an oral interview – in several ways:

1) Keep a copy of your application and review it carefully before the interview

This may be the only document before the oral board, and the starting point of the interview. Know what education and experience you have listed there, and the sequence and dates of all of it. Sometimes the board will ask you to review the highlights of your experience for them; you should not have to hem and haw doing it.

2) Study the class specification and the examination announcement

Usually, the oral board has one or both of these to guide them. The qualities, characteristics or knowledges required by the position sought are stated in these documents. They offer valuable clues as to the nature of the oral interview. For example, if the job involves supervisory responsibilities, the announcement will usually indicate that knowledge of modern supervisory methods and the qualifications of the candidate as a supervisor will be tested. If so, you can expect such questions, frequently in the form of a hypothetical situation which you are expected to solve. NEVER go into an oral without knowledge of the duties and responsibilities of the job you seek.

3) Think through each qualification required

Try to visualize the kind of questions you would ask if you were a board member. How well could you answer them? Try especially to appraise your own knowledge and background in each area, *measured against the job sought*, and identify any areas in which you are weak. Be critical and realistic – do not flatter yourself.

4) Do some general reading in areas in which you feel you may be weak

For example, if the job involves supervision and your past experience has NOT, some general reading in supervisory methods and practices, particularly in the field of human relations, might be useful. Do NOT study agency procedures or detailed manuals. The oral board will be testing your understanding and capacity, not your memory.

5) Get a good night's sleep and watch your general health and mental attitude

You will want a clear head at the interview. Take care of a cold or any other minor ailment, and of course, no hangovers.

What should be done on the day of the interview?

Now comes the day of the interview itself. Give yourself plenty of time to get there. Plan to arrive somewhat ahead of the scheduled time, particularly if your appointment is in the fore part of the day. If a previous candidate fails to appear, the board might be ready for you a bit early. By early afternoon an oral board is almost invariably behind schedule if there are many candidates, and you may have to wait. Take along a book or magazine to read, or your application to review, but leave any extraneous material in the waiting room when you go in for your interview. In any event, relax and compose yourself.

The matter of dress is important. The board is forming impressions about you – from your experience, your manners, your attitude, and your appearance. Give your personal appearance careful attention. Dress your best, but not your flashiest. Choose conservative, appropriate clothing, and be sure it is immaculate. This is a business interview, and your appearance should indicate that you regard it as such. Besides, being well groomed and properly dressed will help boost your confidence.

Sooner or later, someone will call your name and escort you into the interview room. *This is it.* From here on you are on your own. It is too late for any more preparation. But remember, you asked for this opportunity to prove your fitness, and you are here because your request was granted.

What happens when you go in?

The usual sequence of events will be as follows: The clerk (who is often the board stenographer) will introduce you to the chairman of the oral board, who will introduce you to the other members of the board. Acknowledge the introductions before you sit down. Do not be surprised if you find a microphone facing you or a stenotypist sitting by. Oral interviews are usually recorded in the event of an appeal or other review.

Usually the chairman of the board will open the interview by reviewing the highlights of your education and work experience from your application – primarily for the benefit of the other members of the board, as well as to get the material into the record. Do not interrupt or comment unless there is an error or significant misinterpretation; if that is the case, do not hesitate. But do not quibble about insignificant matters. Also, he will usually ask you some question about your education, experience or your present job – partly to get you to start talking and to establish the interviewing "rapport." He may start the actual questioning, or turn it over to one of the other members. Frequently, each member undertakes the questioning on a particular area, one in which he is perhaps most competent, so you can expect each member to participate in the examination. Because time is limited, you may also expect some rather abrupt switches in the direction the questioning takes, so do not be upset by it. Normally, a board member will not pursue a single line of questioning unless he discovers a particular strength or weakness.

After each member has participated, the chairman will usually ask whether any member has any further questions, then will ask you if you have anything you wish to add. Unless you are expecting this question, it may floor you. Worse, it may start you off on an extended, extemporaneous speech. The board is not usually seeking more information. The question is principally to offer you a last opportunity to present further qualifications or to indicate that you have nothing to add. So, if you feel that a significant qualification or characteristic has been overlooked, it is proper to point it out in a sentence or so. Do not compliment the board on the thoroughness of their examination – they have been sketchy, and you know it. If you wish, merely say, "No thank you, I have nothing further to add." This is a point where you can "talk yourself out" of a good impression or fail to present an important bit of information. Remember, *you close the interview yourself.*

The chairman will then say, "That is all, Mr. _____, thank you." Do not be startled; the interview is over, and quicker than you think. Thank him, gather your belongings and take your leave. Save your sigh of relief for the other side of the door.

How to put your best foot forward

Throughout this entire process, you may feel that the board individually and collectively is trying to pierce your defenses, seek out your hidden weaknesses and embarrass and confuse you. Actually, this is not true. They are obliged to make an appraisal of your qualifications for the job you are seeking, and they want to see you in your best light. Remember, they must interview all candidates and a non-cooperative candidate may become a failure in spite of their best efforts to bring out his qualifications. Here are 15 suggestions that will help you:

1) **Be natural – Keep your attitude confident, not cocky**

If you are not confident that you can do the job, do not expect the board to be. Do not apologize for your weaknesses, try to bring out your strong points. The board is interested in a positive, not negative, presentation. Cockiness will antagonize any board member and make him wonder if you are covering up a weakness by a false show of strength.

2) **Get comfortable, but don't lounge or sprawl**

Sit erectly but not stiffly. A careless posture may lead the board to conclude that you are careless in other things, or at least that you are not impressed by the importance of the occasion. Either conclusion is natural, even if incorrect. Do not fuss with your clothing, a pencil or an ashtray. Your hands may occasionally be useful to emphasize a point; do not let them become a point of distraction.

3) **Do not wisecrack or make small talk**

This is a serious situation, and your attitude should show that you consider it as such. Further, the time of the board is limited – they do not want to waste it, and neither should you.

4) Do not exaggerate your experience or abilities

In the first place, from information in the application or other interviews and sources, the board may know more about you than you think. Secondly, you probably will not get away with it. An experienced board is rather adept at spotting such a situation, so do not take the chance.

5) If you know a board member, do not make a point of it, yet do not hide it

Certainly you are not fooling him, and probably not the other members of the board. Do not try to take advantage of your acquaintanceship – it will probably do you little good.

6) Do not dominate the interview

Let the board do that. They will give you the clues – do not assume that you have to do all the talking. Realize that the board has a number of questions to ask you, and do not try to take up all the interview time by showing off your extensive knowledge of the answer to the first one.

7) Be attentive

You only have 20 minutes or so, and you should keep your attention at its sharpest throughout. When a member is addressing a problem or question to you, give him your undivided attention. Address your reply principally to him, but do not exclude the other board members.

8) Do not interrupt

A board member may be stating a problem for you to analyze. He will ask you a question when the time comes. Let him state the problem, and wait for the question.

9) Make sure you understand the question

Do not try to answer until you are sure what the question is. If it is not clear, restate it in your own words or ask the board member to clarify it for you. However, do not haggle about minor elements.

10) Reply promptly but not hastily

A common entry on oral board rating sheets is "candidate responded readily," or "candidate hesitated in replies." Respond as promptly and quickly as you can, but do not jump to a hasty, ill-considered answer.

11) Do not be peremptory in your answers

A brief answer is proper – but do not fire your answer back. That is a losing game from your point of view. The board member can probably ask questions much faster than you can answer them.

12) Do not try to create the answer you think the board member wants

He is interested in what kind of mind you have and how it works – not in playing games. Furthermore, he can usually spot this practice and will actually grade you down on it.

13) Do not switch sides in your reply merely to agree with a board member

Frequently, a member will take a contrary position merely to draw you out and to see if you are willing and able to defend your point of view. Do not start a debate, yet do not surrender a good position. If a position is worth taking, it is worth defending.

14) Do not be afraid to admit an error in judgment if you are shown to be wrong

The board knows that you are forced to reply without any opportunity for careful consideration. Your answer may be demonstrably wrong. If so, admit it and get on with the interview.

15) Do not dwell at length on your present job

The opening question may relate to your present assignment. Answer the question but do not go into an extended discussion. You are being examined for a *new* job, not your present one. As a matter of fact, try to phrase ALL your answers in terms of the job for which you are being examined.

Basis of Rating

Probably you will forget most of these "do's" and "don'ts" when you walk into the oral interview room. Even remembering them all will not ensure you a passing grade. Perhaps you did not have the qualifications in the first place. But remembering them will help you to put your best foot forward, without treading on the toes of the board members.

Rumor and popular opinion to the contrary notwithstanding, an oral board wants you to make the best appearance possible. They know you are under pressure – but they also want to see how you respond to it as a guide to what your reaction would be under the pressures of the job you seek. They will be influenced by the degree of poise you display, the personal traits you show and the manner in which you respond.

ABOUT THIS BOOK

This book contains tests divided into Examination Sections. Go through each test, answering every question in the margin. We have also attached a sample answer sheet at the back of the book that can be removed and used. At the end of each test look at the answer key and check your answers. On the ones you got wrong, look at the right answer choice and learn. Do not fill in the answers first. Do not memorize the questions and answers, but understand the answer and principles involved. On your test, the questions will likely be different from the samples. Questions are changed and new ones added. If you understand these past questions you should have success with any changes that arise. Tests may consist of several types of questions. We have additional books on each subject should more study be advisable or necessary for you. Finally, the more you study, the better prepared you will be. This book is intended to be the last thing you study before you walk into the examination room. Prior study of relevant texts is also recommended. NLC publishes some of these in our Fundamental Series. Knowledge and good sense are important factors in passing your exam. Good luck also helps. So now study this Passbook, absorb the material contained within and take that knowledge into the examination. Then do your best to pass that exam.

EXAMINATION SECTION

EXAMINATION SECTION
TEST 1

DIRECTIONS: Each question or incomplete statement is followed by several suggested answers or completions. Select the one that BEST answers the question or completes the statement. *PRINT THE LETTER OF THE CORRECT ANSWER IN THE SPACE AT THE RIGHT.*

1. Assume that you are making an inspection at a plastics manufacturing factory. The plant manager discusses fire safety procedures with you and tells you that he will be having small-scale bench tests made in order to measure various properties of plastics exposed to fire. The manager tells you he expects to gain certain information from these tests. Of the following, you would be correct in telling him that these tests will be MOST effective in evaluating the   1.____

    A. tendency of the plastic to melt and drip
    B. relative combustibility of plastics
    C. composition of products of combustion
    D. methods of installation of plastic parts

2. Assume that your division commander has asked you to prepare a report on minimizing the hazard of dust explosions. This is one in a series of reports to be used to guide industrial plant managers in your division on fire safety precautions.
Of the following, it would be MOST appropriate for you to point out that generally   2.____

    A. a high level of moisture in the air will be effective in raising the ignition temperature of most dusts and reducing the deflagration once ignition has occurred
    B. relatively small amounts of inert solid powder will be effective in preventing explosions by reducing the combustibility of a dust through heat absorption
    C. removal of high-temperature sources of ignition will be effective in reducing the possibility of explosion because common ignition sources generally do not provide ignition temperatures required for dust explosions
    D. inert gas will be effective in preventing explosions because it dilutes the oxygen to a concentration too low to support combustion

3. The selection of smoke removal and venting procedures in hi-rise buildings depends to a large extent on the factors which affect smoke movement in these structures, such as the *stack effect.*
Which one of the following statements about the stack effect is MOST NEARLY correct?   3.____

    A. When the outside temperature is much lower than the inside temperature and a fire occurs some distance below the neutral pressure plane, the stack effect will not overcome the fire pressure.
    B. The stack effect will cause smoke and toxic gases to flow through stairwells and elevator shafts, except when the doors of these shafts remain closed.
    C. When the outside temperature is greater than the inside temperature, a reverse stack effect occurs with the upper building opening becoming the inlet and the lower opening the outlet.
    D. The magnitude of the stack effect is a function of building height, air leakage between floors, and the differences between inside and outside temperatures, but is not affected by the air leakage through exterior walls.

4. Warehouse fires often present a severe challenge to firefighters. A fire officer inspecting a storage warehouse should be aware of proper indoor storage practices and the use of racks and pallets in such storage.
   Which one of the following statements regarding storage practices in warehouses is generally CORRECT?

   A. The arrangement of commodities stored in racks generally provides greater flue spaces both horizontally and vertically than palletized general storage.
   B. Storage of empty plastic pallets within warehouses should be in piles limited to eight feet in height.
   C. Stacking idle pallets in piles is unlikely to promote rapid spread of fire, heat release, and complete combustion.
   D. Storage of empty wood pallets in an unsprinklered warehouse containing other storage should be limited to buildings of fireproof construction.

4.___

5. The Fire Code provides that, in a dry cleaning establishment, each room where a washing tank is located must be provided with an approved fire extinguishing system.
   The type of system which is specified is a(n) _____ system.

   A. steam
   B. carbon dioxide
   C. foam
   D. ordinary sprinkler

5.___

6. According to the Fire Code, the MAXIMUM quantity of calcium carbide which may be lawfully stored without a permit is _____ lbs.

   A. 60   B. 80   C. 100   D. 120

6.___

7. A Class C refrigerating system, as defined in the Fire Code, is one in which the quantity of refrigerant does NOT exceed _____ lbs.

   A. 20   B. 25   C. 30   D. 35

7.___

8. According to the Building Code, a tank used to provide the required primary water supply to a standpipe system may also be used as a supply for an automatic sprinkler system

   A. in all cases where both have been installed
   B. where there are other acceptable sources of water supply for the sprinkler system
   C. only when the standpipe system has a direct connection to the public water system
   D. provided that its capacity is at least five thousand gallons greater than that required for the sprinkler system

8.___

9. For computing the capacity of water supplies other than the fire pump, the Building Code assumes that the average discharge, in gallons per minute, from a standard one-half inch sprinkler head is

   A. 20   B. 25   C. 30   D. 35

9.___

10. The door that can be closed to separate the bedrooms from the rest of the apartment is the door between the

    A. entrance hall and the bedroom hall
    B. living room and the entrance hall
    C. kitchen and the living room
    D. dining room and the living room

10.___

Questions 11-25.

DIRECTIONS: Questions 11 through 25 are to be answered SOLELY on the basis of the following facts and Building Inspection Form. Each box on the form is numbered. Read the facts and review the form before answering the questions.

Firefighters are required to inspect all buildings within their assigned area of the city. They check conditions within the building for violations of fire safety laws. While inspecting a building, they must fill out a Building Inspection Form as a record of the conditions they observed.

On June 12, 2015, Firefighter Edward Gold, assigned to Engine Company 82, is ordered by Captain John Bailey to inspect the building at 1400 Compton Place as part of the engine company's monthly building inspection duty. The building is a one-story brick warehouse where books of the S & G Publishing Company are stored before shipment to stores.

Firefighter Gold enters the warehouse through the main entrance door in the front of the building. Though an exit sign is present above the door, the sign is unlit because of a burned-out bulb. There is a small office to one side of the main entrance area where Firefighter Gold goes to meet the warehouse manager, Mr. Stevens. The firefighter explains the purpose of the inspection.

Firefighter Gold tells the manager that he will check the automatic sprinkler system first because if a fire got started in a warehouse full of stored books, the fire could spread rapidly. He asks Mr. Stevens for the Certificate of Fitness issued to the company employee certified to maintain the sprinkler system in working order. The certificate is dated June 1, 2002, and Gold observes that it has expired. The manager promises to have the certificate renewed as soon as possible.

The firefighter wants to locate the main control valve of the sprinkler system. He asks Mr. Stevens to go with him and show him its location. Gold and the manager leave through an office door which leads into the main working area of the warehouse. They locate the main sprinkler control valve on the wall in a corner of the work area behind high shelves stocked with books. The firefighter observes that the main control valve is sealed in the open position. Gold next climbs a ladder lying against the storage shelves and measures the distance between the top of the stack of books on the highest shelf and the sprinkler heads suspended on pipes below the ceiling. The distance is three feet.

Firefighter Gold next inspects the remaining exits from the building. A large fire door leads out to the loading dock in the rear of the warehouse. A small door on the side of the warehouse that is used by employees when they leave for the day is partially obstructed by cartons. Lighted exit signs can be clearly seen above both doors. During working hours, only the main entrance door and the fire door to the loading dock are unlocked. Mr. Stevens says he keeps the side door locked to keep employees from leaving early and only unlocks it at closing time.

Firefighter Gold and the manager then walk through the main work area. Gold observes that fireproof rubbish receptacles are placed at frequent intervals. However, they are not covered and the contents are overflowing, resulting in several piles of litter on the floor. *No Smok-*

ing signs are on the walls of the work area, but are difficult to see behind the rows of high storage shelves.

The two fire extinguishers in the work area are found lying on the floor rather than hung on wall racks. The two other fire extinguishers in the warehouse, one in the office and one in the employee lounge, are both correctly hung on wall racks. All four fire extinguishers are fully charged. According to their tags, they were last inspected on March 11, 2015.

Firefighter Gold continues the inspection by checking on the electrical wiring, which appears to be generally in good condition. However, four switch boxes lack covers. The main junction box has a cover, but it cannot be closed because the cover is corroded.

The inspection is now complete, so Firefighter Gold thanks Mr. Stevens for his cooperation and leaves the building. Gold checks that all required information is entered on the Building Inspection Form, including information concerning building violations. Firefighter Gold signs and dates the Building Inspection Form and then submits it to Captain Bailey for his review. After reviewing Firefighter Gold's report, Captain Bailey signs the Building Inspection Form.

BUILDING INSPECTION FORM

DIVISION (1)	BATTALION (2)	COMPANY (3)

BUILDING INFORMATION	Name of Business (4)		Address (5)	
	Type of Business (6)		Occupancy Code Number (7)	
CONDITION OF EXITS	Number of Exits (8)	Exits Obstructed (9)	Exits unlocked (10)	
	Exit Signs (11)	Exit Sign Lights (12)	Fire Doors (13)	
HOUSEKEEPING CONDITIONS	Rubbish Receptacles (14)		No Smoking Signs (15)	
	Clearance of stock in Feet from Sprinkler Heads (16)			
	Electrical Wiring (17)	Switches (18)	Junction Box (19)	
CONDITION OF FIRE EXTINGUISHERS	Charged (20)	Placement (21)	Date of Last Inspection (22)	
CONDITION OF AUTOMATIC SPRINKLER SYSTEM	Color of Siamese (23)	Main Control Valve (24)	Shut-off sign (25)	
	Certificate of Fitness (26)		Date of Last Inspection (27)	
SPECIAL CONDITIONS	Rubbish/Obstructions (28)		Certificate of Occupancy (29)	
			Heavy Load Signs (30)	
FIRE DEPARTMENT INFORMATION	Inspector Name _____ Signature _____ (31)		Rank (32)	Date (33)
	Officer Name _____ (34) Signature _____		Rank (35)	Date (36)

11. Which one of the following should be entered in Box 3?   11._____

    A. Ladder Company 79   B. Engine Company 12
    C. Ladder Company 140   D. Engine Company 82

12. Which one of the following should be entered in Box 4? _____ Company.   12._____

    A. G & R Printing   B. S & G Printing
    C. R & G Publishing   D. S & G Publishing

13. Which one of the following should be entered in Box 8?   13._____

    A. 2   B. 3   C. 4   D. 5

14. Which one of the following should be entered in Box 9? _____ door.   14._____

    A. Office   B. Side   C. Main   D. Fire

15. Which one of the following should be entered in Box 10? _____ door and _____ door.   15._____

    A. Fire; main   B. Side; office
    C. Fire; side   D. Main; cellar

16. The entry in Box 12 should show that replacement bulbs are needed for _____ light (s).   16._____

    A. one   B. two   C. three   D. all

17. The entry in Box 14 should show that covers are missing from _____ of the rubbish   17._____
    receptacles.

    A. two   B. three   C. four   D. all

18. Which one of the following should be entered in Box 16?   18._____

    A. One and one-half   B. Two
    C. Two and one-half   D. Three

19. Which one of the following should be entered in Box 19?   19._____

    A. Faulty circuits   B. Exposed wiring
    C. Corroded cover   D. Good condition

20. Which one of the following entries about the placement of fire extinguishers should   20._____
    appear in Box 21?

    A. One on the floor; three hung on wall racks
    B. Two on the floor; two hung on wall racks
    C. Three on the floor; one hung on wall rack
    D. Four hung on wall racks

21. Which one of the following should be entered in Box 22?   21._____

    A. June 1, 2012   B. May 21, 2014
    C. March 11, 2015   D. May 1, 2015

22. The entry in Box 24 should show that the position of the main control valve is   22._____

    A. open   B. half open
    C. one-third closed   D. closed

23. Which one of the following should be entered in Box 26?　　　　23.____

    A. Expired　　　　　　　　　B. Missing from file
    C. Never issued　　　　　　　D. Current

24. Which one of the following should be entered in Box 28?　　　　24.____

    A. Ceiling plaster cracked
    B. Rubbish piles litter work floor
    C. Second floor stairway blocked
    D. Open paint cans on loading dock

25. Which one of the following should be entered in Box 34?　　　　25.____

    A. John Bailey　　　　　　　B. Edward Gold
    C. John Gold　　　　　　　　D. Edward Bailey

KEY (CORRECT ANSWERS)

1.	D	11.	D
2.	A	12.	D
3.	D	13.	B
4.	C	14.	B
5.	A	15.	A
6.	D	16.	A
7.	A	17.	D
8.	D	18.	D
9.	A	19.	C
10.	A	20.	B

21. C
22. A
23. A
24. B
25. A

TEST 2

DIRECTIONS: Each question or incomplete statement is followed by several suggested answers or completions. Select the one that BEST answers the question or completes the statement. *PRINT THE LETTER OF THE CORRECT ANSWER IN THE SPACE AT THE RIGHT.*

1. The materials of which a building are constructed and the opportunities for the spread of fire are important, but the GREATEST single hazard is usually that of

    A. occupancy
    B. location
    C. fire protective measures
    D. construction

2. A warehouse with a leaky roof contains a large amount of building material. The one of the following materials which is MOST likely to set fire to the warehouse is

    A. gasoline
    B. crude oil
    C. lime
    D. kerosene

3. For the most effective results in conducting a Fire Prevention Week campaign, it would be DESIRABLE to emphasize fire prevention

    A. in its broader community aspects
    B. as a means of lowering insurance rates
    C. as it applies to the individuals' own homes
    D. as a means of lowering operating costs of the fire department

4. Floor or wall openings sometimes prevent the banking up of heated air. This condition, with respect to sprinklers, is considered

    A. advantageous
    B. unimportant
    C. detrimental
    D. good ventilation

5. The BEST all-round fireproofing material, due to its high resistance to heat, its lightness, its great strength, its adaptability to any shape, and which is also very easily repaired when damaged by a severe fire, is

    A. brick
    B. hollow clay tile
    C. gypsum
    D. concrete

6. Commercial storage and industrial occupancies are classified in the Fire Code as

    A. highly hazardous
    B. moderately hazardous
    C. lightly hazardous
    D. all of the above

7. An unusually large number of fires of *unknown cause* is characteristic of the fires involving

    A. restaurants
    B. warehouses
    C. mercantile stores
    D. hospitals

8. It is obvious that where a division wall is not continued through the roof, and where the roof is combustible on both sides of the wall, fire is almost certain to spread beyond the wall if the fire is of any duration. According to the above statement, there is NEED of

    A. parapets
    B. more resistive division walls
    C. fire-stopping of roof spaces
    D. fire-stopping division walls

9. The hazard of flammable gases is generally _____ to that of flammable liquids.

   A. opposite
   B. dissimilar
   C. similar
   D. identical

10. The MOST important factor that would materially decrease large-loss supermarket fires is

    A. education of the general public
    B. separating the utility area from the rest of the building by a fire-resistive wall
    C. maintenance of an adequate supply of fire extinguishers
    D. keeping all aisles clear of merchandise and storage

11. The PRIMARY difference between the large number of small fires that produces a small percentage of total losses, and the smaller number of large fires that accounts for 95 percent of the total loss in the United States is usually

    A. the nature of the material involved in the fire
    B. the type of structure involved
    C. early discovery
    D. availability of personnel to fight the fire

12. From the fire prevention standpoint, air conditioning and air blower systems are of concern MAINLY because they

    A. provide a means for the spread of fire through the building served
    B. severely limit adequate ventilation in case of fire
    C. intensify fires from other sources by providing abnormally large amounts of air
    D. characteristically accumulate hazardous quantities of dust and lints which are subject to spontaneous ignition

13. At what interval of time should rubbish and waste materials be removed from piers, docks, and wharves?

    A. At least daily
    B. Once per week
    C. As often as needed to prevent dangerous condition
    D. As fast as accumulated

14. Of the various rooms found in the average school building, which two places deserve MORE consideration from a point of view of preventing personal injuries that may result from panic?
    The

    A. auditorium and the boiler room
    B. classroom on the highest floor and the room in the lowest (basement) part of the building
    C. auditorium and the cafeteria
    D. classroom nearest the auditorium exit and the auditorium itself

15. The underlying reason behind routine periodic and frequent fire prevention inspection is: 15.____

   A. Occupants, hazards, and code compliances may vary considerably in given buildings over a short period
   B. The need for favorable public opinion
   C. A large city usually has many new buildings being constructed
   D. Most individuals continually and consciously try to evade the fire regulations

16. The FIRST objective of all fire prevention is 16.____

   A. safeguarding life against fire
   B. reducing insurance rates
   C. preventing property damage
   D. confining fire to a limited area

17. Which one of the following is the cause of the GREATEST number of fires? 17.____

   A. Electrical wiring   B. Spontaneous ignition
   C. Sparks on roofs   D. Smoking and matches

18. The type of occupancy in which the LARGEST number of fires occurs is 18.____

   A. restaurants and other mercantile establishments
   B. hospitals, theatres, and other public buildings
   C. dwellings, including apartments and hotels
   D. bakeries, cleaning establishments, and other manufacturing plants

19. Which one of the following factors generally should be given the GREATEST right in estimating the fire risk in a general or mixed public warehouse? 19.____

   A. Availability of water hydrants to the warehouse
   B. Location of warehouse with respect to other buildings in the area
   C. Intensity and direction of prevailing winds in the area
   D. Kind of merchandise stored in the warehouse

20. Of the following, the one which is perhaps the MOST important year-round element in fire prevention in residences is 20.____

   A. proper and regular disposal of combustible waste
   B. care in the operation of heating systems
   C. periodic inspections by members of the fire department
   D. radio announcements calling attention to fire hazards in the home

21. The fire prevention and fire protection problem resolves itself into three phases, each of which must receive attention. The possibility of human or mechanical failure makes it unsafe to place sole reliance on any one method. If two of these phases are preventing the outbreak of fire and preventing the serious spread of fire, then the third phase would be providing for 21.____

   A. extensive research in the cause and prevention of non-incendiary fires
   B. the specialized training of fire department personnel at all levels
   C. the prompt detecting and extinguishing of fire
   D. ample modern firefighting equipment

22. The LARGEST cause of apartment and tenement house fires is 22.____

    A. smoking and matches
    B. electrical
    C. gas stoves and explosions
    D. heating equipment

23. Fire loss statistics show that 90 percent of the losses occur at _____ percent of the fires. 23.____

    A. 10   B. 15   C. 20   D. 30

24. To best analyze the fire prevention and protection problem in a certain section of the city, the MOST basic thing that is necessary to know is the _____ the area. 24.____

    A. number of fire companies in
    B. structural and occupancy data of
    C. number of people living in
    D. available water supply for

25. Of the following, the GREATEST fire hazard in furniture and cabinet shops is 25.____

    A. spontaneous ignition
    B. heating systems in buildings
    C. exposure
    D. misuse of electricity

KEY (CORRECT ANSWERS)

1.	A	11.	C
2.	C	12.	A
3.	C	13.	A
4.	C	14.	C
5.	B	15.	A
6.	D	16.	A
7.	B	17.	D
8.	A	18.	C
9.	C	19.	D
10.	B	20.	A

21.	C
22.	A
23.	A
24.	B
25.	A

TEST 3

DIRECTIONS: Each question or incomplete statement is followed by several suggested answers or completions. Select the one that BEST answers the question or completes the statement. *PRINT THE LETTER OF THE CORRECT ANSWER IN THE SPACE AT THE RIGHT.*

1. On inspection of a 5-story building, you find that only half of the required stairways serving the top floor continue to the roof.
   This condition is legal if the building is a(n)

   A. warehouse
   B. school
   C. office building
   D. department store

   1.____

2. In order to determine whether a building in a county is within the fire limits, one of the sources you should check is the maps that are part of the

   A. Administrative Code
   B. most recent zoning resolution
   C. zoning resolution in force
   D. Sanborn maps

   2.____

3. During inspection of a motion picture theatre, you find 6 reels of safety film in closed containers in the manager's office.
   This condition is

   A. *legal* because the film is safety film
   B. *illegal* because film may not be kept in an office
   C. *legal* because there is less than 25,000 feet of film
   D. *illegal* because the film must be kept in a vented metal cabinet

   3.____

4. A two-story, two-family dwelling has been converted to three-family use. There is only one stairway to the street. There is no fire escape. The stairs are not enclosed with fire-regarded partitions. The doors to the apartments are self-closing, but are not fireproof. Of the following statements, the one that is MOST complete and accurate is that the condition described

   A. *conforms* to the requirements of the Multiple Dwelling Law
   B. *does not conform* to the requirements of the Multiple Dwelling Law because the apartment doors should be fireproof
   C. *does not conform* to the requirements of the Multiple Dwelling Law because the apartment doors should be fireproof and the stair hall should be enclosed
   D. *does not conform* to the requirements of the Multiple Dwelling Law because the apartment doors should be fireproof, the stair hall should be enclosed, and a second means of egress should be provided

   4.____

5. On fire prevention inspection, you find a revolving door being used as a required means of egress from the lobby of a hospital.
   This condition is

   A. *illegal*
   B. *legal* only if the door is a type A revolving door
   C. *legal* only if the door is a type B revolving door
   D. *legal* only if all other required means of egress are swinging doors

   5.____

6. The time of day when the GREATEST number of fires occur is from 6._____

   A. Midnight to 6 A.M.   B. 6 A.M. to 12 Noon
   C. 12 Noon to 6 P.M.   D. 6 P.M. to Midnight

7. Of the following types of industrial organizations, the one in which the GREATEST number of fires occur is 7._____

   A. newspaper and printing shops
   B. carpet and rug factories
   C. foundries, metal works, and machine shops
   D. paint, oil, and varnish factories

8. The fire department and the United States Coast Guard have agreed on a program for coordinating their fire prevention activities on the city waterfront. 8._____
   Part of this agreement provides for notification of the other party whenever

   A. any violation is discovered
   B. any serious violation is discovered
   C. any violation is discovered and is not abated within 10 days
   D. any violation is discovered involving a matter under the jurisdiction of the other party

9. A company on AFID makes a complete inspection of a 12-story commercial building occupied as follows: 9._____
           Alpha Co. - floors 1 through 5 and half of 6
           Beta Co. - half of 6 and all of 7
           Delta Co. - part of 8
           Gamma Co. - part of 8
           Epsilon Co. - part of 8
   All other floors - each occupied by single companies According to Regulations, the number of inspections to be recorded on reports for statistical purposes is MOST NEARLY

   A. 12   B. 13   C. 16   D. 18

10. The division coordinator is authorized to discontinue the use of individual inspectors for inspections generally performed by companies on AFID. This action is to be taken when the company 10._____

    A. is up to date on its inspection schedule for the year
    B. is 10 percent ahead of its inspection schedule for the year
    C. has completed sufficient number of inspections to assure completion of its schedule for the year
    D. has completed its regular inspection schedule for the year

Questions 11-15.

DIRECTIONS: Column I lists five properties of fire extinguishers. Column II lists various types of fire extinguishers. For each property in Column I, select the fire extinguisher from Column II having that property and place the letter next to the extinguisher in the properly numbered space.

COLUMN I	COLUMN II	
11. Contains aluminum sulphate in solution	A. Water gas cartridge expelled	11._____
12. Water in extinguishing agent will cause corrosion of container	B. Antifreeze (water mixed with antifreeze chemical)	12._____
13. Usually contains sodium chloride	C. Carbon dioxide	13._____
	D. Foam	
14. Produces a mass of bubbles filled with CO_2 gas	E. Carbon tetrachloride	14._____
15. Inspection check by weighing extinguisher only		15._____

16. Of the following categories by means of which structured fires were extended during the last few years, the MOST common involved was   16._____

    A. cocklofts B. partitions
    C. stairways D. doors

17. The one of the following which is NOT required by the housing maintenance code for the protection of openings into public halls in old-law tenements less than four stories high is that *every*   17._____

    A. door opening into the public hall shall be fireproof, having a fire-resisting rating of at least one hour
    B. door opening into the public hall shall be self-closing
    C. glazed panel in a door opening into a public hall shall be glazed with wire glass
    D. transom opening upon any public hall shall be glazed with wire glass and firmly secured in a closed position

18. Firestopping of the space above a hung ceiling into areas not exceeding 3,000 square feet is REQUIRED when the   18._____

    A. structural members within the concealed space are individually protected with materials having the required fire resistance
    B. concealed space is sprinklered
    C. ceiling contributes to the required fire resistance of the floor or roof assembly
    D. ceiling is not an essential part of the fire-resistive assembly

19. When a deluge sprinkler system is provided around the perimeter of a theater stage, manual operating devices as well as automatic controls are required by the building code.   19._____
    The MOST complete and accurate statement concerning these manual operating devices is that they should be located

    A. at the emergency control station
    B. adjacent to one exit from the stage
    C. at the emergency control station and adjacent to one exit from the stage
    D. at the emergency control station, adjacent to one exit from the stage, and at the deluge valve

20. Yellow painted Siamese caps on office buildings will indicate that the Siamese serves ONLY

   A. the standpipe in pressurized stairs
   B. the sprinklers in sub-basement locations
   C. a combination standpipe and sprinkler system
   D. as a supply line to the fire pump for the upper level standpipe outlets

21. A fireman, on his way to work, is stopped by a citizen who complains that the employees of a nearby store frequently pile empty crates and boxes in a doorway, blocking passage. The one of the following which would be the MOST appropriate action for the fireman to take is to

   A. assure the citizen that the fire department's inspectional activities will eventually *catch up* with the store
   B. obtain the address of the store and investigate to determine whether the citizen's complaint is justified
   C. obtain the address of the store and report the complaint to his superior officer
   D. ask the citizen for specific dates on which this practice has occurred to determine whether the complaint is justified

22. In the Halon coding system, each digit represents the number of atoms while the position of the digit in the number represents a specific chemical element.
    For Halon number 1202, the number 1 indicates that the molecule contains one atom of

   A. bromine   B. carbon   C. chlorine   D. fluorine

23. A street vault incident described in a department safety bulletin explains how two persons were asphyxiated when they descended into the vault.
    Tests of the atmosphere of the vault showed that the hazard was due to

   A. light smoke and flames generated by burning synthetic insulation
   B. gasoline vapors from a leaking underground tank
   C. replacement of oxygen by carbon dioxide
   D. natural gas entering the vault

24. It is sometimes necessary to make a simple field test to determine the flammability of decorative materials.
    Of the following, the one that generally produces the LEAST reliable results when tested by exposure to a small flame is

   A. all-glass fabric
   B. untreated cotton cloth
   C. flame-retardant treated paper
   D. flexible plastic film

25. The one of the following substances with the LEAST tendency to spontaneous heating is

   A. fish meal   B. lamp black
   C. scrap rubber   D. soap powder

KEY (CORRECT ANSWERS)

1. B
2. C
3. B
4. A
5. A

6. C
7. C
8. B
9. C
10. C

11. D
12. E
13. B
14. D
15. C

16. B
17. A
18. C
19. C
20. C

21. C
22. B
23. D
24. D
25. B

TEST 4

DIRECTIONS: Each question or incomplete statement is followed by several suggested answers or completions. Select the one that BEST answers the question or completes the statement. *PRINT THE LETTER OF THE CORRECT ANSWER IN THE SPACE AT THE RIGHT.*

1. Every applicant for a certificate of license to install underground gasoline storage tanks is required to   1.____

   A. be a resident of the city and maintain a place of business in the city
   B. file a bond and evidence of liability insurance
   C. be a resident of the city or maintain a place of business in the city
   D. pass a written examination given by the fire department

2. After firing a blast, the licensed blaster at a construction site discovered that one charge had not detonated and the exact direction of the drill hole could not be determined. The licensed blaster under the supervision and orders of the walking boss used a metal scraper to remove the tamping, after which the hole was reloaded and fired. This action   2.____

   A. complies with the Fire Prevention Code
   B. violates the Code because a metal scraper was used
   C. violates the Code because the Fire Commissioner's approval is required before charges are removed
   D. violates the Code because no notification was given to the Division of Fire Prevention concerning the incident

3. The Fire Prevention Code specifies that a special permit is required for each of the following EXCEPT   3.____

   A. refining petroleum collected from oil separators or manufacturing plants
   B. loading of small arms ammunition by hand in a retail store selling ammunition
   C. operating a wholesale drug or chemical house
   D. generating acetylene gas

4. The one of the following that is the MOST acceptable statement concerning the fire protection for the truck loading rack in a bulk oil terminal is that the rack must be equipped with a   4.____

   A. water spray system, automatically controlled
   B. foam system, remote manually controlled
   C. water spray system, remote manually controlled
   D. foam system, automatically controlled

5. A fire insurance inspector suggested to the manager of a fireproof warehouse that bags of flour be stacked on skids (wooden platforms 6" high, 6x6 feet in area).
   Of the following, the BEST justification for this suggestion is that, in the event of a fire, the bags on skids are LESS likely to   5.____

   A. topple
   B. be damaged by water used in extinguishment
   C. catch fire
   D. be ripped by fire equipment

6. Permitting piles of scrap paper cuttings to accumulate in a factory building is a bad practice CHIEFLY because they may

   A. ignite spontaneously
   B. interfere with fire extinguishment operations
   C. catch fire from a spark
   D. interfere with escape of occupants if a fire occurs

7. Firefighters are inspecting a furniture factory. During the inspection, they find employees smoking cigarettes in various areas.
   In which area does smoking pose the GREATEST danger of causing a fire?

   A. Employee lounge   B. Woodworking shop
   C. A private office   D. A rest room

8. The MAXIMUM quantity of paints which may be manufactured or stored without a permit, according to the Fire Prevention Code, is _____ gallons.

   A. 20   B. 25   C. 30   D. 50

9. Oil separators are required by the Administrative Code before issuance of a permit to a garage for the storage of volatile inflammable oil if the garage accommodates _____ or more motor vehicles.

   A. four   B. five   C. six   D. ten

10. *The term cellar, as used in the Building Code, shall mean a story having _____ of its height, measured from finished floor to finished ceiling, below the curb level at the center of the street front.*
    The one of the following which, when filled in the blank space, BEST completes the sentence is

    A. more than one-half
    B. no more than one-half
    C. more than three-quarters
    D. no more than three-quarters

11. The Oil Burner Rules of the Board of Standards and Appeals state, *No movable combustible materials shall be stored or maintained within _____ feet of heating apparatus, except where same is protected by fire-retarding material.*
    The one of the following numbers which, when inserted in the blank space above, MOST accurately completes the sentence is

    A. 2   B. 3   C. 4   D. 5

12. As used in the Building Code, the term *horizontal exit* refers to a(n)

    A. exit door on the ground floor which is at the same level as the street grade
    B. corridor or hallway leading to the exit stairs
    C. fire escape with the balcony at the same level as the floor
    D. connection between two floor areas through a fire wall

13. According to the Building Code, a required exit stairway enclosure in a public building MUST have a fire resistance rating of _____ hour(s).

    A. 1   B. 2   C. 3   D. 4

14. A recently enacted section of the Fire Prevention Code places limitations on the use of kerosene-burning equipment.
    When all the provisions of this section of the Code are in full effect, the one of the following uses of kerosene-burning equipment which will NOT be permitted is equipment used exclusively for

    A. cooking purposes
    B. lighting purposes
    C. demonstration and sales purposes
    D. heating purposes in any building in an area not supplied with permanent piped gas

15. The provisions of the Building Code require that in a building more than two stories high, the required stairways must all continue to the roof EXCEPT in a(n)

    A. office building   B. school building
    C. theater   D. storage warehouse

16. The definition of *non-combustible* in the Building Code was recently amended with regard to acoustical and thermal insulation.
    Which one of the following would be *non-combustible* according to the Code?
    Insulation with a flame-spread rating not greater than _____, smoke-developed rating not greater than _____.

    A. 25; 50   B. 50; 50   C. 50; 75   D. 75; 100

17. A new school dormitory is two stories and less than thirty feet in height. Inspection reveals that there is only one stairway from the second floor and the maximum travel distance to the stair enclosure is 80 feet. The stair enclosure and corridors are provided with automatic sprinkler protection.
    With respect to the provisions of the Building Code as it applies to this situation, it would be MOST appropriate to state that this building

    A. complies with the Code
    B. does not comply with the Code because the maximum travel distance is excessive
    C. does not comply with the Code because two exits remote from each other on each story are lacking
    D. does not comply with the Code because the sprinkler system was not extended into the rooms

18. Of the following statements, the one that is LEAST in accord with the material and equipment requirements for oil spill control at bulk storage plants and petroleum product pipelines is that

    A. all material and equipment must be of a type acceptable to the Fire Commissioner
    B. dispersants should be used only when directed by the fire department, Coast Guard, or Corps of Engineers
    C. pipeline operators shall provide at least one vacuum truck
    D. the minimum amount of absorbent material at any plant shall be 2,000 pounds

19. In a high-rise office building over 100 feet in height, the doors opening into interior stair enclosures may NOT be locked from either side at intervals of four stories or less EXCEPT where

    A. the building is equipped with an approved automatic sprinkler system
    B. the doors are equipped with an automatic fail-safe system for opening doors
    C. the second means of egress is a standard fire tower
    D. every floor of the building has a fire warden on duty

20. The Rules of the Board of Standards and Appeals require that combustible materials used for decorative purposes within special occupancy structures be made flameproof. Approval of flameproof materials is

    A. valid for an indefinite period
    B. limited to a period of 6 months
    C. limited to a period of 1 year
    D. limited to a period of 2 years

21. A multiple dwelling, according to the Multiple Dwelling Law, is a dwelling occupied as the residence of _____ or more families living independently of each other.
    The one of the following numbers which, when inserted in the blank space above, MOST accurately completes the sentence is

    A. 2   B. 3   C. 4   D. 5

22. The one of the following statements that is MOST accurate is that in multiple dwellings, windows at grade levels at sidewalks, yards, or courts may

    A. not have bars
    B. have bars provided that they are easily removed from the inside of the window
    C. have bars but at least one window in each room must be without bars
    D. have bars but at least one window in each apartment must be without bars

23. The number of extra sprinkler heads which must be kept in the premises of a building with an automatic sprinkler system, according to the Building Code, is

    A. 10
    B. 10 percent of the number of sprinkler heads in the entire system
    C. 6
    D. 6 percent of the number of sprinkler heads in the entire system

24. The Building Code requires that standpipe systems be equipped with pressure reducing valves where the normal hydrostatic pressure at a 2 1/2" hose outlet valve exceeds _____ lbs. per square inch.

    A. 50   B. 55   C. 60   D. 65

25. Walls of structures used for public entertainment may be covered with combustible wall coverings, according to the Building Code, provided that the

    A. wall covering is pasted or cemented directly to the plaster surfaces of the wall
    B. wall covering does not extend more than six feet in height
    C. building is a Class 1 fireproof structure
    D. building has a seating capacity of 600 people or less

KEY (CORRECT ANSWERS)

1. C
2. A
3. D
4. C
5. B

6. C
7. B
8. A
9. B
10. A

11. D
12. D
13. C
14. D
15. B

16. A
17. A
18. B
19. B
20. C

21. B
22. D
23. C
24. B
25. A

EXAMINATION SECTION
TEST 1

DIRECTIONS: Each question or incomplete statement is followed by several suggested answers or completions. Select the one that BEST answers the question or completes the statement. *PRINT THE LETTER OF THE CORRECT ANSWER IN THE SPACE AT THE RIGHT.*

1. Of the following materials, the one which has the HIGHEST tendency to spontaneous heating is

    A. lanolin
    B. linseed oil
    C. coconut oil
    D. turpentine

    1.____

2. The one of the following fabrics used in the manufacture of clothing that is MOST flammable is

    A. wool   B. acetate   C. cotton   D. linen

    2.____

3. Which of the following substances has the LOWEST boiling point?

    A. Turpentine
    B. Benzene
    C. Mineral spirits
    D. Cellosolve

    3.____

4. Which of the following non-solid fuels has the HIGHEST ignition temperature?

    A. Acetone
    B. Carbon monoxide
    C. Ethylene
    D. Methyl alcohol

    4.____

5. Assume that the cellar of a building is 100 feet long, 100 feet wide, and 10 feet high. If natural gas were distributed evenly throughout the cellar, and all openings from the cellar are closed, which one of the following volumes of natural gas would create an explosive atmosphere if suddenly released into this cellar?
   _____ cubic feet.

    A. 2,500   B. 7,500   C. 17,500   D. 25,000

    5.____

6. A lighted cigarette is LEAST likely to start a fire if dropped and left

    A. on a kapok pillow
    B. on cotton bed clothes
    C. in an explosive vapor-air mixture
    D. on dry grass

    6.____

7. A fire marshal inspecting a number of buildings where explosions are suspected as having been caused by dynamite would find that the scene of the dynamite explosion is MOST likely the one where

    A. a large section of wall has toppled, with its mortar remaining intact
    B. there are fragments of shattered cast iron
    C. a window frame has been pushed out from the wall surface, with some or all of the windows remaining intact
    D. the light bulbs in the building have remained unbroken

    7.____

23

8. During apparatus field inspection of a restaurant located in a building erected in 1972, a fireman finds that the filters for the cooking equipment exhaust system are cleaned every three months and the entire system is cleaned once a year.
   This maintenance procedure is

   A. correct
   B. incorrect, because the filters should be discarded at least every three months and the system cleaned at least once a year
   C. incorrect, because the filters should be discarded at least once a year and the system cleaned at least once a year
   D. incorrect, because both the filters and the entire system should be cleaned at least every three months

9. A group home is a facility for the care and maintenance of not less than three nor more than twelve children and is classified by the building code in the same occupancy group as a one-family dwelling.
   This much of the definition of a group home GENERALLY is

   A. correct
   B. incorrect, because a group home may not have less than seven children
   C. incorrect, because a group home is for adults, not children
   D. incorrect, because a group home is classified in the same occupancy group as a rooming house

10. A fifty-foot high, five-story multiple dwelling built in 1974 has a floor area of 7,000 square feet on each floor. It is equipped with a non-automatic dry standpipe system. During apparatus field inspection duty, a member discovers that a control valve on the standpipe is in closed position with no placard indicating that this was the normal position of the valve. Further investigation reveals that there is no one in the building who has a certificate of fitness to maintain the standpipe system. Of the following statements concerning the above situation, the one that is CORRECT is that the situation as described is

    A. legal
    B. illegal, because an individual with a certificate of fitness must be on the premises
    C. illegal, because an automatic system is required
    D. illegal, because the control valve must be in the open position

11. A tank truck with a capacity of 4,400 gallons is delivering #4 fuel oil to a multiple dwelling. According to the specifications for tank trucks, the person in control of the truck and supervising this delivery

    A. does not require a certificate of fitness because the capacity of the tank is less than 5,000 gallons
    B. does not require a certificate of fitness because the tank has light oil
    C. does not require a certificate of fitness because the delivery is being made to a non-commercial occupancy
    D. requires a certificate of fitness because a fire department permit is needed for all tank trucks delivering #4 fuel oil

12. The multiple dwelling law states that sprinkler systems in lodging houses shall have a supervisory and maintenance service satisfactory to the fire department. The fire department requires a valid inspection of the sprinkler control valve AT LEAST once

A. daily
B. semi-weekly
C. weekly
D. monthly

13. Anhydrous ammonia is being used in a duplicating machine located in a school office. There is no one in the school with a certificate of fitness for the storage and use of ammonia or for the servicing of the duplicating machine. In this situation, a certificate of fitness is GENERALLY

   A. *not* required because the machine is considered office equipment
   B. *not* required unless the quantity of anhydrous ammonia being stored on the premises is more than two 150-lb. cylinders
   C. *not* required because schools, with regular supervised fire drills, are exempt from certain requirements of the fire prevention code
   D. *required* whether or not a permit is needed under the fire prevention code

14. According to the labor law, fire drills are required to be conducted in certain factory buildings.
Which of the following statements is CORRECT with respect to such fire drills?

   A. Fire drills are required to be conducted in every factory building in which there are more than 75 persons above or below the street floor.
   B. Fire drills are not required to be conducted in factory buildings less than 100 feet in height.
   C. Fire drills are required to be conducted in every factory building over two stories in height in which more than twenty-five persons are employed above the ground floor unless the sprinkler system and number of occupants of the building are in accordance with the other provisions of the labor law.
   D. The sprinklering of a factory building is not a factor in determining whether or not a building is required to conduct fire drills.

15. An officer tells members during a drill that a red light and a placard should serve to locate the Siamese hose connection of a temporary standpipe system in a building under construction.
The officer's instructions are

   A. *correct,* because both the red light and a placard are required
   B. *incorrect,* because only the red light is required
   C. *incorrect,* because only a placard is required
   D. *incorrect,* because neither the red light nor a placard is required

16. During apparatus field inspection duty, a fireman inspecting a 40-story office building occupied by 1,000 people is unable to find a fire safety director or deputy fire safety director in the building. The manager of the building states that the fire safety director is out to lunch, that there is no deputy fire safety director, and that he, the manager, is acting as the fire safety director pending the return of the fire safety director. Because the manager does not have a fire safety director certificate of fitness, the fireman issues a violation to him.
The fireman's action in this situation is

A. *correct,* because local law requires a fire safety director with a certificate of fitness in a building this high to be on duty whenever the building is occupied by more than 500 people
B. *incorrect,* because local law permits the fire safety director to be temporarily relieved, for short intervals, by responsible individuals who do not have the required certificate of fitness
C. *correct,* because local law requires a fire safety director with a certificate of fitness to be on duty in a building this high, regardless of the occupancy of the building
D. *incorrect,* because whenever local law is not complied with, a referral report should be forwarded, and no violation issued

17. A commercial vehicle without a fire department permit is transporting 500 pounds of dynamite from a neighboring outside county through the city to another out-of-town county without stopping to make any deliveries enroute. There is no department pumping engine escort. The situation as described is

    A. *legal,* because the shipment contains less than 1,000 pounds of dynamite
    B. *illegal,* because a pumping engine escort is required whenever explosives are transported without a fire department permit through the city
    C. *legal,* even though a fire department permit has not been issued, because the shipment does not contain any blasting caps
    D. *illegal,* because dynamite may not be transported through the city from one out-of-town location to another

18. Of the following exit doors in buildings erected in 1976, the one that does NOT have to swing outward is a(n)

    A. corridor door from a room used for office purposes with an occupancy of 80 persons
    B. corridor door from a lecture room in a school building where the room has an occupancy of 80 persons
    C. exterior street-floor exit door from a space 2,000 square feet in area in a business building, where the space is occupied by fewer than 50 persons and the maximum travel distance to the door is 50 feet
    D. exterior street-floor exit door from a lobby in a hotel, where the lobby will not be occupied by more than 50 persons and the maximum travel distance to the door is 50 feet

19. During apparatus field inspection duty, a fireman inspecting a 90-foot high apartment house erected in 1972 finds that the standpipe hose is missing from every hose rack in the building. Of the following statements concerning this situation, the one that is CORRECT is that

    A. the situation as described may be legal but the fire-man needs additional information to make a final decision
    B. all such buildings, regardless of when erected, must have the standpipe hose racks equipped with hose
    C. all such buildings, if erected under the new building code, must have their standpipe hose racks equipped with hose
    D. the situation as described would be acceptable for an office building but not for an apartment house

20. A permit is required to store empty combustible packing boxes in a building whenever the   20.____

    A. boxes occupy more than two thousand cubic feet
    B. storage space is less than 50 feet from the nearest wall of a building occupied as a hospital, school, or theater
    C. boxes are of cardboard or similarly combustible material
    D. building is of non-fireproof construction

21. An inspector, taking some clothing to a dry cleaner in his neighborhood, noticed that   21.____
    inflammable cleaning fluid was stored in a way which created a fire hazard. The fireman called this to the attention of the proprietor, explaining the danger involved.
    This method of handling the situation was

    A. *bad;* the fireman should not have interfered in a matter which was not his responsibility
    B. *good;* the proprietor would probably remove the hazard and be more careful in the future
    C. *bad;* the fireman should have reported the situation to the fire inspector's office without saying anything to the proprietor
    D. *good;* since the fireman was a customer, he should treat the proprietor more leniently than he would treat other violators

22. According to the Building Code, a vertical iron ladder to an escape manhole opening in   22.____
    the sidewalk is required from a cellar room when the room is being used as a

    A. coal storage room   B. restaurant kitchen
    C. boiler room   D. factory

23. In a building of public assembly, the provisions of the Fire Prevention Code prohibit the   23.____
    use of decorations, drapes, or scenery made of combustible material which have not been rendered fireproof.
    Of the following types of occupancies, the one that is exempt from the provisions of this section is a

    A. school   B. hospital   C. church   D. museum

24. As used in the Building Code, a *4-hour fire rating* of a wall means that in a standard fire   24.____
    test of four hours duration, the

    A. wall will not collapse
    B. unexposed side of the wall will not char or smolder
    C. temperature on the unexposed side of the wall will not rise
    D. temperature on the unexposed side of the wall will not rise more than a predetermined amount

25. The prohibition against smoking in retail stores applies   25.____

    A. to all stores
    B. only to stores employing more than 25 persons
    C. only to stores accommodating more than 300 persons
    D. only to stores employing more than 25 persons or accommodating more than 300 persons

KEY (CORRECT ANSWERS)

1.	C	11.	D
2.	D	12.	C
3.	B	13.	D
4.	D	14.	C
5.	C	15.	A
6.	C	16.	D
7.	A	17.	B
8.	D	18.	C
9.	B	19.	A
10.	D	20.	A

21. B
22. C
23. C
24. D
25. A

TEST 2

DIRECTIONS: Each question or incomplete statement is followed by several suggested answers or completions. Select the one that BEST answers the question or completes the statement. *PRINT THE LETTER OF THE CORRECT ANSWER IN THE SPACE AT THE RIGHT.*

1. The one of the following which is NOT required by the Code for the protection of openings into public halls in old-law tenements less than four stories high is that every   1.____

    A. door opening into the public hall shall be fireproof, having a fire-resisting rating of at least one hour
    B. door opening into the public hall shall be self-closing
    C. glazed panel in a door opening into a public hall shall be glazed with wire glass
    D. transom opening upon any public hall shall be glazed with wire glass and firmly secured in a closed position

2. Firestopping of the space above a hung ceiling into areas not exceeding 3,000 square feet is REQUIRED when the   2.____

    A. structural members within the concealed space are individually protected with materials having the required fire resistance
    B. concealed space is sprinklered
    C. ceiling contributes to the required fire resistance of the floor or roof assembly
    D. ceiling is not an essential part of the fire-resistive assembly

3. When a deluge sprinkler system is provided around the perimeter of a theater stage, manual operating devices as well as automatic controls are required by the Building Code.
The MOST complete and accurate statement concerning these manual operating devices is that they should be located   3.____

    A. at the emergency control station
    B. adjacent to one exit from the stage
    C. at the emergency control station and adjacent to one exit from the stage
    D. at the emergency control station, adjacent to one exit from the stage, and at the deluge valve

4. Yellow painted Siamese caps on office buildings will indicate that the Siamese serves ONLY   4.____

    A. the standpipe in pressurized stairs
    B. the sprinklers in sub-basement locations
    C. a combination standpipe and sprinkler system
    D. as a supply line to the fire pump for the upper level standpipe outlets

5. Of the following buildings, the one that MUST have emergency smoke-venting equipment is a   5.____

    A. new office building, 275 feet high, equipped throughout with automatic sprinklers
    B. new office building, 175 feet high, without an air conditioning system

29

C. new office building, 75 feet high, without sprinklers and with a central air conditioning system serving more than the floor on which the equipment is located
D. one-story building, classified in occupancy group B-1, greater in depth than 100 feet from a frontage space

6. A factory building was erected in 1912 and was occupied continuously as such until 1950 when it became completely vacant. After many years, it was reoccupied with factory occupancies.
This structure

   A. must comply with the State Labor Law affecting factory buildings erected after October 1, 1913
   B. may be reoccupied as a factory building without changing its classification as one erected before October 1, 1913
   C. may be reoccupied as a factory building erected before October 1, 1913 provided an automatic sprinkler system is installed
   D. cannot be reoccupied as a factory unless it is of fireproof construction

6.___

7. A five-story fireproof factory building erected in 1909 has the following occupancies:
   First floor - dress manufacturing
   Second floor - tannery
   Third floor - artificial flower manufacturing
   Fourth floor - machine shop
   Fifth floor - vacant
Under the State Labor Law, an automatic extinguishing system is

   A. *not required* because the building is classed as fireproof
   B. *required* for the artificial flower factory and all floors above
   C. *not required* if the tannery is moved to the fifth floor
   D. *required* throughout

7.___

8. Which one of the following statements does NOT correctly describe the protection requirements for vertical separation of openings?
In buildings classified in occupancy group

   A. E exceeding three stories or 40 feet in height, openings located vertically above one another in exterior walls except in stairway enclosures required to have a fire resistance rating of one hour or more shall be separated by a spandrel wall at least three feet high between the top of one opening and the bottom of the opening immediately above
   B. D exceeding three stories or 40 feet in height, openings located vertically above one another in exterior walls except in stairway enclosures shall have each such opening above the lower one protected against fire by an opening protective
   C. C exceeding three stories or 40 feet in height, openings located vertically above one another in exterior walls except in stairway enclosures shall be protected by a fire canopy of non-combustible materials extending out at least two feet horizontally from the wall and at least as long as the width of the lower opening
   D. B, spandrels and fire canopies shall be constructed to provide at least the fire-resistance rating required for the exterior wall, but in no event less than one hour

8.___

9. It is MOST complete and accurate to state that, according to the Manual of Fire Communications, in the event the officer in command of a fire or emergency operation requires additional manpower, in lieu of transmitting additional alarms or special calls, he may

   A. telephone the Office of the Chief of Department, specifying the kind of aid required and when it should be sent
   B. notify the dispatcher by radio of the assistance required, specifying the number of officers and fire-men, and the location to which they shall report
   C. telephone the dispatcher specifying the assistance required, including the number of officers and fire-men needed, location to which they shall report, and the expected time additional manpower will be released
   D. notify the Office of the Chief of Department, specifying the assistance required, the location to which they shall report, the reason for calling additional manpower, and the amount of time they can be expected to be detained

10. While inspecting a sprinklered building, a fire officer is asked by the building manager for his opinion about painting the wooden water tank on the roof. The manager explains it is his understanding that painting the tank will extend its useful life.
    Of the following, it would probably be MOST appropriate for the fire officer to indicate that

    A. painting the interior of the tank below water level will prolong the life of the tank, but painting the exterior may tend to hide structural defects
    B. painting a wooden tank may be desirable from the standpoint of appearance, but it is of questionable value in increasing the life of the tank
    C. the use of paint is undesirable for any purpose on either the exterior or interior of the tank
    D. the manager should consult a painting contractor to find out what his experience and recommendations are

11. In a large warehouse facility, the GREATEST fire hazard potential will result if rubber automotive tires are stored on the

    A. side in stacked piles   B. tread in racks
    C. side on pallets   D. tread in stacked piles

12. During a fire prevention inspection, a firefighter may find a condition which could be the immediate cause of death in the event of a fire.
    Which one of the following conditions in a restaurant is the MOST dangerous?

    A. Blocked exit doors
    B. A crack in the front door
    C. A window that does not open
    D. A broken air conditioning system

13. Firefighters must regularly inspect office buildings to determine whether fire prevention laws have been obeyed. Some of these fire prevention laws are as follows: DOORS: Doors should be locked as follows:
    I. Doors on the ground floor may be locked on the street side to prevent entry into the stairway.
    II. Doors in office buildings that are less than 100 feet in height may be locked on the stairway side on each floor above the ground floor.
    III. Doors in office buildings that are 100 feet or more in height may be locked on the stairway side except for every fourth floor.

    The doors in an office building which is less than 100 feet in height may be locked on the stairway side

    A. on all floors including the ground floor
    B. on all floors above the ground floor
    C. except for every fourth floor
    D. on all floors above the fourth floor

14. SIGNS: Signs concerning stairways should be posted in the following manner:
    I. A sign shall be posted near the elevator on each floor, stating, *IN CASE OF FIRE, USE STAIRS UNLESS OTHERWISE INSTRUCTED.* The sign shall contain a diagram showing the location of the stairs and the letter identification of the stairs.
    II. Each stairway shall be identified by an alphabetical letter on a sign posted on the hallway side of the stair door.
    III. Signs indicating the floor number shall be attached to the stairway side of each door.
    IV. Signs indicating whether re-entry can be made into the building, and the floors where re-entry can be made, shall be posted on the stairway side of each door.

    Which one of the following CORRECTLY lists the information which should be posted on the stairway side of a door?

    A sign will indicate the
    A. floor number, whether re-entry can be made into the building, and the floors where re-entry can be made
    B. alphabetical letter of the stairway, whether re-entry can be made into the building, and the floors where re-entry can be made
    C. alphabetical letter of the stairway and the floor number
    D. alphabetical letter of the stairway, the floor number, whether re-entry can be made into the building, and the floors where re-entry can be made

15. The Fire Department now uses companies on fire duty, with their apparatus, for fire prevention inspection in commercial buildings.
    The one of the following changes which was MOST important in making this inspection procedure practicable was the

    A. reduction of hours of work of firemen
    B. use of two-way radio equipment
    C. use of enclosed cabs on fire apparatus
    D. increase in property values during the post-war period

16. The MAXIMUM length of unlined linen hose which shall be permitted at any standpipe hose outlet valve is

    A. 50' B. 75' C. 100' D. 125'

17. The State Labor Law requires that fire drills be conducted monthly in factory buildings over two stories in height in which more than 25 persons are employed above the ground floor.
    The one of the following statements that is MOST complete and accurate is that the law provides for automatic exemption from this requirement to factory buildings which are

    A. completely sprinklered
    B. completely sprinklered by a system having two adequate sources of water supply
    C. completely sprinklered by a system having two adequate sources of water supply and a maximum number of occupants of any one floor not more than 50 percent above the capacity of the exits required for the same building if unsprinklered
    D. completely sprinklered by a system having two adequate sources of water supply, a maximum number of occupants of any one floor not more than 50 percent above the capacity of the exits required for the same building if unsprinklered and an interior fire alarm system

18. Automatic sprinkler systems installed in the public halls of converted multiple dwellings with a required Siamese are subjected to a hydrostatic pressure test before acceptance. The test pressure for such systems is to be NOT less than

    A. 30 pounds per square inch
    B. 30 pounds per square inch in excess of the normal pressure required for such systems when in service
    C. 200 pounds per square inch
    D. 200 pounds per square inch in excess of the normal pressure required for such systems when in service

19. According to the rules of the Board of Standards and Appeals, when flameproofed materials are subjected to prescribed tests, they shall meet established standards for each of the following properties EXCEPT

    A. flashing   B. duration of flame
    C. duration of glow   D. temperature of flame

20. Each year many children die in fires which they have started while playing with matches. Of the following measures, the one that would be MOST effective in preventing such tragedies is to

    A. warn the children of the dangers involved
    B. punish parents who are found guilty of neglecting their children
    C. keep matches out of the reach of children
    D. use only safety matches

21. Sparks given off by welding torches are a serious fire hazard. 21.____
    The BEST of the following methods of dealing with this hazard is to conduct welding operations

    A. only in fireproof buildings protected by sprinkler systems
    B. only out-of-doors on a day with little wind blowing
    C. only on materials certified to be non-combustible by recognized testing laboratories
    D. only after loose combustible materials have been cleared from the area and with a man standing by with a hose line

22. A two-story, Class 3, non-fireproof building was originally occupied as a store on the first 22.____
    floor and one apartment on the second floor. Upon inspection, you find that the second floor is now being used for offices. The building is 20' x 50'. There is one stairway made of wood, enclosed with fire-retarded stud partitions, leading directly to the street from the second floor.
    The one of the following statements that is MOST complete and accurate is that the situation as described

    A. complies with applicable laws
    B. is illegal because the stair should be of incombustible material
    C. is illegal because there should be two means of egress
    D. is illegal because there should be two means of egress and the stair should be of incombustible material

Questions 23-25.

DIRECTIONS: Questions 23 through 25 are to be answered SOLELY on the basis of the following passage.

Automatic sprinkler systems are installed in many buildings. They extinguish or keep from spreading 96% of all fires in areas they protect. Sprinkler systems are made up of pipes which hang below the ceiling of each protected area and sprinkler heads which are placed along the pipes. The pipes are usually filled with water, and each sprinkler head has a heat sensitive part. When the heat from the fire reaches the sensitive part of the sprinkler head, the head opens and showers water upon the fire in the form of spray. The heads are spaced so that the fire is covered by overlapping showers of water from the open heads.

23. Automatic sprinkler systems are installed in buildings to 23.____

    A. prevent the build-up of dangerous gases
    B. eliminate the need for fire insurance
    C. extinguish fires or keep them from spreading
    D. protect 96% of the floor space

24. If more than one sprinkler head opens, the area sprayed will be 24.____

    A. flooded with hot water
    B. overlapped by showers of water
    C. subject to less water damage
    D. about 1 foot per sprinkler head

25. A sprinkler head will open and shower water when 25._____
    A. it is reached by heat from a fire
    B. water pressure in the pipes gets too high
    C. it is reached by sounds from a fire alarm
    D. water temperature in the pipes gets too low

KEY (CORRECT ANSWERS)

1.	A	11.	B
2.	C	12.	A
3.	C	13.	B
4.	C	14.	A
5.	D	15.	B
6.	B	16.	D
7.	D	17.	C
8.	A	18.	C
9.	B	19.	D
10.	B	20.	C

21. D
22. A
23. C
24. B
25. A

TEST 3

DIRECTIONS: Each question or incomplete statement is followed by several suggested answers or completions. Select the one that BEST answers the question or completes the statement. *PRINT THE LETTER OF THE CORRECT ANSWER IN THE SPACE AT THE RIGHT.*

1. The one of the following which is the MOST valid statement in the Fire Prevention Code regarding height restrictions on combustible fiber storage is that   1.___

    A. a clearance of at least 18 inches shall be maintained below the sprinkler head
    B. storage shall be no higher than 20 feet above the floor
    C. storage shall be no higher than 2/3 of the distance from floor to ceiling
    D. storage shall be piled to a height not greater than 6 inches below the top of the enclosing wall

2. The one of the following which is NOT among the Fire Prevention Code protection requirements for the storage of television special effects is that   2.___

    A. partitions in the storage room shall have at least a one-hour fire resistive rating
    B. the roof of the storage room shall have at least a 1 1/2 hour fire resistive rating
    C. there shall be one sprinkler head for each 80 square feet of floor space in the storage room
    D. there shall be mechanical ventilation providing at least four air changes per hour

3. According to the Fire Prevention Code, of the following containers, the ones which are NOT legal for the transportation of gasoline are   3.___

    A. 5-gallon cans with metal seals
    B. glass bottles not exceeding 4 ounces each
    C. 55-gallon steel barrels or drums
    D. 10-gallon safety cans

4. The following conditions have been found during an inspection: 4.___
    I. 10,000 small arms cartridges in a store authorized to sell gunpowder
    II. 500 small arms cartridges in a pawn shop
    III. 200 small arms cartridges in a liquor store
    IV. 100 small arms cartridges in a drug store

    Which of the following choices lists ONLY those of the above conditions that comply with the Fire Prevention Code either because a permit may be issued or because a pernit is not required?

    A. I, II, III   B. I, II, IV
    C. I, III, IV   D. II, III, IV

5. While inspecting a building, an officer notices that a standard enclosure having a three-hour fire resistance rating has been constructed above ground on the lowest floor of the building.   5.___
    According to the Building Code, the MAXIMUM size fuel oil storage tank that can be placed in this enclosure is one with a capacity of _____ gallons.

    A. 1,100   B. 2,500   C. 10,000   D. 20,000

6. The one of the following which is NOT a Class B multiple dwelling is a

   A. hotel
   B. boarding school
   C. clubhouse
   D. hospital

7. When inspecting an industrial plant, an officer discovers a conveyor passing through a fire wall with no fire shutter for the opening.
   The MOST valid of the following statements concerning alternate forms of protection is that

   A. no alternate is acceptable; a shutter having fire resistance equal to the wall fire resistance is required
   B. a sprinkler head located in the opening to provide at least 3 gallons per square foot per minute is acceptable
   C. two sprinkler heads to provide a water curtain for the entire opening is acceptable
   D. four water spray nozzles on each side of the opening controlled by an automatic valve actuated by a heat detector is acceptable

8. A new restaurant in a multiple-story building of Class I construction has a false front on the outside of the building representing an English castle.
   The one of the following which meets the Building Code requirement for this condition to be legal is that the false front is of

   A. fire retardant treated wood not over 40 feet high
   B. fire retardant treated wood covering less than 2,000 square feet of surface
   C. slow burning plastic, not over 25 feet high, covering not over 1,000 square feet of surface
   D. slow burning plastic, not over 40 feet high, covering less than 5% of the building surface

9. At a recent fire on the third floor of a building, firemen could not open the locked windows nor could they break the plastic glazing.
   For such conditions, the Building Code requires that

   A. keys to the windows be available in the lobby
   B. one window for each 50 feet of street front be openable from the inside or outside
   C. all plastic glazing be replaced by glass
   D. all locks be removed and replaced with spring latches

10. Showroom spaces located in office buildings over 100 feet high are required to be sprinklered when the

    A. building air conditioning system serves more than the floor in which the equipment is located, and the showroom space exceeds 7,500 square feet in area and is located more than 40 feet above curb level
    B. showroom space is over 1,000 square feet in area and is located more than 40 feet above curb level
    C. showroom space is over 7,500 square feet in area, is not equipped with an approved smoke detection alarm system, and is served by a one-floor mechanical ventilation system
    D. showroom space exceeds 2,500 square feet in area and is located more than 75 feet above curb level

11. In a building classified as occupancy group E, occupied or arranged to be occupied for an occupant load of more than one hundred persons above or below the street level or more than a total of five hundred persons in the entire building, a building evacuation supervisor performs his training activities under the direction of

    A. the battalion chief on duty
    B. the building fire safety director
    C. the building fire brigade supervisor
    D. someone other than any of the above

11.___

12. The one of the following which BEST identifies where a Class E fire alarm signal system will sound continuously upon operation of a manual station is only on the floor where

    A. actuated
    B. actuated and the floor above
    C. actuated and the next two floors above
    D. actuated, the floor above, and the floor below

12.___

13. The ONLY one of the following occupancies in which portable kerosene space heaters approved by the Board of Standards and Appeals may be used in the event of failure of the central heating unit is in

    A. private dwellings
    B. multiple dwellings
    C. places of public assembly
    D. schools

13.___

14. The one of the following which is NOT a requirement relating to oxygen and acetylene torch operations in a building under demolition is that there be

    A. one fire guard in the area of torch operation equipped with a 2 1/2" hose line
    B. one fire guard for each torch operator and an addi-tional fire guard on the floor or level below
    C. fire guards to make an inspection of the exposed area one half hour after completion of torch operations
    D. fire guards to make an inspection of the exposed area one hour after completion of torch operations

14.___

15. Upon responding to an alarm of fire in a building, an officer notes that the Siamese connections are painted yellow.
    This color coding indicates that

    A. the sprinkler system protects only showrooms located not over 40 feet above the curb line
    B. the standpipe riser is only four inches in size
    C. a floor control valve is provided for the sprinkler system on each floor
    D. the Siamese connection supplies a high-expansion foam system

15.___

16. The one of the following which does NOT correctly describe what can happen during manual operation of an elevator with the keyed switch in the *Fireman Service* position is that the

    A. doors will open on all floors but the fire floor
    B. direction of travel can be changed after a floor selection has been made

16.___

C. doors will open only in response to the *Door Open* button in the car
D. doors can be automatically reclosed while in the process of opening

17. The Building Code places restrictions on the suspension of new ceilings below existing suspended ceilings in construction group II in order to restrict the travel of fire in hidden spaces.
The one of the following requirements which BEST describes the nature of this restriction is that the

   A. concealed space shall be provided with firestops to divide the space into sections not exceeding 3,000 square feet each
   B. new ceiling shall be supported directly from the ceiling carrying channels and shall have no openings from the concealed space to the area below
   C. new ceiling shall be of non-combustible construction or have a flame spread rating of 25 or less, and a smoke developed rating of 50 or less
   D. existing ceiling shall be completely removed before the new ceiling is suspended

17.____

18. While inspecting a 125-foot-high factory building constructed in 1912 within 20 feet of an adjacent one-story fireproof garage 12 feet in height, an officer notices that the fire windows in the factory wall facing the garage are glazed with wireglass only to the fourth floor or 65-foot level. Windows above that level are 60 feet higher vertically than the roof of the garage and are glazed with inch plate glass lights 400 square inches in area.
The one of the following which is the PROPER conclusion for the officer to draw is that

   A. such windows comply with the State Labor Law
   B. a violation exists since all fire windows in the wall of a factory building facing any building within 30 feet must be glazed with wireglass
   C. a violation exists since the fire windows in all factory buildings erected before 1913 must have wireglass
   D. none of the fire windows in the factory wall need be wireglass if there are no openings in the garage wall facing it

18.____

19. An officer submits for review a referral report containing statements about the exterior screened stairway of a factory building he has recently inspected which he considers to be in violation of the State Labor Law.
Of the officer's observations listed below, the one that is NOT a violation of the State Labor Law is:

   A. No balcony connecting with the stairs at the fourth floor
   B. Door connecting with the balcony at the third floor opens inward
   C. Stair terminates in rear yard not communicating to a street
   D. Access to balcony at second floor via sliding door

19.____

20. A five story non-fireproof factory building erected in 1908 has an area on all floors of 900 square feet with two exits remote from each other on all floors, except for the fourth floor which is used entirely as a raw material storeroom. No one is regularly employed on that floor. For security reasons, the fourth floor has only one exit.
It would be CORRECT to say that, according to the State Labor Law,

   A. this arrangement is expressly forbidden, as every floor must have two exits
   B. one exit from the fourth floor would be acceptable provided it is protected by an automatic sprinkler system

20.____

C. the one exit from the fourth floor is acceptable provided it conforms to the criteria for a factory exit
D. one exit from the fourth floor is acceptable provided the longest distance to the exit from any point on the floor does not exceed 75 feet

21. Buildings which have been vacated by order of the fire department are kept under surveillance.
    When such buildings have been boarded up, surveillance may, with approval, be reduced to once each

    A. week
    B. month
    C. quarter-year
    D. half-year

22. Overly detailed fire prevention inspections are to be avoided CHIEFLY because they

    A. unduly interfere with the normal activities of the occupancy, causing public resentment
    B. require excessive time which could be used to better advantage inspecting other occupancies
    C. tend to result in oversight of some fundamental hazards
    D. are beyond the capabilities of many firemen who are not specifically trained in inspectional techniques

23. Requests for sprinkler re-evaluation are accepted by the fire department, and a re-inspection made, if the petitioner states that substantial changes have been made in the sprinkler system.
    The one of the following statements that is MOST accurate and complete is that such re-inspections are made by the division commander

    A. in all instances
    B. except when he has endorsed the original sprinkler order
    C. except when he has endorsed the original sprinkler order or when his workload is excessive
    D. except when he has endorsed the original sprinkler order, his workload is excessive, or the re-evaluation is extremely complex

24. Department regulations require the forwarding of reports to the Fire Commissioner relating to demolition work adjacent to or adjoining company quarters.
    The one of the following statements that is MOST accurate and complete is that such reports should be forwarded when notice of the proposed demolition is

    A. received
    B. received and when the work is completed
    C. received, when the work actually starts, and when the work is completed
    D. received, when the work actually starts, when any interruption of work occurs, and when the work is completed

25. The one of the following statements that is MOST complete and accurate is that when a building inspector issues a Violation Order, the time allowed for compliance

    A. must be the specific number of days indicated on the Standard Form of Orders
    B. may be less than the specific number of days indicated on the Standard Form of Orders

C. may be more than the specific number of days indicated on the Standard Form of Orders
D. may be more or less than the specific number of days indicated on the Standard Form of Orders, depending upon the circumstances

KEY (CORRECT ANSWERS)

1.	C	11.	B
2.	D	12.	B
3.	D	13.	D
4.	C	14.	A
5.	D	15.	C
6.	D	16.	A
7.	D	17.	D
8.	C	18.	A
9.	B	19.	D
10.	A	20.	C

21.	C
22.	B
23.	D
24.	A
25.	B

TEST 4

DIRECTIONS: Each question or incomplete statement is followed by several suggested answers or completions. Select the one that BEST answers the question or completes the statement. *PRINT THE LETTER OF THE CORRECT ANSWER IN THE SPACE AT THE RIGHT.*

1. Of the following substances, the one that would MOST appropriately be protected with a sprinkler installation is

    A. cellulose acetate
    B. quicklime
    C. magnesium powder
    D. calcium carbide

    1.___

2. Providing clearance around unprotected steel columns in storage occupancies is a practice which is GENERALLY

    A. *desirable,* chiefly because the quantity of combustibles stored is reduced
    B. *undesirable,* chiefly because flue-like conditions will prevail
    C. *desirable,* chiefly because it will allow water from sprinklers to keep the column wet
    D. *undesirable,* chiefly because stock can topple if not supported

    2.___

3. National fire records indicate that over the years restaurant fires have increased in number and in total dollar loss despite technological improvements.
   The large increase in the number of restaurant fires is PRIMARILY attributable to

    A. fires of incendiary origin
    B. duct fires
    C. the use of open flames for cooking
    D. careless handling of smoking materials

    3.___

4. When serving a summons for a violation of the Building Code, it is most important that proper procedure be followed.
   Of the following statements, the one that is MOST acceptable is that a summons may be

    A. mailed to the residence of the building's owner if he is not on the premises
    B. given to a superintendent to be forwarded to the owner if he is not on the premises
    C. placed on the desk or in the immediate vicinity of the owner if he refuses to accept it
    D. made out with the initials of the owner if the full name is not known

    4.___

5. A dry-pipe sprinkler system is generally not considered acceptable protection for an occupancy utilizing flammable liquids MAINLY because

    A. corrosion tends to weaken these systems
    B. water is a poor extinguishing agent for flammable liquids
    C. the systems are too expensive for the purpose
    D. a fast spreading fire may be out of control by the time water arrives

    5.___

6. In order to enforce the fire safety laws, firefighters must inspect buildings and stores.
   It is NOT a good idea for firefighters to let owners of buildings and stores know when they are coming because

    6.___

A. firefighters will waste valuable time if the owner breaks the appointment
B. owners might try to hide fire hazards from the fire-fighters
C. firefighters can make the inspection faster without an appointment
D. owners would be angry if the firefighters were unable to keep the appointment

7. Many older buildings are modernized to give a blank wall appearance by being *wrapped*. It is INACCURATE to state, with reference to *wrapped* buildings, that

   A. the use of expanded metal panels reduces the hazard from exposure fires
   B. they are essentially windowless buildings
   C. solid metal panels may be blown loose and scale a considerable distance
   D. expanded metal panels may be hung or mounted a foot or more from the original exterior wall

8. According to the Administrative Code, it is unlawful to manufacture within the city all of the following EXCEPT

   A. blank cartridges   B. railroad track torpedoes
   C. flashlight compositions   D. ship signal rockets

9. A newly appointed firefighter is assigned to go with an experienced firefighter to inspect a paint store. The paint store owner refuses to allow the inspection, saying that he is closing the store early that day and going on vacation. The new firefighter demands rudely that the inspection be allowed, even though it would be permissible to delay it.
Of the following, it would be BEST for the experienced firefighter to

   A. repeat the demand that the inspection be allowed and quote the law to the store owner
   B. tell the new firefighter that it would be best to schedule the inspection after the store owner's vacation
   C. tell the store owner to step aside, and instruct the new firefighter to enter the store and begin the inspection
   D. tell the new firefighter to forget about the inspection because the store owner is uncooperative

10. One person shall be permitted to supervise more than one interior fire alarm system. The one of the following that is NOT in accord with the restrictions placed on this permission is that

    A. the buildings in which the interior fire alarm systems are located must be within an area whose diameter does not exceed six hundred feet
    B. the interior fire alarms in all buildings in the group can be tested within thirty minutes of commencing work daily
    C. the addresses of all buildings shall be listed on the one certificate of fitness
    D. records and logbooks must be kept on each premises

11. The one of the following which is NOT in accord with the Regulations for Use of Halon 1301, Extinguishing Agent, is that

    A. maximum concentration shall not exceed 10 percent where human habitation is present in the volume to be flooded
    B. minimum concentration of FE 1301 used shall not be less than 10 percent

C. a discharge rate which results in attaining the design concentration in 8 seconds is acceptable
D. a central office connection must be provided for fire detection or systems operation where human habitation is present in the volume to be flooded

12. According to the Fire Prevention Code, a person who holds a permit for the manufacture of inflammable mixtures and who wishes to manufacture combustible mixtures is   12.___

    A. *required* to obtain another permit
    B. *not required* to obtain another permit
    C. *not required* to obtain another permit unless the mixtures include stove polishes or insecticides
    D. *not required* to obtain another permit unless the mixtures include medicinal and toilet preparations

13. The one of the following statements which is MOST accurate and complete is that the Fire Prevention Code permits the hanging of fresh-cut decorative greens in places of public assembly only if they do not contain   13.___

    A. pitch
    B. pitch and are hung by means of non-combustible material
    C. pitch, are hung by means of non-combustible material, and do not remain for a period in excess of 24 hours
    D. pitch, are hung by means of non-combustible material, have been treated with an approved evaporation-retarding product, and do not remain for a period in excess of 48 hours

14. In any automatic wet-pipe sprinkler system which has standard one-half inch sprinkler heads exposed to cold and subject to freezing, shut-off valves may be provided and the water supply discontinued   14.___

    A. under no circumstances
    B. from November 15 to March 15 when there are five or less such exposed heads
    C. from November 1 to April 1 when there are ten or less such exposed heads
    D. from November 15 to April 15 when there are fifteen or less such exposed heads

15. At an inspection of a building, one floor of which is used for combustible fiber storage, the following facts are revealed: 15.___
    I. The safe bearing capacity of the floor, as certified by the Department of Buildings, is 250 lbs./sq.ft. The weight of the combustible fiber is 75 lbs./sq.ft.
    II. The floor is 10,000 sq.ft. in area, of which 6,000 sq.ft. is occupied by the fiber bales.
    III. The height from floor to ceiling is 16', and the stacked bales stand 10' high.
    In this situation, _____ of the Fire Prevention Code.

    A. Item I is in   B. Item II is in
    C. Item III is in   D. there is no

16. Carelessness in smoking is a very common cause of fire.   16.___
    A lighted cigarette placed on top of most upholstery will GENERALLY

    A. cause no damage
    B. burn to the end without starting a fire

C. cause a gradually increasing fire
D. start a fire rapidly

17. The one of the following that is the type of automatic sprinkler system MOST commonly found in museums, art galleries, and storage places for records or valuable merchandise is the _____ system.

    A. deluge
    B. pre-action
    C. dry pipe
    D. sypho-chemical

17.____

18. The Fire Prevention Code requires that a permit be obtained for the storage of more than the equivalent of five barrels of oils and fats.
    The one of the following which is excluded from this requirement is

    A. lubricating oils
    B. grease
    C. edible oils
    D. soap stock

18.____

19. The Fire Prevention Code requires that rooms in dry cleaning establishments in which washing tanks are located be equipped with

    A. asbestos cloths or blankets
    B. carbon dioxide or dry chemical extinguishers
    C. buckets of sand
    D. automatic fire alarm device

19.____

20. The one of the following occupancies which is required to have a two-source water supply for its sprinkler system is one containing

    A. combustible fiber storage
    B. a motion picture film studio
    C. oils and fats storage
    D. a theater

20.____

21. The one of the following statements that is MOST accurate is that the Fire Prevention Code prohibits the storage of distilled liquors and alcohols in

    A. quantities aggregating more than 50 gallons, without a permit
    B. any building of wooden construction
    C. excess of one barrel for each five square feet of floor space
    D. barrels stacked more than one high

21.____

22. A special permit issued by the Fire Commissioner is required for the operation of certain businesses. Concerning parking lots, technical establishments, retail drug stores, and dry cleaning establishments, it is MOST accurate to say that special permits are required for all

    A. four of them
    B. of the above except parking lots
    C. of the above except technical establishments
    D. of the above except retail drug stores

22.____

23. The one of the following chemicals which may NOT be manufactured or stored in a drug and chemical supply house in any quantity is   23.___

    A. acetone
    B. benzole
    C. chloride of nitrogen
    D. metallic magnesium

24. A permit is required for the storage of empty wooden packing boxes in buildings if the quantity stored exceeds   24.___

    A. one ton
    B. 2,000 square feet of area
    C. 2,000 cubic feet of space
    D. one ton or 2,000 square feet of area, whichever is the smaller amount

25. The MAXIMUM number of excess liquefied petroleum gas cylinders that may be stored in a single structure protected by an approved dry sprinkler system is   25.___

    A. 25   B. 50   C. 75   D. 100

KEY (CORRECT ANSWERS)

1. A		11. B
2. C		12. B
3. A		13. C
4. C		14. C
5. D		15. D
6. B		16. B
7. A		17. B
8. D		18. C
9. B		19. A
10. C		20. B

21. B
22. A
23. C
24. C
25. B

EXAMINATION SECTION
TEST 1

DIRECTIONS: Each question or incomplete statement is followed by several suggested answers or completions. Select the one that BEST answers the question or completes the statement. *PRINT THE LETTER OF THE CORRECT ANSWER IN THE SPACE AT THE RIGHT.*

1. During an inspection of a plant which manufactures paper products, the officer observes completed work being placed in paper cartons. The cartons are then stacked on wooden skids in a separate storage area awaiting shipment.
   The one of the following which is generally the MOST appropriate evaluation of the practice described in this situation is that skids

   A. are highly combustible, adding much fuel to the fire
   B. permit excess air flow to fires
   C. minimize water damage losses by raising stock off the floor
   D. provide space under the stock, thus permitting fire to be more readily extinguished

2. Assume that a three-story, Class 3 non-fireproof building has been converted to two-family use. There is one stairway to the street, 2'8" wide. The doors to the apartments all swing in. There are no fire escapes.
   The one of the following statements that is MOST accurate is that the situation as described

   A. complies with all applicable laws
   B. is illegal because the stairs are too narrow
   C. is illegal because two means of egress are required
   D. is illegal because the doors do not swing in the direction of egress

3. The flammability limits of aviation fuels are of little significance in understanding their fire hazard properties CHIEFLY because the fuels

   A. have practically the same limits
   B. form flammable vapor-air mixtures at all temperatures
   C. ignite readily under tank failure conditions
   D. resist flashing to vapor when in the gelled form

4. An inspector enters a luncheonette and discovers that the owner, the only person on duty, apparently does not understand English.
   The one of the following which would be the BEST action for the inspector to take in this situation is to attempt to

   A. make the owner understand by speaking English in a loud, clear voice
   B. make the owner understand by using sign language
   C. find a customer or passerby who can act as an interpreter
   D. question the owner closely to determine whether he really does not understand English

5. For proper protection of low flash point flammable liquid processes, automatic sprinkler protection with a strong water supply is essential.
   The BEST justification of this statement is that

47

A. a sprinkler system with a strong water supply will extinguish most fires involving such processes
B. water from sprinklers will reduce the intensity of burning of the liquid and the danger to exposures
C. although the sprinklers are ineffective on flammable liquid fires, they provide protection in the event of other types of fires
D. water from the sprinklers will dilute the flammable liquid and make extinguishment easier

6. According to the regulations, company commanders shall cause a thorough inspection of all schools within their administrative district.
Such inspections shall be made

    A. annually
    B. semi-annually
    C. at the beginning of each school term
    D. within 60 days after school opens for the fall term

7. While inspecting a garage, a fire inspector notices that a garage license has not been issued for the premises by the Department of Licenses.
The inspector should

    A. discontinue his inspection pending a determination by the Department of Licenses of the allowable motor vehicle occupancy
    B. complete his inspection and forward it (including a statement of the allowable motor vehicle occupancy) with a request that a copy be sent to the Department of Licenses
    C. discontinue his inspection and request that a communication (inquiry form) be sent to the Department of Licenses asking for an explanation
    D. complete his inspection and forward it with a request that the Department of Licenses be asked to determine the allowable motor vehicle occupancy

Questions 8-11.

DIRECTIONS: Questions 8 through 11 are to be answered on the basis of the information given in the following paragraph.

The principal value of inspection work is in the knowledge obtained relating to the various structural features of the building and the protective features provided. Knowledge of the location of stairways and elevators, the obstruction provided by merchandise, the danger from absorption of water by baled stock, the potential hazard of rupture of containers such as drums or cylinders, and the location of protective equipment, all are essential features to be noted and later discussed in company school and officer's college.

8. According to the above paragraph, the CHIEF value of inspection work is to gather information which will aid in

    A. fixing responsibility for fires
    B. planning firefighting operations
    C. training new firemen
    D. obtaining compliance with the Building Code

9. The one of the following objects which would be the MOST help in accomplishing the objective of the inspection as stated in the above paragraph is a

    A. copy of the Building Code
    B. chemical analysis kit
    C. plan of the building
    D. list of the building's tenants

10. An example of a *structural feature* contained in the above paragraph is the

    A. location of stairways and elevators
    B. obstruction provided by merchandise
    C. danger of absorption of water by baled stock
    D. hazard of rupture of containers such as drums or cylinders

11. Of the following, the BEST example of what is meant by a *protective feature,* as used in the above paragraph, is

    A. a fire extinguisher   B. a burglar alarm
    C. fire insurance   D. a medical first-aid kit

12. When a violation order is to be served and the owner or person in charge of the premises cannot readily be located, every effort shall be made to serve such order. Of the following statements concerning the attempts to serve such an order, the one that is NOT correct is:

    A. Attempt to ascertain from occupants or people in the area the name and address of the owner or management
    B. Send a member to effect service if the owner or management is located in the city but out of the company district
    C. Make an appointment by telephone for service of the order
    D. Post the violation notice prominently in or on the premises and mail a copy to the owner or management

13. Every applicant for a certificate of license to install underground gasoline storage tanks is required to

    A. be a resident of the city and maintain a place of business in the city
    B. file a bond and evidence of liability insurance
    C. be a resident of the city or maintain a place of business in the city
    D. pass a written examination given by the fire department

14. The Fire Prevention Code specifies that a special permit is required for each of the following EXCEPT

    A. refining petroleum collected from oil separators or manufacturing plants
    B. loading of small arms ammunition by hand in a retail store selling ammunition
    C. operating a wholesale drug or chemical house
    D. generating acetylene gas

15. The one of the following that is the MOST acceptable statement concerning the fire protection for the truck loading rack in a bulk oil terminal is that the rack must be equipped with a

A. water spray system, automatically controlled
B. foam system, remote manually controlled
C. water spray system, remote manually controlled
D. foam system, automatically controlled

16. The one of the following which is NOT in accord with the regulations for the use of Halon 1301, extinguishing agent, is that

    A. maximum concentration shall not exceed 10 percent where human habitation is present in the volume to be flooded
    B. minimum concentration of FE 1301 used shall not be less than 10 percent
    C. a discharge rate which results in attaining the design concentration in 8 seconds is acceptable
    D. a central office connection must be provided for fire detection or systems operating where human habitation is present in the volume to be flooded

17. Members of the uniformed force are authorized to issue summonses where fire perils exist, although it is generally preferable to first issue a violation order to correct the illegal condition.
However, members must issue a summons immediately in a licensed place of public assembly upon noting

    A. an obstructed revolving exit door in a crowded cabaret
    B. the absence of a certified standpipe system operator in a theatre
    C. an inoperative fire extinguishing system in a restaurant cooking duct
    D. standees in a motion picture theatre

18. During the course of an inspection at a blasting site, an officer notes that the magazine has been provided with electrical security devices, and that it contains eight 10-pound cartons of explosives which are to be stored overnight, overhead wires run from the magazine to the watchman's shanty, and the driller, without a C. of F., loads holes under the direct supervision of the blaster. The condition as described is generally ILLEGAL because

    A. explosives must be in original and unbroken packages of 50 or 25 pound capacity only
    B. storage of explosives between the hours of 10 P.M. and 6 A.M. is prohibited
    C. all electrical wiring must be protected by heavy wall conduit and be buried at least 12 inches deep
    D. no person may load holes in blasting operations unless they hold a certificate of fitness

19. The one of the following that is LEAST in accord with the regulations for the use of Halon 1301 extinguishing agent systems is that

    A. these systems are limited to applications as automatic total flooding systems for interior Class B and C fires and Class A fires that are not deep-seated
    B. abort systems are permitted for smoke detector activated systems which provide the manual capacity to *dump* the Halon 1301 immediately
    C. actuation of only one products-of-combustion device will fail to initiate the *dump* of Halon 1301 but will actuate the local and central office company alarms
    D. concentrations used shall not exceed 10 percent in areas where human habitation is present in the volume to be flooded

20. Interstate transportation of petroleum products into and through the city in tank trucks which do NOT conform to fire department requirements is GENERALLY

    A. *not permitted* even when the pickups are all made outside the city and no pickups are made in the city
    B. *permitted* without restriction if the vehicles comply with United States Department of Transportation regulations governing interstate commerce
    C. *not permitted* where deliveries are to be made in the city
    D. *permitted* during non-business hours, along regularly established commercial routes

21. Of the following occupancies constructed and occupied in 1962, each of which accommodates less than 300 persons, the one that CANNOT be described as a *place of assembly*, according to the applicable building code, is a

    A. college assembly hall
    B. motion picture theatre
    C. courtroom
    D. legitimate theatre

22. According to the labor law, the one of the following conditions that is generally considered to be LEGAL in a 5-story building constructed and occupied as a factory since 1911 is that

    A. a single means of egress is provided from a floor of 2500 sq.ft. or less where no person is regularly employed
    B. no point on the upper floor which is equipped with an approved sprinkler system is more than 200 feet distant from an exit
    C. one of the two required stairways extends to the roof from which there is egress to an adjacent building
    D. there are double swinging doors leading to an exit on an upper floor where more than 5 persons are employed

23. Certain old factory buildings may be found to have some fire escapes which are not in accordance with the requirements of the labor law.
    It is generally CORRECT to state of these substandard factory exits that they

    A. may be used in computing occupancy exit requirements if maintained in good repair and the building is equipped with an automatic sprinkler
    B. must be provided with a counterbalanced stairway in lieu of the former drop ladder in guides
    C. shall be kept clear of all obstructions and periodically used during required fire drills
    D. may not be equipped with any exit or directional sign at the openings leading thereto

24. According to the labor law, the use of plate glass in fire windows in fireproof buildings is

    A. *prohibited,* except in buildings less than 75 feet in height
    B. *permitted,* if the fire windows are located more than 30 feet horizontally from the nearest opening in the wall of another building
    C. *prohibited* for use in all fire windows in fireproof buildings
    D. *permitted* if the fire windows are more than 30 feet above the roof of a building within a horizontal distance of 25 feet

25. Under certain conditions, a newsstand may be located in a street floor lobby which serves as an exit passageway for a building constructed after 1976.
The one of the following which is NOT one of these conditions is that the newsstand must

    A. occupy no more than 100 square feet or 5 percent of the net floor area of the lobby, whichever is greater
    B. not reduce the clear width of the lobby at any point
    C. be located at least 30 feet from an exit door
    D. be protected by at least 2 automatic sprinkler heads if constructed of combustible material

---

KEY (CORRECT ANSWERS)

1.	C	11.	A
2.	A	12.	D
3.	C	13.	C
4.	C	14.	D
5.	B	15.	C
6.	A	16.	B
7.	D	17.	C
8.	B	18.	D
9.	C	19.	D
10.	A	20.	D

21.	C
22.	B
23.	A
24.	B
25.	B

TEST 2

DIRECTIONS: Each question or incomplete statement is followed by several suggested answers or completions. Select the one that BEST answers the question or completes the statement. *PRINT THE LETTER OF THE CORRECT ANSWER IN THE SPACE AT THE RIGHT.*

1. Suppose that a factory has stored within it a number of substances. 1.____
   If the owner asked you which of the following is MOST likely to constitute a fire hazard, you would reply

   A. sodium chloride
   B. calcium chloride
   C. chromium
   D. silicon dioxide

2. Vertical openings, such as dumbwaiters, elevators, and chutes, are the bane of a fire- 2.____
   fighting force.
   This condition arises MAINLY because the existence of such openings in a burning building facilitates

   A. accidental falls
   B. generation of gases
   C. spread of the fire
   D. the perpetration of arson

3. Suppose that a neighbor were to ask you whether there is more hazard in the use of ker- 3.____
   osene than gasoline at ordinary room temperature.
   You should reply that there is MORE hazard in the use of

   A. *kerosene,* because it gives off dangerous quantities of explosive vapors which are lighter than air
   B. *gasoline,* because gasoline vapor may flow along the floor and be ignited at a long distance from its point of origin
   C. *kerosene,* because its flash point is very low
   D. *gasoline,* particularly because when ignited it burns

4. Steel supporting beams in buildings often are surrounded by a thin layer of concrete to 4.____
   keep the beams from becoming hot and collapsing during a fire.
   The one of the following statements which BEST explains how collapse is prevented by this arrangement is that concrete

   A. becomes stronger as its temperature is increased
   B. acts as an insulating material
   C. protects the beam from rust and corrosion
   D. reacts chemically with steel at high temperatures

5. It has been suggested that property owners should be charged a fee each time the Fire 5.____
   Department is called to extinguish a fire on their property.
   Of the following, the BEST reason for *rejecting* this proposal is that

   A. delay in calling the Fire Department may result
   B. many property owners don't occupy the property they own
   C. property owners may resent such a charge as they pay real estate taxes
   D. it may be difficult to determine on whose property a fire started

6. An officer inspecting buildings in a commercial area came to one whose outside surface appeared to be of natural stone. The owner told the officer that it was not necessary to inspect his building as it was *fireproof*. The officer, however, completed his inspection of the building.
Of the following, the BEST reason for continuing the inspection is that

   A. stone buildings catch fire as readily as wooden buildings
   B. the Fire Department cannot make exceptions in its inspection procedures
   C. the building may have been built of imitation stone
   D. interiors and contents of stone buildings can catch fire

7. From the viewpoint of fire safety, the CHIEF advantage of a foam rubber mattress compared to a cotton mattress is that the foam rubber mattress

   A. is slower burning
   B. generates less heat when burning
   C. does not smolder
   D. is less subject to water damage

8. At a social gathering, a fire chief hears a man who describes himself as the owner of the XYZ factory state that he *pays off* fire department inspectors who visit his establishment. When the chief asks the man whether he will repeat his statement under oath, the man refuses with the remark, *I am not looking for trouble.*
In this situation, the chief should

   A. forget the incident since the factory owner is not willing to give evidence
   B. investigate the background and reputation of the man to determine whether he really owns the factory and has any reason for making false statements about the fire department
   C. report the incident to police authorities
   D. report the incident to higher authorities in the fire department

9. The one of the following methods of storing large piles of coal which is undesirable because it increases the danger of spontaneous heating is

   A. making the pile compact by use of a roller
   B. storing the coal on smooth, solid ground
   C. covering the sides and top of the pile with road tar
   D. mixing coal of various sizes in one pile

10. The one of the following materials which has the LEAST tendency to spontaneous heating is

    A. baled hides   B. bagged charcoal
    C. bulk fish scrap   D. boxed mineral wool

11. In most buildings in which lighting is provided by artificial means and an auxiliary system for emergency exit lighting is not provided, phosphorescent exit and directional signs are required.
Of the following occupancies, the one which is generally EXCLUDED from this requirement is a

    A. warehouse   B. school dormitory
    C. hospital   D. library

12. In determining overcrowding or adequacy of means of egress, a fire officer must be aware that the minimum number of persons to be provided for in any floor area shall be the number which can be accommodated within the net floor area at a given occupancy and area per person.
Accordingly, the GREATEST concentration of persons to be provided for will be generally found in a

    A. basement sales area
    B. high school classroom
    C. dance hall
    D. work room

13. Of the following statements, the one that is generally ACCURATE concerning the installation of combustible luminous suspended ceilings is that they may

    A. not be installed below an existing suspended ceiling
    B. be installed below existing sprinkler heads
    C. not be used in any room in occupancy group F (assembly)
    D. be installed in corridors not exceeding 100 sq.ft.

14. The building code exempts from the sprinkler requirements those floors which are generally unventilated but are equipped with a given openable area.
A fixed window will be considered openable if it is

    A. equipped with an interior heat sensitive device to actuate the automatic fire shutters
    B. of frangible glass panels and located 15 feet below grade
    C. within 8 feet of an openable window of at least 3 feet x 3 feet dimension
    D. readily broken and not more than 110 feet above grade

15. Of the following, the MOST complete and accurate statement about exit requirements is that there shall be at least two door openings, remote from each other and leading to exits from every room or enclosed space, in a business occupancy (E) in which the total occupant load *exceeds*

    A. 25   B. 50   C. 75   D. 100

16. On October 23, 1976, 25 persons died and many were injured as a result of an arson fire in an illegal social club in the Bronx.
Of the following, the MOST probable contributory cause of this multiple loss of life was the

    A. door to the club was not self-closing and was opened in the direction of egress when the fire occurred
    B. front windows had been bricked-up and prevented access by department ladders
    C. confusing layout caused many patrons to bypass the secondary means of egress and become trapped in the toilet rooms
    D. original lath and plaster had been replaced by combustible wood paneling and there had been an extensive use of highly flammable decorations

17. It is INCORRECT for a fire officer giving training on the protection of electronic data processing (EDP) units and ancillary equipment against fire damage to state that

A. the design features of EDP units make them relatively resistant to damage by temperatures under 600° F
B. smoke and acids produced by fire can adversely affect the operation of computer equipment and magnetic components
C. the heat and steam produced by a fire and its extinguishment that would not normally damage ordinary paper records may easily damage magnetic tapes
D. in cases where fire can spread throughout or beyond the computer's housing, a fixed CO_2 system may be required

18. Of the following exit and access requirements relating to dead-end corridors in various occupancy group buildings, it is generally MOST accurate to state that

A. no more than one classroom shall be permitted on a dead-end corridor in an educational occupancy
B. storage of combustible materials in non-combustible lockers is permitted in dead-end corridors in an institutional occupancy
C. dead-end corridors are not permitted in an assembly occupancy
D. no more than one patient bedroom is permitted in a dead-end corridor in an institutional occupancy

19. In the past, building marquee collapses have resulted in the injury or death of firefighters. According to the new building code, marquees are generally

A. not permitted
B. permitted if supported by incombustible piers at the curb line
C. not permitted to project beyond the street line
D. permitted on buildings of a public nature but may have to be removed if the building occupancy is changed

20. When a standpipe system is altered, extended, or extensively repaired, it must undergo certain inspections and tests.
Of the following, it is generally MOST accurate to state that the

A. entire system shall be subjected to the hydrostatic test pressure
B. altered, new or repaired section shall be subjected to the pressure test and the entire system subjected to the flow test
C. flow test shall be confined to a determination that water is available at the top outlet of each riser
D. pressure test in buildings not exceeding 3 stories or 40 feet in height need only sustain 150 percent of the normal hydrostatic pressure at the topmost hose outlet

21. A substance which is subject to *spontaneous combustion* is one that

A. is explosive when heated
B. is capable of catching fire without an external source of heat
C. acts to speed up the burning of material
D. liberates oxygen when heated

Questions 22-25.

DIRECTIONS: Questions 22 through 25 are to be answered on the basis of the following paragraph.

For the five-year period 2006-2010, inclusive, the average annual fire loss in the United States amounted to approximately $1,354,830,000. Included in this estimate is $1,072,666,000 damage to buildings and contents, and $282,164,000 average annual loss in aircraft, motor vehicles, forest and other miscellaneous fires not involving buildings. Preliminary estimates indicate that the total United States fire loss in 2011 was $1,615,000,000. These are property damage fire losses only and do not include indirect losses resulting from fires which are just as real and sometimes far more serious than property damage losses. But because evaluation of indirect monetary losses is usually very difficult, their importance in the national fire waste picture is often overlooked.

22. According to the data in the above paragraph, the BEST of the following estimates of the total direct fire loss in the United States for the six-year period 2006-2011, inclusive, is

    A. $1,400,000,000
    B. $2,700,000,000
    C. $7,000,000,000
    D. $8,400,000,000

23. The BEST example of an indirect fire loss, as that term is used in the above paragraph, is monetary loss due to

    A. smoke or water damage to exposures
    B. condemnation of foodstuffs following a fire
    C. interruption of business following a fire
    D. forcible entry by firemen operating at a fire

24. Suppose that during the period 2011-2015 the average annual fire loss to buildings and contents increases 10 percent, and the average annual loss due to fires not involving buildings decreases 10 percent. The MOST valid of the following conclusions is that the average annual fire loss for the 2011-2015 period, compared to the losses for the 2006-2011 period,

    A. will increase
    B. will decrease
    C. will be unchanged
    D. cannot be calculated from the information given

25. If a comparison is made between total annual direct and indirect fire losses on the basis of the information given in the above paragraph, the MOST valid of the following conclusions is that

    A. generally, direct losses are higher
    B. generally, indirect losses are higher
    C. generally, direct and indirect losses are approximately equal
    D. there is not sufficient information to determine which is higher or if they are approximately equal

KEY (CORRECT ANSWERS)

1. D
2. C
3. B
4. B
5. A

6. D
7. C
8. D
9. D
10. D

11. D
12. A
13. C
14. A
15. D

16. A
17. C
18. A
19. D
20. C

21. B
22. D
23. C
24. A
25. D

TEST 3

DIRECTIONS: Each question or incomplete statement is followed by several suggested answers or completions. Select the one that BEST answers the question or completes the statement. *PRINT THE LETTER OF THE CORRECT ANSWER IN THE SPACE AT THE RIGHT.*

1. It has been suggested that companies be given additional Apparatus Field Inspection Duty and other inspectional duties as punishment for poor performance of evolutions, poor condition of equipment or quarters, etc.
   Of the following, the MOST valid objection to this proposal is that

   A. the punishment does not directly improve the skills or functions which are found to be deficient
   B. inspectional activities would be degraded by making such assignments a form of punishment
   C. the punishment is imposed on a group rather than on an individual basis
   D. scheduling of regular inspectional activities would be disrupted

   1.____

2. The Administrative Code authorizes members to issue summonses in cases arising under laws relating to fires and to fire peril.
   Departmental regulations require that such summonses be returnable in the appropriate court _____ than 14 calendar days, _____ Sundays and holidays.

   A. not less; including   B. not less; excluding
   C. not more; including   D. not more; excluding

   2.____

3. When conducting an Apparatus Field Inspection of an occupancy with a required and approved sprinkler system, it is MOST important, of the following, for firemen to make certain that

   A. feeder lines are adequate to supply the number of sprinkler heads
   B. sprinkler heads are sufficient and properly spaced
   C. stock does not interfere with the proper distribution of water from sprinkler heads
   D. records of monthly hydrostatic pressure tests are properly kept and are up to date

   3.____

4. While inspecting an above-ground storage tank installation, an inspector notices leakage of the contents through *weep* holes in a tank.
   This is a sign that the

   A. tank contents are under excessive pressure
   B. strength of the entire tank may be endangered by corrosion
   C. volumetric capacity of the tank has been exceeded
   D. tank is *breathing* as intended

   4.____

5. A member on inspectional duty came across, in a building under construction, a propane gas heater with its safety valve negated by means of wire and tape across the buttons at the top of the safety assembly.
   Of the following actions taken by the member in this situation, the one that is NOT in accord with departmental orders is the

   5.____

59

A. serving of a violation order to discontinue use of devices to negate safety features on propane gas heaters on premises
B. picking up of the permits for storage and use of propane
C. notification of the Battalion Chief of the administrative district concerned
D. impounding of the propane heater

6. Of the following, the PRIMARY purpose of holding fire tests at a high-rise office building is to

    A. determine the hazard of polyurethane insulation
    B. evaluate the effectiveness of sprinklers with a limited water supply
    C. test the effectiveness of stair pressurization
    D. develop procedures for venting the fire floor by window vents

7. At the first sign of a fire, the manager of a motion picture theatre had the lights turned on and made the following announcement: *Ladies and gentlemen, the management has found it necessary to dismiss the audience. Please remain seated until it is time for your aisle to file out. In leaving the theatre, follow the directions of the ushers. There is no danger involved.*
The manager's action in this situation was

    A. *proper*
    B. *improper,* chiefly because he did not tell the audience the reason for the dismissal
    C. *improper,* chiefly because he did not permit all members of the audience to leave at once
    D. *improper,* chiefly because he misled the audience by saying that there was no danger

8. Generally, sprinkler heads must be replaced each time they are used.
The BEST explanation of why this is necessary is that the sprinkler heads

    A. are subject to rusting after discharging water
    B. may become clogged after discharging water
    C. have a distorted pattern of discharge of water after use
    D. are set off by the effect of heat on metal and cannot be reset

9. A fire insurance inspector suggested to the manager of a fireproof warehouse that bags of flour be stacked on skids (wooden platforms 6" high, 6x6 feet in area). Of the following, the BEST justification for this suggestion is that in the event of a fire, the bags on skids are less likely to

    A. topple
    B. be damaged by water used in extinguishment
    C. catch fire
    D. be ripped by fire equipment

10. Permitting piles of scrap paper cuttings to accumulate in a factory building is a bad practice CHIEFLY because they may

    A. ignite spontaneously
    B. interfere with fire extinguishment operations
    C. catch fire from a spark or smoldering match
    D. interfere with escape of occupants if a fire occurs

11. High grass and weeds should not be permitted to grow near a building CHIEFLY because, in the event of a grass fire, the weeds and grass may

    A. give off toxic fumes
    B. limit maneuverability of firemen
    C. interfere with the escape of occupants from the building
    D. bring the fire to the building and set it on fire

12. Visitors near patients in *oxygen tents* are not permitted to smoke.
    The BEST of the following reasons for this prohibition is that

    A. the flame of the cigarette or cigar may flare dangerously
    B. smoking tobacco is irritating to persons with respiratory disease
    C. smoking in bed is one of the major causes of fires
    D. diseases may be transmitted by means of tobacco smoke

13. A MAJOR difference between the building code currently in effect and the one in effect prior to it is that in the current code

    A. doors to the outside grade must be the same size as corridor doors
    B. sprinklering of a building will permit a reduction in total door width
    C. the width of an exit door is based on the width of the corridor leading to it
    D. the width of exit doors is based on both the number of persons and the type of occupancy

14. While inspecting a one-story factory building erected in 1962, you notice that an exit door has been relocated. The size, location, and lighting of all exits in the building comply with the old building code in effect before.
    To determine whether the relocated exit is a legal one, it is necessary to check the provisions of

    A. the State Labor Law and the new building code for the relocated exit *only*
    B. the State Labor Law *only*
    C. the new building code for the relocated exit *only*
    D. none of the foregoing since checking the old building code is sufficient

15. The new building code divides the construction clauses into two major construction groups.
    These two groups are called

    A. fireproof and non-fireproof
    B. rigid frame and flexible frame
    C. commercial and residential
    D. combustible and noncombustible

16. The State Labor Law requires that the balconies and stairways of outside fire escapes be able to safely sustain a live load, in pounds per square foot, of _____ with a safety factor of _____.

    A. 75; two   B. 90; four   C. 105; two   D. 120; four

17. A plant manufacturing nitro-cellulose products has 100 employees. The Fire Prevention Code requires that these premises be equipped with fire pails filled with water. The required MINIMUM number of such pails must be

    A. 25   B. 50   C. 75   D. 100

18. The MAIN purpose of an oil separator is to

    A. separate volatile inflammable oils from other oils
    B. provide a fireproof block between a spark or flame device and an oil storage tank
    C. prevent volatile inflammable oils from flowing into a sewer
    D. make it impossible for the wrong kind of oil to be delivered from a bulk storage plant

19. The MAXIMUM quantity of fuel oil permitted to be stored in an exposed tank in the cellar of a two-family dwelling is _____ gallons.

    A. 225   B. 550   C. 750   D. 875

20. According to the Fire Prevention Code, the MAXIMUM quantity of paint (other than water base) that may be stored without a permit is _____ gallons.

    A. 10   B. 15   C. 20   D. 25

21. Of the following licenses, certificates of qualification, or certificates of fitness, the Fire Department does NOT issue the one authorizing the holder to

    A. operate refrigerating machines (unlimited capacity)
    B. install underground storage tanks for gasoline
    C. operate low pressure boilers using #6 oil
    D. install oil burning equipment

22. In the course of your work in a residential area, you see a wood frame, brick veneer dwelling, two-stories and attic in height, erected in 1965. The building is occupied by two families, with a living room in the attic.
    Without special approval by the Board of Standards and Appeals, this condition could

    A. not be legal
    B. be legal provided that there is a fire escape from the attic
    C. be legal provided the stair enclosure is properly fire retarded
    D. be legal provided that the attic living room is not used as a bedroom

23. A typical occupancy falling into the Assembly occupancy group as used in the building code would be a

    A. radio station   B. library
    C. nursing home   D. tavern

24. Of the following situations, the one in which a fire escape may NOT be considered a legal means of egress is in a three-story

    A. factory building erected in 1912
    B. mixed occupancy building with a store on the first floor and one family on each of the floors above, erected in 1965
    C. multiple dwelling erected in 1971
    D. office building erected in 1950 and altered in 1972

25. A storage garage is one that has 25.____
    A. a stock room for repair parts for vehicles
    B. an area for vehicles that are not used on a daily basis
    C. a gasoline tank to supply gasoline to the vehicles
    D. room only for vehicles that are to be sold

KEY (CORRECT ANSWERS)

1.	B	11.	D
2.	A	12.	A
3.	C	13.	D
4.	B	14.	B
5.	A	15.	D
6.	C	16.	B
7.	A	17.	B
8.	D	18.	C
9.	B	19.	B
10.	C	20.	C

21. D
22. A
23. D
24. C
25. C

TEST 4

DIRECTIONS: Each question or incomplete statement is followed by several suggested answers or completions. Select the one that BEST answers the question or completes the statement. *PRINT THE LETTER OF THE CORRECT ANSWER IN THE SPACE AT THE RIGHT.*

1. A violation order is to be served requiring the immediate removal of liquefied petroleum gas cylinders when such cylinders are found on construction sites without a permit issued by the Fire Department.
Pending removal of such cylinders,

   A. vacate procedures are to be instituted
   B. a fireman is to be detailed to the site to safeguard the illegally stored gas cylinders
   C. the contractor is to be ordered to provide a watchman to safeguard the illegally stored gas cylinders
   D. the Police Department is to be notified so that a patrolman can be assigned to the site to safeguard the illegally stored gas cylinders

   1.___

2. A four-story loft building is now occupied as follows: Street level - furniture repair and refinishing shop; 2nd story - one apartment occupied by an artist-in-residence, wife, and 5 young children; 3rd story - two apartments each occupied by an artist-in-residence and his wife; 4th story - one apartment occupied by an artist-in-residence, his wife, and his mother-in-law. The building is non-fireproof construction, 40' x 70', is 50' in height, and has an automatic wet sprinkler system protecting the furniture shop. The occupancy as described is

   A. *legal*
   B. *illegal,* because the sprinkler system does not extend throughout the building
   C. *illegal,* because the number of occupants exceeds the permissible limits
   D. *illegal,* because of the presence of the furniture repair and refinishing shop

   2.___

3. Some organizations have adopted the National Fire Protection Association diamond-shaped coding system for identifying characteristics of hazardous materials. The diamond shown in the diagram at the right has its boxes labeled W, X, Y, and Z.
Under the National Fire Protection Association coding system, the lettered boxes represent, respectively,

   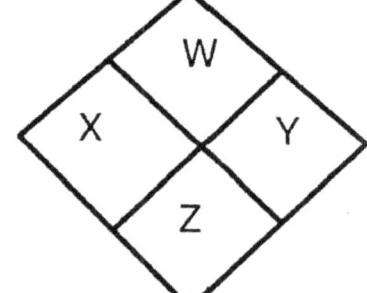

   A. X - Health, Y - Reactive, W - Flammable
   B. X - Reactive, Y - Flammable, W - Health
   C. X - Health, Y - Reactive, Z - Flammable
   D. X - Flammable, Y - Health, Z - Reactive

   3.___

4. The shut sprinkler control valve is one of industry's greatest fire hazards. When it is necessary to shut down a system for repairs or other reasons, certain precautions should be taken.
Of the following statements regarding such precautions, the LEAST acceptable is to

   A. have the system shut down during non-working hours
   B. have the system shut down during working hours while normal operations are going on
   C. notify the Fire Department of the intended shutdown
   D. prepare to supply the system through the two-inch drain in the event of an emergency or fire

Questions 5-8.

DIRECTIONS: Questions 5 through 8 are to be answered on the basis of the information given in the following paragraph.

A mixture of a combustible vapor and air will burn only when the proportion of fuel to air lies within a certain range, i.e., between the upper and lower limits of flammability. If a third, non-combustible gas is now added to the mixture, the limits will be narrowed. As increasing amounts of diluent are added, the limits come closer until, at a certain critical concentration, they will converge. This is the peak concentration. It is the minimum amount of diluent that will inhibit the combustion of any fuel-air mixture.

5. If additional diluent is added beyond the peak concentration, the flammable limits of the mixture will

   A. converge rapidly
   B. diverge slowly
   C. diverge rapidly
   D. not be affected

6. If the four numbers listed below were peak concentration values obtained in a test of four diluents, then the MOST efficient diluent would have the value of

   A. 7.5   B. 10   C. 12.5   D. 15

7. The word *inhibit,* as used in the last sentence of the above paragraph, means MOST NEARLY

   A. slow the rate of
   B. prevent entirely the occurrence of
   C. reduce the intensity of
   D. retard to an appreciable extent the manifestation of

8. The one of the graphs shown below which BEST represents the process described in the paragraph is

A.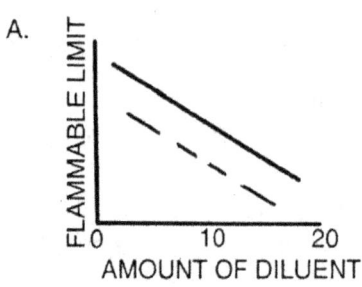
B.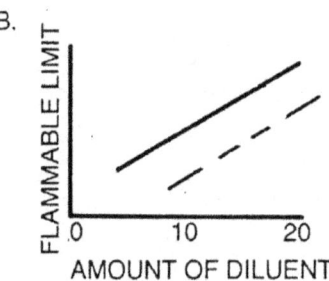
C.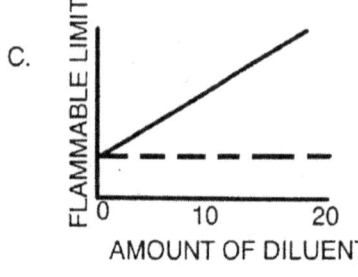
D.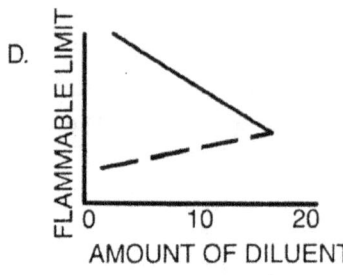

——————— UPPER FLAMMABLE LIMITS

— — — — — — LOWER FLAMMABLE LIMITS

9. Of the following metals, the one which is LEAST acceptable as a non-sparking metal for tools is

   A. hardened copper
   B. bronze
   C. brass
   D. copper alloys

10. Of the heating defects responsible for hotel fires, the MAJOR defect is

    A. defective flues
    B. overheated appliances
    C. defective appliances
    D. inadequate clearance

11. Community relations and fire prevention education efforts must be concentrated in residential neighborhoods, particularly in the depressed areas of the city.
    The one of the following which does NOT provide support for this point of view is that

    A. residential occupants are exposed to more serious occupancy hazards than industrial workers
    B. open hydrants, excessive false alarms, and hostile acts are concentrated in depressed areas
    C. rubbish fires and vacant building fires are most frequent in these areas
    D. the primary incidence of fire takes place in residential areas

12. The State Multiple Dwelling Law allows a *family* to have four boarders, and the City Multiple Dwelling Law allows a *family* to have only two boarders.
    In the city, a *family* is allowed

A. two boarders because the Multiple Dwelling Code is the more restrictive requirement
B. four boarders because the State law takes precedence over the city code
C. two or four boarders, depending upon whether the Law or Code applies to a given situation
D. two or four boarders, at the discretion of the Fire Commissioner

13. Fire Department regulations governing the issuance of city-wide permits for the use of combustible gases during temporary torch operations require fire guards to make inspections after completion of torch operations for the purpose of detecting fire. Signed inspection reports are to be filed and available for examination by the Fire Department.
The one of the following which is MOST accurate and complete is that such inspections are to be made _____ after completion of operations.

   A. every 15 minutes, for a period of one hour,
   B. one-half hour and one hour
   C. every half hour, for a period of two hours,
   D. one half hour, one hour, and two hours,

14. On an A.F.I.D., a company comes upon the following garages:
   I. Adjacent to a dwelling occupied by one family, storing two cars, one owned by the family and the other by the next door neighbor who pays a monthly rental
   II. In a dwelling outside the fire limits, occupied by one family storing three cars owned by the family
   III. In a fireproof dwelling occupied by three families in two stories above the garage, with two means of egress and no entrances to any apartment through the garage, storing two cars owned by tenants

   A Fire Department permit is required for

   A. none of these garages   B. garages I and III
   C. garages II and III   D. all three garages

15. If a building is altered under the provisions of the building code, and the building is not provided with sprinkler protection, the one of the following actions that the company officer should take is to

   A. transmit an A-8 report for referral to the Department of Buildings
   B. issue a summons to the owner of the building
   C. prepare a report on Department letterhead and send it to the Division of Fire Prevention
   D. call the Department of Buildings and notify them about the violation

16. The one of the following fibers that can be made into fabric which can be effectively treated with common water-soluble-salt flame-retardant solutions is

   A. dacron   B. nylon   C. rayon   D. nomex

17. The inspection of public assembly occupancies classified as theatres in company administrative districts should be scheduled so that each such premises is inspected AT LEAST once every

   A. 30 days, approximately one half hour before scheduled performances
   B. 30 days, at irregular time periods when premises are open to the public

C. three months, approximately one half hour before scheduled performances
D. three months, at irregular time periods when premises are open to the public

18. The one of the following automatic fire alarm detectors that works on the principle of uneven expansion of bi-metallic strips is the _____ device.

    A. rate compensation
    B. ionization type
    C. rate of rise type
    D. fixed temperature

19. The one of the following which is probably the MOST frequent source of ignition of flammable vapors in hospital operating rooms is

    A. static electricity
    B. x-ray equipment
    C. sterilizing machinery
    D. electric cauterizing devices

20. At an open demonstration, polyurethane foam, widely used in furniture, was exposed to fire.
    In this demonstration, it was shown that the foam

    A. was self-extinguishing
    B. flamed and gave off acrid smoke
    C. could not be ignited
    D. melted but would not flame

Questions 21-23.

DIRECTIONS: Questions 21 through 23 are to be answered on the basis of the following paragraph.

Shafts extending into the top story, except those stair shafts where the stairs do not continue to the roof, shall be carried through and at least two feet above the roof. Every shaft extending above the roof, except open shafts and elevator shafts, shall be enclosed at the top with a roof of materials having a fire resistive rating of one hour and a metal skylight covering at least three-quarters of the area of the shaft in the top story, except that skylights over stair shafts shall have an area not less than one-tenth the area of the shaft in the top story, but shall be not less than fifteen square feet in area. Any shaft terminating below the top story of a structure and those stair shafts not required to extend through the roof shall have the top enclosed with materials having the same fire resistive rating as required for the shaft enclosure.

21. The above paragraph states that the elevator shafts which extend into the top story are

    A. not required to have a skylight but are required to extend at least two feet above the roof
    B. neither required to have a skylight nor to extend above the roof
    C. required to have a skylight covering at least three-quarters of the area of the shaft in the top story and to extend at least two feet above the roof
    D. required to have a skylight covering at least three-quarters of the area of the shaft in the top story but are not required to extend above the roof

22. The one of the following skylights which meets the requirements of the above paragraph is a skylight measuring

    A. 4' x 4' over a stair shaft which, on the top story, measures 20' x 9'
    B. 4 1/2' x 3 1/2' over a pipe shaft which, on the top story, measures 5' x 4'
    C. 2 1/2' x 1 1/2' over a dumbwaiter shaft which, on the top story, measures 2 1/2' x 2 1/2'
    D. 4' x 3' over a stair shaft which, on the top story, measures 15' x 6'

23. Suppose that in a Class I building, a shaft which does not go to the roof is required to have a three-hour fire resistive rating.
    In regard to the material enclosing the top of this shaft, the above paragraph

    A. states that a one-hour fire resistive rating is required
    B. states that a three-hour fire resistive rating is required
    C. implies that no fire resistive rating is required
    D. neither states nor implies anything about the fire resistive rating

Questions 24-25.

DIRECTIONS: Questions 24 and 25 are to be answered SOLELY on the basis of the following passage.

The four different types of building collapses are as follows:

1. <u>Building Wall Collapse</u> - An outside wall of the building collapses but the floors maintain their positions.

2. <u>Lean-to Collapse</u> - One end of a floor collapses onto the floor below it. This leaves a sheltered area on the floor below.
3. <u>Floor Collapse</u> - An entire floor falls to the floor below it but large pieces of machinery in the floor below provide spaces which can provide shelter.
4. <u>Pancake Collapse</u> - A floor collapses completely onto the floor below it, leaving no spaces. In some cases, the force of this collapse causes successive lower floors to collapse.

24. The MOST serious injuries are likely to occur at _____ collapses.

    A. pancake   B. lean-to
    C. floor   D. building wall

25. Of the following, a floor collapse is MOST likely to occur in a(n)

    A. apartment building   B. private home
    C. factory building   D. hotel

26. When using a standardized survey report during AFID, it generally is NOT advisable to make an inspection of the facilities in the strict sequence of the items on the form PRIMARILY because the

    A. sequence of the items in the form may not correspond to the physical arrangement of the occupancy or structure
    B. members performing inspection duty will be more likely to make errors of omission rather than commission on the forms

C. occupancy or structure may require a multi-inspector, multi-page form inspectional approach
D. procedure does not permit distribution of tasks among all the members participating in the inspection

27. Sparks given off by welding torches are a serious fire hazard.
The BEST of the following methods of dealing with this hazard is to conduct welding operations only

A. in fireproof buildings protected by sprinkler systems
B. out-of-doors on a day with little wind blowing
C. on materials certified to be non-combustible by recognized testing laboratories
D. after loose combustible materials have been cleared from the area and with a man standing by with a hose line

28. Two types of steel hoops are commonly found on older wooden gravity tanks - round hoops and flat ones.
The one of the following statements concerning such hoops that is MOST accurate is that hidden corrosion is a serious problem with _____ hoops.

A. the round hoops but not with the flat
B. the flat hoops but not with the round
C. both types of
D. neither type of

29. While on AFID, you come across a clothing factory which shows evidence of poor housekeeping practices.
For you to imply to the owner that the Fire Department will conduct frequent inspections of his premises until satisfactory conditions are maintained is

A. *proper,* mainly because the owner may be persuaded by it to maintain satisfactory conditions
B. *improper,* mainly because the owner may feel that he is being harassed
C. *proper,* mainly because any means which result in the elimination of hazardous conditions are permissible
D. *improper,* mainly because threats which may not be carried out should not be made

30. Generally, officers on fire prevention inspection duty do not inspect the living quarters of private dwellings unless the occupants agree to the inspection.
The BEST of the following explanations of why private dwellings are excluded from compulsory inspections is that

A. private dwellings seldom catch fire
B. fires in private dwellings are more easily extinguished than other types of fires
C. people may resent such inspections as an invasion of privacy
D. the monetary value of private dwellings is lower than that of other types of occupancies

KEY (CORRECT ANSWERS)

1. C	11. A	21. A
2. D	12. A	22. B
3. A	13. B	23. B
4. B	14. B	24. A
5. D	15. A	25. C
6. A	16. C	26. A
7. B	17. A	27. D
8. D	18. D	28. B
9. C	19. A	29. A
10. A	20. B	30. C

EXAMINATION SECTION
TEST 1

DIRECTIONS: Each question or incomplete statement is followed by several suggested answers or completions. Select the one that BEST answers the question or completes the statement. *PRINT THE LETTER OF THE CORRECT ANSWER IN THE SPACE AT THE RIGHT.*

1. A television receiver has a GREATER inherent fire hazard than a conventional radio receiver because

    A. of greater electrical leakage
    B. cabinets are inadequately ventilated
    C. higher voltage is used in the system
    D. they are operated for longer periods of time
    E. the coaxial cable lead-in is covered with a highly flammable coating

    1.____

2. Of the following, the MOST frequent factor contributing to conflagrations in the United States and Canada in the last 25 years has been

    A. high winds
    B. lack of exposure protection
    C. delayed alarms
    D. congestion of hazardous occupancies
    E. inadequate water distribution system

    2.____

3. If, upon reinspection of a plant which has 30 days to comply with a previous order, you find that the order has not been completely obeyed but that some work has taken place, you SHOULD

    A. report to proper authorities to obtain legal action
    B. assume the delay is unavoidable and check again in 30 days
    C. inform the person in charge that a 10-day extension will be granted and that legal action will be taken if the order has not been followed
    D. issue a summons for failure to comply
    E. none of the above

    3.____

4. An analysis of loss records in one city showed that one-third of the total loss in building fires was in residence buildings and that, of the total loss in such buildings, in the year under study, nearly 80 percent was in multiple dwelling buildings.
The one of the following courses of action for the Fire Department which should be taken IMMEDIATELY on the basis of this report is to

    A. relocate companies
    B. recommend sprinkler protection for multiple dwellings
    C. institute special training fighting multiple dwelling fires
    D. reduce the protection given to other than multiple dwelling residences
    E. inspect multiple dwellings more thoroughly

    4.____

5. It is good practice to so install heating devices that under conditions of maximum heat (long-continued exposure) they will not cause the temperature of exposed woodwork to exceed 160° F. This practice is

    5.____

A. *correct*, because of the possibility that wood and other combustible materials, after long-continued exposure to relatively moderate heat, may ignite at temperatures far below their usual ignition temperatures
B. *not correct*, because no wood in ordinary use will ignite at a temperature of less than 400°F and, consequently, the requirement is needlessly severe
C. *correct*, because oxidation proceeds much more rapidly at higher temperatures
D. *not correct*, because oxidation proceeds much more slowly at higher temperatures
E. *correct*, because under prolonged heating the temperature of the air in the room will build up until the ignition point is reached unless the applied temperature is kept sufficiently low

6. Analysis of the causes of fires is important, as only by knowing the causes of fires is it possible to effectively prevent fire.
An analysis of fires in rooms used for spraying flammable paints and finishes has shown that the MOST important of the following causes is

   A. smoking by employees
   B. defective electrical equipment
   C. spontaneous ignition of paint deposits, rubbish, and wiping rags
   D. static electricity resulting from friction
   E. cutting and welding operations

7. The flammability or combustibility of radioactive materials has little or no direct effect on the fire hazard of a laboratory PRIMARILY because

   A. the unusual structural characteristics of such a laboratory serve to limit possible fire spread from such hazards
   B. water or water spray are effective on most radioactive substances
   C. the quantities of such material in any one laboratory are usually small
   D. laboratory fire prevention and firefighting facilities usually exceed maximum fire hazards
   E. such materials are inherently of a low order of combustibility

8. Comparison of the burning qualities of foam rubber and cotton mattresses shows that GENERALLY

   A. a cotton mattress burns faster but cooler
   B. a foam rubber mattress burns slower but hotter
   C. a foam rubber mattress burns faster and hotter
   D. a cotton mattress burns faster and hotter
   E. the potential fire hazard of a foam rubber mattress is higher

9. During Christmas and other holiday shopping seasons, it is required that frequent inspections shall be made of department stores at irregular intervals. Of the following, the MOST important reason for this inspection procedure is to

   A. prevent unnecessary interference with store operations
   B. check characteristic holiday operations
   C. permit more frequent and thorough coverage of the stores in question
   D. avoid delay in urgent fire operations
   E. permit more flexible scheduling of inspection

10. The fire load computation of a building indicates, for the most part, the

    A. risk of a fire breaking out
    B. rate at which a fire is likely to grow
    C. combustibility of the various parts of the building rather than its contents
    D. amount of combustibles and the method of protection
    E. maximum fire stress to which the building might be subjected

11. It is far more important that escape routes from multistory buildings should be protected against smoke and hot gases than from direct flame or heat.
    This statement is

    A. *not correct;* resistive construction is likely to be smoke-resistive as well
    B. *correct;* adequate means for ventilation is essential to prevent cutting off escape routes
    C. *not correct;* unless corridors and escape stairs are constructed of fire resistive materials, progress of fire cannot be blocked
    D. *correct;* unless properly protected from smoke and hot gases, escape stairs would be unusable by occupants
    E. *not correct;* unless properly protected against direct flame or heat, escape routes cannot resist smoke or hot gases

12. The MINIMUM width of exit usually required for a single file of persons is MOST NEARLY _____ inches.

    A. 15-17   B. 18-20   C. 21-23
    D. 24-27   E. 27-30

13. The MOST pronounced method of reducing the fire and life hazards in public buildings is by

    A. ample exits of any type
    B. ample stairways inside the buildings
    C. the use of exit signs and panic locks
    D. fire-resisting construction suitable for the occupancy
    E. installing fire extinguishers in every hallway

14. From all viewpoints, the MOST hazardous materials that could be stored, constituting a life as well as a fire hazard, would be

    A. second-hand niter bags
    B. used motor vehicles
    C. loose or baled vegetable fibers
    D. pyroxylin and pyroxylin plastic products
    E. foam rubber mattresses

15. The CHIEF fire hazard of welding and cutting operations is

    A. flames of the torch igniting nearby material
    B. broken hose line
    C. flying sparks
    D. backfiring of torch
    E. tank explosion

16. Of the following items associated with motion picture theatres, the PRIMARY hazard is

    A. misuse of electricity
    B. heating defects
    C. smoking and matches
    D. projection booth fires
    E. improperly lit exits

17. The MOST hazardous method of fumigation is by the use of

    A. heat (125° F)
    B. carbon tetrachloride mixture with flammable fumigant
    C. carbon dioxide mixture with flammable fumigant
    D. carbon bisulphide
    E. carbon monoxide

18. The combined use of inspections, periodic reports of activities, follow-up procedures, special reports from subordinates, and a rating system comprise a system of

    A. coordination
    B. command
    C. control
    D. representation
    E. on-the-job training

19. What should be provided in air conditioning ducts to PREVENT the spread of fire and smoke through a property?

    A. Automatic dampers
    B. Intake screens
    C. Steel wool air filters
    D. Heat actuated devices
    E. Halon extinguishers

20. The OUTSTANDING fire hazard of boarding and rooming houses is

    A. misuse of electricity
    B. smoking and matches
    C. heating defects
    D. incendiary
    E. kitchen fires

21. The SIMPLEST and MOST feasible method of avoiding the overheating of woodwork near any high temperature heating appliance is by

    A. filling the intervening space with insulating material
    B. covering the woodwork with sheet metal
    C. providing an air space between the woodwork and the appliance
    D. covering the woodwork with asbestos sheets
    E. painting the woodwork with varnish

22. The PRINCIPLE source of fire hazard in connection with heating equipment in mercantile buildings comes from

    A. defective wiring
    B. insufficient clearance from combustible materials
    C. the storage and handling of fuel
    D. defective motors
    E. none of the above

23. More ink has been spilled on the item of smoking as a cause of fire than on any other, but the total result has been negligible.
    This situation is BEST accounted for by the fact that

A. smoking is generally an automatic act performed unthinkingly
B. truly effective facilities for elimination of smoking hazards are exceedingly cumbersome or expensive
C. most people regard smoking as a personal prerogative and resent control measures
D. smoking is practiced by many individuals with defective intelligence and social attitudes
E. individual behavior cannot be controlled

24. There are two basic factors in assessing building construction from the fire prevention standpoint. One is the combustibility of materials.
The other is

   A. extinguishment facilities
   B. excess structural strength
   C. ventilation control
   D. limitation of fire spread
   E. means of access and egress

25. The LEAST accurate statement concerning the protection of openings in walls and partitions is:

   A. Protection of wall openings may prevent either the horizontal or the vertical spread of fire
   B. The general features of a building have no bearing on the extent to which such protection is necessary
   C. The protection secured by fire doors and fire windows cannot be better than the fire resistant value of the walls
   D. Good solid walls are preferable to those with fire doors in restricting the spread of fire
   E. Sprinkler systems may provide adequate protection

26. The one of the following which is NOT included among the six categories in which all structures are classified by the Administrative Code with respect to type of construction is _____ structures.

   A. heavy timber   B. metal   C. wood frame
   D. fire-resistant E. fireproof

27. All storage tanks, comprising or forming a part of an oil storage plant, shall be buried so that the tops thereof shall be a distance below the grade level of AT LEAST

   A. 1'   B. 2'   C. 3'   D. 4'   E. 6'

28. According to the Administrative Code, a Class B refrigeration system is one

   A. capable of less than 15 tons capacity
   B. containing not more than 20 lbs. of refrigerant
   C. capable of less than 30 tons capacity
   D. containing 1000 pounds or over of refrigerant
   E. capable of 40 tons capacity or over

29. According to the Administrative Code, it shall be unlawful to transport or store guncotton EXCEPT in

    A. strong wooden cases lined with liquid-proof paper
    B. strong wooden cases
    C. carboys so tinted as to exclude light
    D. water-tight metal vessels
    E. aluminum or other non-tarnishing metal

30. One purpose of building inspections is to enable the Fire Department to plan its operations before a fire starts.
    This statement is

    A. *incorrect;* no two fires are alike
    B. *correct;* many firefighting problems can be anticipated
    C. *incorrect;* fires should be prevented, not extinguished
    D. *correct;* the Fire Department should have detailed plans for every possible emergency
    E. *incorrect;* fires are not predictable

KEY (CORRECT ANSWERS)

1. C	11. D	21. C	
2. A	12. C	22. B	
3. A	13. D	23. A	
4. E	14. D	24. D	
5. A	15. C	25. B	
6. C	16. D	26. D	
7. C	17. D	27. B	
8. C	18. C	28. C	
9. B	19. A	29. D	
10. E	20. C	30. B	

TEST 2

DIRECTIONS: Each question or incomplete statement is followed by several suggested answers or completions. Select the one that BEST answers the question or completes the statement. *PRINT THE LETTER OF THE CORRECT ANSWER IN THE SPACE AT THE RIGHT.*

1. According to the Fire Prevention Code, an essential oil is defined as an oil   1.____

    A. needed to provide the viscosity of a given grade of oil
    B. derived from animal life and not from mineral sources
    C. which has low volatility at room temperature
    D. used for flavoring or perfuming purposes
    E. required as the base of lubricating compounds

2. According to the Fire Prevention Code, it shall be UNLAWFUL to sell or deliver for use   2.____

    A. sticks or cartridges of explosives which are packed so as to lie on their sides
    B. any explosive except in original and unbroken packages
    C. dynamite in cases of 25 and 50 lbs.
    D. nitroglycerine in liquid form under any circumstances
    E. any explosives packed in quantities in excess of 50 lbs.

3. The Fire Prevention Code requires that a storage garage containing more than four motor vehicles shall be continuously under the supervision of one or more persons, each holding a certificate of fitness.   3.____
   The MAXIMUM number of such certificated persons required for any garage shall be

    A. 7   B. 6   C. 5   D. 4   E. 3

4. According to the annual report statistics for the last years, the floor of multiple dwellings where fires started MOST frequently was the   4.____

    A. cellar   B. 1st floor   C. 2nd floor
    D. 3rd floor   E. roof

5. You are assigned to inspect buildings for fire hazards. The one of the following MOST appropriately used for fire-retardant coating of wood is   5.____

    A. varnish   B. shellac   C. wood stain
    D. lacquer   E. white wash

6. An officer taking some clothing to a dry cleaner in his neighborhood noticed that inflammable cleaning fluid was stored in a way which created a fire hazard. The officer called this to the attention of the proprietor, explaining the danger involved.   6.____
   This method of handling the situation was

    A. *bad;* the officer should not have interfered in a matter which was not his responsibility
    B. *good;* the proprietor would probably remove the hazard and be more careful in the future
    C. *bad;* the officer should have reported the situation to the fire inspector's office without saying anything to the proprietor

D. *good;* since the officer was a customer, he should treat the proprietor more leniently than he would treat other violators
E. *bad;* the officer should have ordered the proprietor to remove the violation immediately and issued a summons

7. Automobile fires are caused MOST frequently by

   A. overheating of the motor
   B. gasoline explosion
   C. defective carburetor
   D. defective or overheated brakes
   E. faulty ignition wiring

8. The PRINCIPAL fire hazard in connection with heating equipment in mercantile buildings comes from

   A. failure to operate and clean equipment properly
   B. insufficient clearance from combustible material
   C. use of improper types or grades of fuel
   D. defective flues
   E. exposed wiring in heating controls

9. Supermarket fires have in common the fact that MOST fires occur in the

   A. utility area
   B. sales area
   C. basement storage area
   D. check-out and packaging area
   E. shelves containing paper products

10. Of the following, the LEAST accurate statement concerning Field Violation Cards is that

    A. when all the violations listed on a Field Violation Card have been complied with, such card shall be placed in the Occupancy Folder
    B. not more than two Minor Violation Orders shall be recorded on any one card
    C. not more than two Major Violation Orders shall be recorded on any one card
    D. when the space on both sides is completely used for entries, such card is placed on file in the Occupancy Folder
    E. when subsequent violations are found for a building which previously complied with violations found, the additional entries shall be made on the same Field Violation Card

11. Of the following statements concerning coal storage, the one that is ACCEPTABLE is:

    A. Coal for storage should preferably be deposited in horizontal layers
    B. Alternate wetting and drying will prevent development of heat in the pile
    C. The desirable height of a properly stored coal pile is 25 to 30 feet
    D. Storage of mixed sizes of coal together will reduce spontaneous ignition to a minimum
    E. Standing timbers should be placed in coal piles to provide air access and circulation

12. The Multiple Dwelling Law provides that, in every multiple dwelling erected after April 18, 1929, every stair, fire stair, and fire tower beyond a specified width shall be provided with a handrail on each side.

    This specified width is

    A. 3'2"   B. 3'8"   C. 4'2"   D. 4'10"   E. 5'6"

13. The one of the following for which the Official Action Guide provides that a permit is required for storage, regardless of quantity and purpose, is

    A. shale oil
    B. heavy lubricating oil
    C. machine oil
    D. kerosene
    E. illuminating oil

Questions 14-16.

DIRECTIONS: Questions 14 through 16, inclusive, are to be answered on the basis of the following paragraph.

A flameproof fabric is defined as one which, when exposed to small sources of ignition, such as sparks or smoldering cigarettes, does not burn beyond the vicinity of the source of ignition. Cotton fabrics are the materials commonly used that are considered most hazardous. Other materials, such as acetate rayons and linens, are somewhat less hazardous, and woolens and some natural silk fabrics, even when untreated, are about equal to the average treated cotton fabric insofar as flame spread and ease of ignition are concerned. The method of application is to immerse the fabric in a flame-proofing solution. The container used must be large enough so that all the fabric is thoroughly wet and there are no folds which the solution does not penetrate.

14. According to the above paragraph, a flameproof fabric is one which

    A. is unaffected by heat and smoke
    B. resists the spread of flames when ignited
    C. burns with a cold flame
    D. cannot be ignited by sparks or cigarettes
    E. may smolder but cannot burn

15. According to the above paragraph, woolen fabrics which have not been flameproofed are as likely to catch fire as _____ fabrics.

    A. treated silk
    B. treated acetate rayon
    C. untreated linen
    D. untreated synthetic
    E. treated cotton

16. In the method described above, the flameproofing solution is BEST applied to the fabric by _____ the fabric.

    A. sponging
    B. spraying
    C. dipping
    D. brushing
    E. sprinkling

17. The daily peak time for the number of fires in the city, in general,

    A. varies from day to day
    B. is about 9 A.M.

C. is at about 5 P.M.
D. is at about 1 A.M.
E. varies from season to season

18. According to the Multiple Dwelling Law, a part of a building is *fire-retarded* if it is protected against fire in an approved manner with materials of fire-resistive ratings of AT LEAST _____ hour(s).

    A. one   B. two   C. three   D. four   E. five

19. The Multiple Dwelling Law permits the conduct of business in any multiple dwelling EXCEPT that

    A. no space in a non-fireproof multiple dwelling may be used for a bakery or business where fat is boiled under any condition
    B. the number of persons employed in manufacturing enterprises in multiple dwellings shall be limited to a maximum of seven persons
    C. exits of the dwelling portion and the business space may be common if the number of persons employed is limited to ten persons or less
    D. when the ground story of any non-fireproof multiple dwelling is extended for business purposes, the underside of the roof of such extension shall be fire-retarded if there are fire escapes above such extension
    E. there shall be no manufacturing business conducted above the second floor of any non-fireproof multiple dwelling

20. According to the Building Code, a sprinkler system is NOT required in

    A. garages in cellars of multiple dwellings if area is less than 5,000 square feet
    B. dressing rooms and stage of auditoriums of large public high schools where seating capacity is less than 1,500
    C. furnished rooms of converted non-fireproof multiple dwellings if the public hall has sprinkler protection
    D. non-fireproof lodging houses if equipped with an automatic, closed-circuit fire alarm system
    E. department stores if each floor does not exceed 10,000 square feet

21. The Building Code requires that in all newly constructed loft buildings used for mercantile purposes,

    A. 8 inch standpipe risers shall be installed in buildings 150 feet or more in height
    B. standpipes be installed if 75 feet in height or over
    C. the minimum size of standpipe riser in a building 100 feet high be at least 3 inches
    D. when a standpipe is required, no point on a floor be more than 75 feet from a riser
    E. multiple standpipe risers may not be cross-connected

22. The proscenium of a theatre is MOST closely associated with the

    A. stage
    B. special entrance for scenery
    C. street entrance and exit
    D. passageways to boxes
    E. balcony arch over the orchestra section

23. The MAXIMUM quantity of kerosene fuel oil that may be stored for heating and cooking use without a permit from the Fire Commissioner is _____ gallons. 23.____

   A. 10   B. 25   C. 50   D. 100   E. 150

24. An ACCEPTABLE method of absorbing waste oils in a dry cleaning establishment is, according to the Fire Prevention Code, 24.____

   A. a quantity of sand spread on the floor
   B. use of thin asbestos fibre flooring
   C. non-combustible cloth on the floor
   D. diatomaceous earth or equivalent absorbent material spread on the floor
   E. woven glass fibre mats

25. Suppose you are making an inspection of a factory. During the inspection, the factory manager asks you a technical question which you cannot answer.
Of the following, the BEST procedure for you to follow is to 25.____

   A. tell him you are not there to answer his questions but to make an inspection
   B. guess at the answer so that he won't doubt your competency
   C. tell him you don't know the answer but that you will look it up and notify him
   D. give him the title of a textbook that probably would contain the information
   E. change the subject by asking him a question

26. While performing building inspections, a fireman finds a janitor in the basement checking for a gas leak by holding a lighted match to the gas pipes.
Of the following, the fireman's FIRST action should be to 26.____

   A. reprimand the janitor for endangering life and property
   B. explain the hazards of this action to the janitor
   C. report the janitor to his superior as incompetent
   D. tell the janitor to put out the match
   E. issue a summons for this action

27. According to the Administrative Code, a refrigerant is defined as the chemical agent used to produce refrigeration other than 27.____

   A. brine
   B. a chemical of the hydrocarbon clan
   C. the compressor
   D. methyl bromide
   E. ammonia

28. The Administrative Code defines as a combustible mixture any substance which, when tested in a Tagliabue open cup tester, emits an inflammable vapor at temperatures 28.____

   A. below 100° F   B. above 300° F
   C. between 100° F and 300° F   D. below 125° F
   E. above 125° F

29. A partially filled gasoline drum is a more dangerous fire hazard than a full one. Of the following, the BEST justification for this statement is that

   A. a partially filled gasoline drum contains relatively little air
   B. gasoline is difficult to ignite
   C. when a gasoline drum is full, the gasoline is more explosive
   D. gasoline vapors are more explosive than gasoline itself
   E. air is not combustible

30. The tendency of this substance to spontaneous heating is very slight. It is usually shipped in bulk. This substance should be kept dry, and storing or loading in hot wet piles should be avoided.
    This description applies MOST closely to

   A. metal powder
   B. soft coal
   C. charcoal
   D. scrap film
   E. jute

KEY (CORRECT ANSWERS)

1. D	11. A	21. B
2. B	12. B	22. A
3. E	13. A	23. A
4. A	14. B	24. A
5. E	15. E	25. C
6. B	16. C	26. D
7. E	17. C	27. A
8. B	18. A	28. C
9. A	19. E	29. D
10. E	20. E	30. E

TEST 3

DIRECTIONS: Each question or incomplete statement is followed by several suggested answers or completions. Select the one that BEST answers the question or completes the statement. *PRINT THE LETTER OF THE CORRECT ANSWER IN THE SPACE AT THE RIGHT.*

1. An inspector is denied access to a building by the building manager after presenting his identification. Of the following actions, it would be MOST appropriate for the captain to

    A. post an official notice of inspection on the premises
    B. notify the enforcement unit of the division of fire prevention
    C. give orders to have three routine inspections of premises made before taking special measures to gain access
    D. contact the building owner by telephone to request access

1.____

Questions 2-5.

DIRECTIONS: Questions 2 through 5 are to be answered on the basis of the information given in the following paragraph.

Old buildings are liable to possess a special degree of fire risk merely because they are old. Outmoded electrical wiring systems and installation of new heating appliances for which the building was not designed may contribute to the increased hazard. Old buildings have often been altered many times; parts of the structure may antedate building codes; dangerous defects may have been covered up. On the average, old buildings contain more lumber than comparable new buildings which, in itself, makes old buildings more susceptible to fire. It is not true, though, that sound lumber in old buildings is drier than new lumber. Moisture content of lumber varies with that of the atmosphere to which it is exposed.

2. According to the above paragraph, old buildings present a special fire hazard CHIEFLY because of the

    A. poor planning of the buildings when first designed
    B. haphazard alteration of the buildings
    C. failure to replace worn out equipment
    D. inadequate enforcement of the building codes

2.____

3. We may conclude from the above paragraph that lumber

    A. should not be used in buildings unless absolutely necessary
    B. should not be used near electrical equipment
    C. is more inflammable than newer types of building materials
    D. tends to lose its moisture at a constant rate

3.____

4. According to the above paragraph, the amount of moisture in the wooden parts of a building depends upon the

    A. age of the building
    B. moisture in the surrounding air

4.____

C. type of heating equipment used in the building
D. quality of lumber used

5. In regard to building codes, the above paragraph implies that

   A. old buildings are exempt from the provisions of building codes
   B. some buildings now in use were built before building codes were adopted
   C. building codes usually don't cover electrical wiring systems
   D. building codes generally are inadequate

6. According to Department Regulations, the *Monthly Statistical Report - Field Inspection Activity* should include company field inspection duty of all

   A. types
   B. types except re-inspection duty on violation orders
   C. types except surveillance inspection duty
   D. types except inspectional duty relative to complaints

7. During field inspection of a building containing an automatic sprinkler system, you note that the shut-off valves are located where they are not readily accessible. The one of the following procedures to follow in this situation, according to department regulations, is to

   A. write an order to the owner or occupant requiring correction of the physical defect
   B. require no action by the owner or occupant but make special note of the valve location in the building record file
   C. bring to the attention of the owner or occupant the potential water damage hazard inherent in this situation
   D. write an order to the owner or occupant for a sign indicating valve location

8. The difficulties encountered in fighting fire in the cellar of a pool supply occupancy were compounded by bulk storage of calcium hypochlorite.
   This bleaching and sanitizing agent is LEAST likely to

   A. be unstable and highly combustible when finely divided
   B. form a mixture that spontaneously bursts into flame on contact with oxidizable material
   C. decompose when involved in fire, by liberating oxygen and intensifying the fire
   D. have an increased fire and explosion potential when pre-mixed with algaecides and fungicides as an all-purpose water treatment

9. Acetylene is a particularly hazardous flammable gas because, in addition to its flammability, it is reactive and unstable. Consequently, its storage and handling in some respects differs from other flammable gases. The following statements may be pertinent to acetylene and its storage:
   I. Acetylene is not toxic but can have an anesthetic effect
   II. Copper must be avoided in most acetylene piping and equipment
   III. Acetylene gas can explode if subjected to more than 15 psi
   Which one of the following choices lists only those of the abovementioned statements that are generally CORRECT?

   A. I, II   B. II, III   C. I, III   D. I, II, III

10. Before leaving quarters to perform apparatus field inspection duty (AFID) at a hospital, a company officer holds a drill on institutional fire safety.
It would be MOST appropriate for the officer to tell the members that the MAJORITY of fires in hospitals generally occur in

   A. storage rooms
   B. lounges
   C. patients' rooms
   D. corridors

11. Special fire hazards in industry are sometimes diminished by automatic carbon dioxide fixed-pipe extinguishing systems. While difficult to check an existing system for compliance with design and installation standards, certain of the following conditions can be noted during a building inspection to determine whether it is apparently operative and in good order:
   I. Have cylinders been weighed within the past five years and is there a visible record of such weighing?
   II. Are automatic-closing doors and shutters unobstructed and free to close upon actuation?
   III. Are there means accessible during a fire of manually actuating the system?

   Which of the following choices contains only those of the above conditions that are generally VALID?

   A. I, II
   B. II, III
   C. I, III
   D. I, II, III

12. A considerable number of serious burn injuries and fatalities result from fires involving clothing being worn. The following may or may not be correct statements concerning Fire Department experience gained from such fires:
   I. Cotton and rayon have proved to be relatively nonflammable fibers
   II. Nylon and acetate melt and liquefy under fire exposure, thereby tending to aggravate the severity of burn injuries
   III. Victims of clothing fires are more likely to be persons over 60 years of age than children under 10

   Which of the following choices contains only those of the above-mentioned statements that are generally CORRECT?

   A. I, II
   B. I, III
   C. II, III
   D. I, II, III

13. Some communities have a program for inspecting dwellings, conducted as a courtesy and service to householders.
   The USUAL effect of a dwelling-house inspection campaign is

   A. annoyance on the part of homeowners and their refusal to admit firemen
   B. anticipation of firemen's visits by cleaning up before their arrival
   C. avoidance of major problems found by firemen and their stressing instead the easily corrected conditions
   D. embarrassment of both firemen and homeowners by the procedure and their seeking premature termination of the visit

14. Of the following agents for transferring flammable and combustible liquids, the BEST one is

   A. air pressure
   B. hydraulic or inert gas
   C. straight gravity discharge systems
   D. positive displacement pumps

15. The effect of applying wallpaper to a new interior finish surface on the flame propagation characteristics of that surface is GENERALLY considered

    A. minimal
    B. moderate
    C. considerable
    D. severe

16. While you are on apparatus field inspection duty, one of your members reports that he has issued an order to a building owner to remedy a violation forthwith. The member states that the owner seems agitated and hostile and refuses to correct the condition. You decide to speak to the owner yourself.
    In discussing this situation with the owner, it is MOST advisable for you to

    A. inform the owner firmly but bluntly that he is incorrect in insisting the condition does not require correction
    B. try to convince the owner that you are an expert in this area and that your knowledge should not be questioned
    C. express an appropriate degree of anger at the owner's refusal to correct an unsafe condition
    D. stick to discussion of the specific violation and avoid trying to convince the owner of the importance of correcting all fire hazards

17. Experience with the city fire prevention program GENERALLY demonstrates that

    A. fires have increased in the public areas of ghetto multiple dwellings despite intensive inspections
    B. inspections are ineffective in both loft buildings and ghetto multiple dwellings
    C. the extensive educational program in the schools in the 1950's resulted in decreases in the number of fires and false alarms when the children reached adulthood
    D. fires have increased in the living areas of ghetto multiple dwellings

18. It is common to find self-closing doors kept open with wooden wedges or other fastenings. To eliminate such unsafe hazards, hooks, fitted with fusible links, have been designed to hold the doors open.
    GENERALLY, these hooks are

    A. *desirable,* if placed low enough for convenient use
    B. *undesirable,* unless placed behind doors, where they would not be subject to damage
    C. *desirable,* if used only on stair and corridor doors
    D. *undesirable* under practically all conditions

19. While supervising an inspection of a commercial building, an officer notices some wooden packing cases resting against a steam riser. He advises the owner to move the stock at least 12 inches away from the riser to permit air to circulate.
    This advice GENERALLY is

    A. *proper;* however, a clearance of 36 inches should have been suggested
    B. *improper;* steam risers do not reach the ignition temperature of wood
    C. *proper;* standard practice uses a rise of 90F above room temperature as the maximum permissible temperature on surrounding woodwork
    D. *improper;* the air space suggested may permit hidden fire to travel behind the stock

20. Realistic fire tests to determine the actual burning characteristics of several rigid foam plastic wall and roof assemblies have been conducted within recent years. Of the following conclusions, the one BEST supported by this research is that

    A. low flame spread, rigid polystyrene foam, encased in aluminum skins, required automatic sprinkler protection for satisfactory performance under fire conditions
    B. low flame spread, rigid polyurethane foam, encased in aluminum skins, required automatic sprinkler protection for satisfactory performance under fire conditions
    C. rigid, foamed polyurethane products produce minimum fire contribution when sprayed on walls
    D. materials with a small-scale flame spread rating of 25 are practically self-extinguishing

21. At a neighborhood community organization meeting and discussion on *Fire Safety in the Home,* a woman asked the officer representing the Fire Department where spot-type heat detectors should be placed in a room to give an alarm properly if fire should occur. The officer responded that the center of the ceiling was the best location. He added that any point on the ceiling was the next best, and, if it were necessary to mount the detector on a side wall, it should be placed at least 6 inches but no more than 12 inches from the ceiling. The officer's instructions to the citizen were

    A. *correct*
    B. *incorrect* in his statement of *any point on the ceiling;* spot-type detectors should not be placed on ceilings in the corner of rooms
    C. *incorrect* in his statement *at least 6 inches from the ceiling*
    D. *incorrect;* side wall locations for spot-type detectors are preferable to ceiling locations

22. Safety cans for indoor handling of small quantities of flammable liquids are approved when equipped with pouring outlets that have tight-fitting caps or valves which are normally kept closed by springs, except when manual pressure is applied to keep them open. During apparatus field inspection, a company officer finds that small unsafe containers are being utilized at a certain location. Wishing to use this discovery to convince the occupants of the premises of the superiority of the authorized container, the officer decides to explain the advantages of the approved type.
Of the following, the MOST complete and accurate explanation he could give is that the approved container

    A. prevents spillage if accidentally tipped over
    B. is self-venting if exposed to fire and prevents spillage if accidentally tipped over
    C. provides relief venting in case of explosion, is self-venting if exposed to fire, and prevents spillage if accidentally tipped over
    D. prevents a static charge from building up during pouring operations, provides relief venting in case of explosion, is self-venting if exposed to fire, and prevents spillage if accidentally tipped over

23. While inspecting a cylindrical gravity tank for an automatic sprinkler system, a chief observes that the water in the tank is 10 feet deep and that the tank has a diameter of 9 feet. He asks the building manager how many gallons are in the tank and receives the reply, *About 10,000.*
Based on his own observation and calculations, the chief should

A. *agree* that the manager's answer is probably correct
B. *disagree* with the manager's answer; the answer is more nearly 20,000 gallons
C. *disagree* with the manager's answer; the answer is more nearly 15,000 gallons
D. *disagree* with the manager's answer; the answer is more nearly 5,000 gallons

24. The one of the following that is NOT an accurate statement with respect to the findings of a survey conducted by a member of the National Commission on Fire Prevention and Control concerning the public's knowledge of fire safety is that   24.____

    A. many youngsters indicated that they were likely to do something dangerous if a frying pan caught fire
    B. many adults and most youngsters did not know that a 15-ampere fuse is the safest for ordinary household lighting circuits
    C. most youngsters and adults indicated they would make the mistake of opening a hot door
    D. most youngsters and adults did not know that carbon monoxide can rob them of their judgment and coordination

25. You are inspecting a building for violations. You must perform the following steps in the order given: 25.____
    I. Find the manager of the building and introduce yourself.
    II. Have the manager accompany you during the inspection.
    III. Start the inspection by checking the Fire Department permits which have been issued to the building. The permits are located in the office of the building.
    IV. Inspect the building for violations of the Fire Prevention Laws. Begin at the roof and work down to the basement or cellar.
    V. As you inspect, write on a piece of paper any violations you find and explain them to the building manager.

    You are inspecting a supermarket. After entering the building, you identify yourself to the store manager and ask him to come along during the inspection. Which one of the following actions should you take NEXT?

    A. Start inspecting the supermarket, beginning at the basement.
    B. Start inspecting the supermarket, beginning at the roof.
    C. Ask to see the Fire Department permits which have been issued to the supermarket.
    D. Write down any violations which are seen while introducing yourself to the manager.

26. Many fires are caused by improper use of oxyacetylene torches.   26.____
    The MAIN cause of such fires is the

    A. high pressure under which the gases are stored
    B. failure to control or extinguish sparks
    C. high temperatures generated by the equipment
    D. explosive nature of the gases used

Questions 27-29.

DIRECTIONS: Questions 27 through 29 are to be answered on the basis of the following paragraph.

The only openings permitted in fire partitions except openings for ventilating ducts shall be those required for doors. There shall be but one such door opening unless the provision of additional openings would not exceed in total width of all doorways 25 percent of the length of the wall. The minimum distance between openings shall be three feet. The maximum area for such a door opening shall be 80 square feet, except that such openings for the passage of motor trucks may be a maximum of 140 square feet.

27. According to the above paragraph, openings in fire partitions are permitted only for

    A. doors
    B. doors and windows
    C. doors and ventilation ducts
    D. doors, windows, and ventilation ducts

28. In a fire partition 22 feet long and 10 feet high, the MAXIMUM number of doors 3 feet wide and 7 feet high is

    A. 1   B. 2   C. 3   D. 4

29.

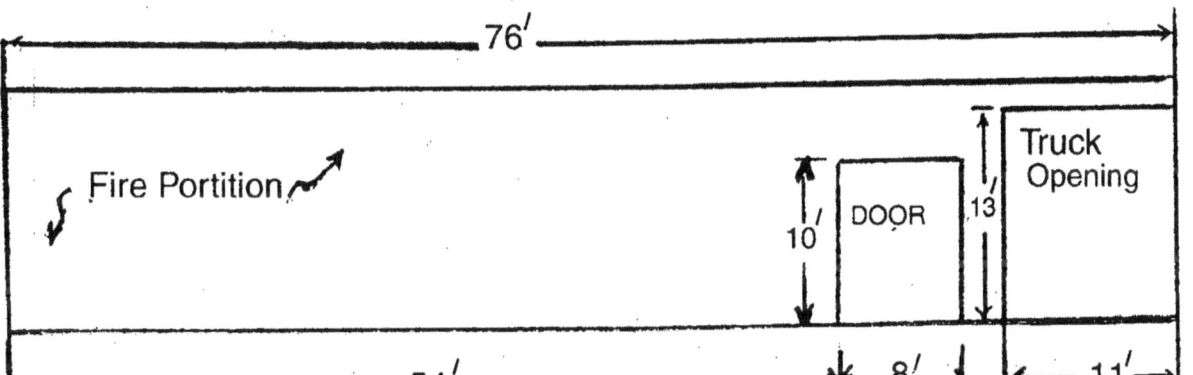

The one of the following statements about the layout shown on the preceding page that is MOST accurate is that the

    A. total width of the openings is too large
    B. truck opening is too large
    C. truck and door openings are too close together
    D. layout is acceptable

30. The Rules of the Board of Standards and Appeals provide that in a coin-operated dry-cleaning establishment spotting and sponging may be done by

    A. the general public or a qualified operator if water only is used
    B. a qualified operator if water only is used
    C. the general public if water only is used or by a qualified operator if inflammable liquids are used
    D. neither the general public nor a qualified operator

KEY (CORRECT ANSWERS)

1. B	11. B	21. B
2. B	12. C	22. B
3. C	13. B	23. D
4. B	14. D	24. C
5. B	15. A	25. C
6. A	16. D	26. B
7. D	17. D	27. C
8. A	18. D	28. A
9. D	19. C	29. B
10. C	20. A	30. B

TEST 4

DIRECTIONS: Each question or incomplete statement is followed by several suggested answers or completions. Select the one that BEST answers the question or completes the statement. *PRINT THE LETTER OF THE CORRECT ANSWER IN THE SPACE AT THE RIGHT.*

1. An officer is performing a routine quarterly inspection in a large motion picture theatre. Which one of the following actions taken by the officer during his inspection would generally be CORRECT? 1.____

    A. His first action is to proceed to the box office to review the theatre inspection log book.
    B. He informs the theatre owner that daily entries made by the owner in the log book should contain the name of the person designated to prevent any undue excitement or possible panic and indicate the location of the nearest street fire alarm box.
    C. Upon finding that the theatre owner has failed to maintain the log in the prescribed manner, the officer serves him with a summons.
    D. He examines the entries made since the previous inspection by an officer and records the results of this examination.

2. The owner of a building which comes under the jurisdiction of the Housing Maintenance Code would be in compliance with the Code if he 2.____

    A. installs, in a dwelling unit, a gas-fired refrigerator which is equipped with a flue assembly composed of non-metallic material
    B. obtains combustion air for the gas-fueled water heater in a bedroom in his new law tenement directly from the outer air
    C. connects each gas-fueled heater to the rigid gas piping supply line by means of a metallic flexible gas connection
    D. arranges to have the gas appliance in his old law tenement inspected by a licensed plumber on a biennial basis

3. Of the following activities, the one the code specifically permits bulk or waste oil recovery plants to do is 3.____

    A. refine waste oil for resale without a permit
    B. mix waste oil with No. 6 fuel oil for use in approved fuel oil burners
    C. transport waste oil in the vendor's container in 220 gallon quantities without a permit
    D. store waste oil in premises other than storage plants or buried tank systems in quantities greater than those restricting other combustible oils

4. A chief, visiting a company performing apparatus field inspection, is informed by the lieutenant in command of a hazardous situation just encountered in a fur processing plant. In the presence of the factory manager, the two officers discussed various sections of the Administrative Code which might be relevant and several approaches to the problem that could be taken by the fire department to abate the hazard. Finally, the chief directed the lieutenant to issue certain orders to the manager. Discussing this problem in the presence of the manager was 4.____

93

A. *proper,* mainly because he probably would realize that the fire department was not acting arbitrarily or unreasonably
B. *improper,* mainly because he might prefer one of the approaches which was suggested and rejected
C. *proper,* mainly because the activities of the fire department should, whenever possible, be open to the public
D. *improper,* mainly because inaccurate statements may have been made during the preliminary discussion

5. A chief supervising apparatus field inspection duty activities comes upon a company just as it is completing inspection of a clothing manufacturing plant. The lieutenant in command reports that the company has issued minor violation orders for five conditions which they discovered. The chief considers four of the conditions cited clear violations of the Administrative Code. The fifth condition he considers a borderline case which he, himself, would not have handled by issuing a violation order.
In this situation, the BEST of the following courses for the chief to take is to

A. direct the lieutenant to cancel the violation order for the borderline situation
B. say nothing to the lieutenant at this time but later warn him against unduly strict interpretation of the Administrative Code
C. accept the lieutenant's findings without any comment at this time or later
D. question the lieutenant closely about various sections of the Administrative Code to determine whether he has a proper understanding of its requirements

Questions 6-7.

DIRECTIONS: Questions 6 and 7 are to be answered SOLELY on the basis of the following passage.

Following is a list of rules for fire extinguishers which are required in different types of public buildings in the city:

Rule 1: Hospitals, nursing homes, hotels, and motels must have one 2 1/2 gallon water extinguisher for every 2,500 square feet, or part thereof, of floor area on each floor.

Rule 2: Stores with floor areas of 1,500 square feet or less must have one 2 1/2 gallon water extinguisher. Stores with floor areas of over 1,500 square feet must have one 2 1/2 gallon water extinguisher for every 2,500 square feet, or part thereof, of floor area on each floor.

Rule 3: Kitchens must have one 2 1/2 gallon foam extinguisher or one 5 pound dry chemical extinguisher for every 1,250 square feet, or part thereof, of floor area on each floor. For kitchen areas, this rule is in addition to Rules 1 and 2.

6. An inspector is inspecting a one-story nursing home which has a total of 3,000 square feet of floor area. This includes a kitchen, which is 1,500 square feet in area, in the rear of the floor.
Of the following, the inspector should conclude that the nursing home should be equipped with _____ extinguisher(s) and _____ extinguisher(s).

A. 1 water; 1 foam
B. 1 water; 1 dry chemical
C. 2 water; 2 foam
D. 2 foam; 1 dry chemical

7. An inspector is inspecting a store which has two floors. The first floor has 2,600 square feet. The second floor has 1,450 square feet.
   The store should be equipped with AT LEAST

   A. two 2 1/2 gallon water extinguishers, one for each floor
   B. three 2 1/2 gallon water extinguishers, two for the first floor and one for the second floor
   C. two 2 1/2 gallon foam extinguishers, one for each floor
   D. two 2 1/2 gallon extinguishers, either foam or water, one for each floor

7._____

8. A recycling sprinkler head called *The Aquamatic* has been developed that will turn itself off after the fire is extinguished and turn itself on again if the fire should rekindle.
   Of the following, it would generally be INACCURATE to state that this recycling sprinkler head

   A. has been approved by the Underwriters' Laboratories for installation where there is high risk of flash fires
   B. is capable of discharging 30 gpm and is approved by the Underwriters' Laboratories for use in systems engineered to make maximum use of available water
   C. eliminates the need to turn off the main valve to replace Aquamatic elements
   D. has a 165° temperature rating, the usual 1/2 inch national pipe thread, is mounted in the pendant position and is approved for installation in any sprinkler system, new or old

8._____

9. Assume that you are supervising a scheduled inspection of auxiliary fire protection equipment in a tunnel in the absence of a deputy chief.
   In supervising the inspection, it would be appropriate for you to do all of the following EXCEPT

   A. utilize the members of the Rescue Company in carrying out specific inspectional duties
   B. notify the dispatcher of the units participating, the designated radio contact, and the units which are not available for response to their assigned alarms
   C. make a written recommendation suggesting a corrective procedure to upgrade a particular piece of inadequate equipment
   D. forward referrals and recommendations through official channels to the division of fire prevention for transmittal to the various agencies concerned and for necessary follow-up

9._____

10. What was formerly known as the *spray sprinkler* is now designated as the *standard sprinkler* and is generally similar in appearance to the old type head.
    Of the following, the MOST NEARLY accurate statement about the modern one-half inch sprinkler head is that

    A. a larger area of coverage is secured by directing all the water downward and horizontally
    B. the present upright spray sprinkler operates on the direct spray principle

10._____

C. major changes in deflector design have reduced discharge capacities, but have increased particle division
D. there is increased exposure to the ceiling, but more direct discharge on the burning materials

11. The one of the following which is generally a CORRECT statement about automatic deluge sprinkler systems is that they are

    A. installed in properties when there is a danger of serious water damage due to accidental functioning
    B. equipped with quartzoid bulb type activators in lieu of fusible links
    C. controlled by a quick-opening valve known as the deluge valve
    D. ineffective where ceilings are unusually high and heads would not open quickly enough

11.____

12. An inspection of the private class 3 box cards of the computerized alarm assignment system should reveal that the cards PROPERLY list the

    A. company numbers of those engine and ladder companies responding to each terminal under the *Response Policy* column
    B. battalion number of the battalion chief assigned to respond to each terminal under the *B.C.* column
    C. company numbers of the engine and ladder companies assigned to the associated street box
    D. address of the alarm service company

12.____

13. The General Accounting Office in Washington publicized the fact that there is a possible defect in some models of a certain smoke detector.
The one of the following which BEST describes this defect is that these detectors

    A. failed to signal an alarm under heavy smoke conditions
    B. expected battery life is only three months or less
    C. have smoke entry vents which are too narrow so that dust tends to render the detectors ineffective
    D. are overheating and, in time, tend to self-ignite

13.____

14. Assume that you are a fire officer who has been asked to address a local community group on the relative merits of smoke and heat detectors and the proper placement, operation, and maintenance of the various types of detectors. During this meeting, it would be MOST appropriate for you to point out that

    A. it is more advisable to install a smoke detector than a heat detector in the kitchen
    B. placement of a smoke detector in a room below an insulated attic should be on the ceiling towards the center of the room
    C. placing a smoke detector in the hallway near each sleeping area and on every floor level not containing a sleeping area will provide minimal protection
    D. a smoke detector installed on the ceiling near a doorway should be placed closer to the wall above the doorway than the distance from the ceiling to the top of the door

14.____

15. The basic multiple-death fire safety problem in nursing home facilities is GENERALLY considered to be the failure to   15.____

    A. confine the fire's resultant products of combustion to the room of origin
    B. conduct and properly supervise comprehensive fire exit and evacuation drills
    C. adequately service and maintain existing smoke-detection and smoke-control systems
    D. reduce the combustible contents of patients' rooms and enforcement of the no-smoking restrictions by a trained staff

16. The basic assumption of fire prevention educational programs is that people frequently   16.____

    A. must be forced into obeying fire laws
    B. are unaware of the dangers involved in some of their actions
    C. don't care whether or not their actions are dangerous
    D. assume that fire insurance protects them against all fire loss

Questions 17-19.

DIRECTIONS: Questions 17 through 19 are to be answered on the basis of the following paragraph.

Unlined linen hose is essentially a fabric tube made of closely woven linen yarn. Due to the natural characteristics of linen, very shortly after water is introduced, the threads swell after being wet, closing the minute spaces between them making the tube practically watertight. This type of hose tends to deteriorate rapidly if not thoroughly dried after use or if installed where it will be exposed to dampness or the weather. It is not ordinarily built to withstand frequent service or for use where the fabric will be subjected to chafing from rough or sharp surfaces.

17. Seepage of water through an unlined linen hose is observed when the water is first turned on.   17.____
    From the above paragraph, we may conclude that the seepage

    A. indicates that the hose is defective
    B. does not indicate that the hose is defective provided that the seepage is proportionate to the water pressure
    C. does not indicate that the hose is defective provided that the seepage is greatly reduced when the hose becomes thoroughly wet
    D. does not indicate that the hose is defective provided that the seepage takes place only at the surface of the hose

18. Unlined linen hose is MOST suitable for use   18.____

    A. as a garden hose
    B. on fire department apparatus
    C. as emergency fire equipment in buildings
    D. in fire department training schools

19. The use of unlined linen hose would be LEAST appropriate in a(n)   19.____

    A. outdoor lumber yard
    B. non-fireproof office building

C. department store
D. cosmetic manufacturing plant

20. Doors in theatres and other places of public assembly usually open outwardly. The MAIN reason for this requirement is, in the event of fire, to

   A. provide the widest possible passageway for escape of the audience
   B. prevent panic-stricken audience from jamming the doors in a closed position
   C. indicate to the audience the safe direction of travel
   D. prevent unauthorized persons from entering the building

21. Fire prevention inspections should be conducted at irregular hours or intervals. The BEST justification for this *irregularity* is that it permits the firemen to

   A. make inspections when they have free time
   B. see the inspected establishments in their normal condition and not in their *dressed-up* condition
   C. avoid making inspections at times which would be inconvenient for the inspected establishments
   D. concentrate their inspectional activities on those establishments which present the greatest fire hazard

22. Static electricity is a hazard in industry CHIEFLY because it may cause

   A. dangerous or painful burns
   B. chemical decomposition of toxic elements
   C. sparks which can start an explosion
   D. overheating of electrical equipment

Questions 23-25.

DIRECTIONS: Questions 23 through 25 are to be answered on the basis of the following paragraph.

A plastic does not consist of a single substance, but is a blended combination of several. In addition to the resin, it may contain various fillers, plasticizers, lubricants, and coloring material. Depending upon the type and quantity of substances added to the binder, the properties, including combustibility, may be altered considerably. The flammability of plastics depends upon the composition and, as with other materials, upon their physical size and condition. Thin sections, sharp edges, or powdered plastics will ignite and burn more readily than the same amount of identical material in heavy sections with smooth surfaces.

23. According to the above paragraph, all plastics contain a

   A. resin
   B. resin and a filler
   C. resin, filler, and plasticizer
   D. resin, filler, plasticizer, lubricant, and coloring material

24. The one of the following conclusions that is BEST supported by the above paragraph is that the flammability of plastics   24._____

    A. generally is high
    B. generally is moderate
    C. generally is low
    D. varies considerably

25. According to the above paragraph, *plastics* can BEST be described as   25._____

    A. a trade name
    B. the name of a specific product
    C. the name of a group of products which have some similar and some dissimilar properties
    D. the name of any substance which can be shaped or molded during the production process

26. While on inspection duty, an inspector discovers the superintendent of a tenement just starting to remove boxes and other material which are blocking hallways. Apparently, the superintendent started removal as soon as he saw the inspector approach.   26._____
    In this situation, it is MOST important that the inspector

    A. warn the superintendent of the penalties for violation of the Fire Prevention Code
    B. help the superintendent remove the material blocking the hallways
    C. commend the superintendent for his efforts to maintain a safe building
    D. check again, after completing the inspection, to see whether the material has been removed completely

27. Persons engaged in certain hazardous activities are required to obtain a Fire Department permit or certificate for which a fee is charged.   27._____
    The MAIN reason for requiring permits or certificates is to

    A. obtain revenue for the city government
    B. prevent unqualified persons from engaging in these activities
    C. obtain information about these activities in order to plan for fire emergencies
    D. warn the public of the hazardous nature of these activities

28. An inspector, on his way to work, is stopped by a citizen who complains that the employees of a nearby store frequently pile empty crates and boxes in a doorway, blocking passage.   28._____
    The one of the following which would be the MOST appropriate action for the inspector to take is to

    A. assure the citizen that the fire department's inspectional activities will eventually *catch up* with the store
    B. obtain the address of the store and investigate to determine whether the citizen's complaint is justified
    C. obtain the address of the store and report the complaint to his superior officer
    D. ask the citizen for specific dates on which this practice has occurred to determine whether the complaint is justified

29. While inspecting a business building, you discover an oil burner installation with the following features:
    I. Installed on the third story, whose floor is 40' above the street level
    II. Oil delivery lines to the burner are one and one-half inches iron pipe size, and
    III. Pressure in the oil lines to the burner is 25 lbs. per square inch

    The one of the following statements concerning this installation and the applicable sections of the rules of the Board of Standards and Appeals that is MOST accurate is that

    A. feature I is a violation of the rules
    B. feature II is a violation of the rules
    C. feature III is a violation of the rules
    D. the installation complies with the rules

30. The Fire Department now uses companies on fire duty, with their apparatus, for fire prevention inspection in commercial buildings.
    The one of the following changes which was MOST important in making this inspection procedure practicable was the

    A. reduction of hours of work of firemen
    B. use of two-way radio equipment
    C. use of enclosed cabs on fire apparatus
    D. increase in property values during the post-war period

KEY (CORRECT ANSWERS)

1. C	11. D	21. B
2. D	12. B	22. C
3. D	13. B	23. A
4. D	14. B	24. D
5. C	15. A	25. C
6. C	16. B	26. D
7. B	17. C	27. B
8. C	18. C	28. C
9. D	19. A	29. D
10. A	20. B	30. B

READING COMPREHENSION
UNDERSTANDING AND INTERPRETING WRITTEN MATERIAL
EXAMINATION SECTION
TEST 1

DIRECTIONS: Each question or incomplete statement is followed by several suggested answers or completions. Select the one that BEST answers the question or completes the statement. *PRINT THE LETTER OF THE CORRECT ANSWER IN THE SPACE AT THE RIGHT.*

Questions 1-3.

DIRECTIONS: Questions 1 through 3 are to be answered SOLELY on the basis of the following paragraph.

The aging housing inventory presents a broad spectrum of conditions, from good upkeep to unbelievable deterioration. Buildings, even relatively good buildings, are likely to have numerous minor violations rather than the gross and evident sanitary violations of an earlier age. Except for the serious violations in a relatively small number of slum buildings, the task is to deal with masses of minor violations that, though insignificant in themselves, amount in the aggregate to major deprivations of health and comfort to tenants. Caused by wear and tear, by the abrasions of time, and aggravated by neglect, these conditions do not readily yield to the dramatic *vacate and restore* measures of earlier times. Moreover, the lines between *good* and *bad* housing have become blurred in many parts of our cities; we find a range of *shades of gray* blending into each other. Different kinds of code enforcement efforts may be required to deal with different degrees of deterioration.

1. The above passage suggests that code enforcement efforts may have to be   1.____
   A. developed to cope with varying levels of housing dilapidation
   B. aimed primarily at the serious violations in slum buildings
   C. modeled on the *vacate and restore* measures of earlier times
   D. modified to reduce unrealistic penalties for petty violations

2. According to the above passage, during former times some buildings had sanitary violations which were   2.____
   A. irreparable and minor
   B. blurred and gray
   C. flagrant and obvious
   D. insignificant and numerous

3. According to the above passage, the aging housing stock presents a   3.____
   A. great number of rent-controlled buildings
   B. serious problem of tenant-caused deterioration
   C. significant increase in buildings without intentional violations
   D. wide range of physical conditions

Questions 4-5.

DIRECTIONS: Questions 4 and 5 are to be answered SOLELY on the basis of the following passage.

In general, housing code provisions relating to the safe and sanitary maintenance of dwelling units prescribe the maintenance required for foundations, walls, ceilings, floors, windows, doors, stairways, and also the facilities and equipment required in other sections. The more recent codes have, in addition, extensive provisions designed to ensure that the unit be maintained in a rat-free and rat-proof condition. Also, as an example of new approaches in code provisions, one proposed Federal model housing code prohibits the landlord from terminating vital services and utilities except during temporary emergencies or when actual repairs or maintenance are in process. This provision may be used to prevent a landlord from turning off utility services as a technique of self-help eviction or as a weapon against rent strikes.

4. According to the above passage, the more recent housing codes have extensive provisions designed to

    A. maintain a reasonably fire-proof living unit
    B. prohibit tenants from participating in rent strikes
    C. maintain the unit free from rats
    D. prohibit tenants from using lead-based paints

5. According to the above passage, one housing code would permit landlords to terminate vital services during

    A. a rent strike
    B. an actual eviction
    C. a temporary emergency
    D. the planning of repairs and maintenance

Questions 6-8.

DIRECTIONS: Questions 6 through 8 are to be answered SOLELY on the basis of the following passage.

City governments have long had building codes which set minimum standards for building and for human occupancy. The code (or series of codes) makes provisions for standards of lighting and ventilation, sanitation, fire prevention, and protection. As a result of demands from manufacturers, builders, real estate people, tenement owners, and building-trades unions, these codes often have established minimum standards well below those that the contemporary society would accept as a rock-bottom minimum. Codes often become outdated so that meager standards in one era become seriously inadequate a few decades later as society"s concept of a minimum standard of living changes. Out-of-date codes, when still in use, have sometimes prevented the introduction of new devices and modern building techniques. Thus, it is extremely important that building codes keep pace with changes in the accepted concept of a minimum standard of living.

6. According to the above passage, all of the following considerations in building planning would probably be covered in a building code EXCEPT

   A. closet space as a percentage of total floor area
   B. size and number of windows required for rooms of differing sizes
   C. placement of fire escapes in each line of apartments
   D. type of garbage disposal units to be installed

6._____

7. According to the above passage, if an ideal building code were to be created, how would the established minimum standards in it compare to the ones that are presently set by city governments?
   They would

   A. be lower than they are at present
   B. be higher than they are at present
   C. be comparable to the present minimum standards
   D. vary according to the economic group that sets them

7._____

8. On the basis of the above passage, what is the reason for difficulties in introducing new building techniques?

   A. Builders prefer techniques which represent the rock-bottom minimum desired by society.
   B. Certain manufacturers have obtained patents on various building methods to the exclusion of new techniques.
   C. The government does not want to invest money in techniques that will soon be outdated.
   D. New techniques are not provided for in building codes which are not up-to-date.

8._____

Questions 9-11.

DIRECTIONS: Questions 9 through 11 are to be answered SOLELY on the basis of the following paragraph.

When constructed within a multiple dwelling, such storage space shall be equipped with a sprinkler system and also with a system of mechanical ventilation in no way connected with any other ventilating system. Such storage space shall have no opening into any other part of the dwelling except through a fireproof vestibule. Any such vestibule shall have a minimum superficial floor area of fifty square feet, and its maximum area shall not exceed seventy-five square feet. It shall be enclosed with incombustible partitions having a fire-resistive rating of three hours. The floor and ceiling of such vestibule shall also be of incombustible material having a fire-resistive rating of at least three hours. There shall be two doors to provide access from the dwelling, to the car storage space. Each such door shall have a fire-resistive rating of one and one-half hours and shall be provided with a device to prevent the opening of one door until the other door is entirely closed.

9. According to the above paragraph, the one of the following that is REQUIRED in order for cars to be permitted to be stored in a multiple dwelling is a(n)

   A. fireproof vestibule   B. elevator from the garage
   C. approved heating system   D. sprinkler system

9._____

10. According to the above paragraph, the one of the following materials that would NOT be acceptable for the walls of a vestibule connecting a garage to the dwelling portion of a building is   10.____

    A. 3" solid gypsum blocks
    B. 4" brick
    C. 4" hollow gypsum blocks, plastered both sides
    D. 6" solid cinder concrete blocks

11. According to the above paragraph, the one of the following that would be ACCEPTABLE for the width and length of a vestibule connecting a garage that is within a multiple dwelling to the dwelling portion of the building is   11.____

    A. 3'8" x 13'0"   B. 4'6" x 18'6"
    C. 4'9" x 14'6"   D. 4'3" x 19'3"

Questions 12-13.

DIRECTIONS: Questions 12 and 13 are to be answered SOLELY on the basis of the following paragraph.

It shall be unlawful to place, use, or maintain in a condition intended, arranged, or designed for use, any gas-fired cooking appliance, laundry stove, heating stove, range or water heater or combination of such appliances in any room or space used for living or sleeping in any new or existing multiple dwelling unless such room or space has a window opening to the outer air or such gas appliance is vented to the outer air. All automatically operated gas appliances shall be equipped with a device which shall shut off automatically the gas supply to the main burners when the pilot light in such appliance is extinguished. A gas range or the cooking portion of a gas appliance incorporating a room heater shall not be deemed an automatically operated gas appliance. However, burners in gas ovens and broilers which can be turned on and off or ignited by non-manual means shall be equipped with a device which shall shut off automatically the gas supply to those burners when the operation of such non-manual means fails.

12. According to the above paragraph, an automatic shut-off device is NOT required on a gas   12.____

    A. hot water heater   B. laundry dryer
    C. space heater   D. range

13. According to the above paragraph, a gas-fired water heater is permitted   13.____

    A. only in kitchens   B. only in bathrooms
    C. only in living rooms   D. in any type of room

Questions 14-18.

DIRECTIONS: Questions 14 through 18 are to be answered SOLELY on the basis of the information contained in the statement below.

No multiple dwelling shall be erected to a height in excess of one and one-half times the width of the widest street on which it faces, except that above the level of such height, for each one foot that the front wall of such dwelling sets back from the street line, three feet shall be added to the height limit of such dwelling, but such dwelling shall not exceed in maximum height three feet plus one and three-quarter times the width of the widest street on which it faces.

Any such dwelling facing a street more than one hundred feet in width shall be subject to the same height limitations as though such dwelling faced a street one hundred feet in width.

14. The MAXIMUM height of a multiple dwelling set back five feet from the street line and facing a 60 foot wide street is ___ feet.

    A. 60   B. 90   C. 105   D. 165

15. The MAXIMUM height of a multiple dwelling set back six feet from the street line and facing a 120 foot wide street is _____ feet.

    A. 198   B. 168   C. 120   D. 105

16. The MAXIMUM height of a multiple dwelling is

    A. 100 ft.   B. 150 ft.   C. 178 ft.   D. unlimited

17. The MAXIMUM height of a multiple dwelling set back 10 feet from the street line and facing a 110 foot wide street is ___ feet.

    A. 178   B. 180   C. 195   D. 205

18. The MAXIMUM height of a multiple dwelling set back eight feet from the street line and facing a 90 foot wide street is ___ feet.

    A. 135   B. 147   C. 178   D. 159

Questions 19-23.

DIRECTIONS: Questions 19 through 23 are to be answered SOLELY on the basis of the following statement.

The number of persons accommodated on any story in a lodging house shall not be greater than the sum of the following components,

   a. 22 persons for each full multiple of 22 inches in the smallest clear width for each means of egress approved by the department, other than fire escapes
   b. 20 persons for each lawful fire escape accessible from such story.

19. The MAXIMUM number of persons that may be accommodated on a story in a lodging house depends on the

    A. number of lawful fire escapes *only*
    B. number of approved means of egress *only*
    C. smallest clear width in each approved means of egress *only*
    D. number of lawful fire escapes and sum total of smallest clear widths in each approved means of egress

20. The MAXIMUM number of persons that may be accommodated on a story of a lodging house having one lawful fire escape and a sum total of 44 inches in the smallest clear widths of the two approved means of egress is

    A. 20   B. 22   C. 42   D. 64

21. The MAXIMUM number of persons that may be accommodated on a story of a lodging house having two lawful fire escapes and a sum total of 60 inches in the smallest clear width of the approved means of egress is

    A. 64 B. 84 C. 100 D. 106

22. The MAXIMUM number of persons that may be accommodated on a story of a lodging house having one lawful fire escape and a sum total of 33 inches in the smallest clear width of the approved means of egress is

    A. 42 B. 53 C. 64 D. 73

23. The MAXIMUM number of persons that may be accommodated on a story of a lodging house having two lawful fire escapes and two approved means of egress, with 40 inches and 44 inches in the smallest clear widths, respectively, is

    A. 84 B. 104 C. 106 D. 108

Questions 24-25.

DIRECTIONS: Questions 24 and 25 are to be answered SOLELY on the basis of the following paragraph.

Though the recent trend toward apartment construction may appear to be the Region's response to large-lot zoning and centralized industry, it really is not. It is mainly a function of the age of the population. Most of the apartments are occupied by one- and two-person families young people out of school but without a family of their own and older people whose children have grown. Both groups have been increasing in number; and, in this Region, they characteristically live in apartments. It is this increased demand for apartments and the simultaneous decrease in demand for one-family houses that dramatically raised the percentage of building permits issued for multi-family housing units from 36 percent in 1977 to 67 percent in 1981. The fact that three-fourths of the apartments were built in the Core between 1977 and 1981 at the same time as the Core was losing population underscores the failure of the apartment boom to slow the outward spread of the population.

24. According to the above paragraph, one of the reasons for the increase in the number of building permits issued for multi-family construction in the City Metropolitan Region is

    A. that workers in industry want to live close to their jobs
    B. an increase in the number of elderly people living in the Region
    C. the inability of many families to afford the large lots necessary to build private homes
    D. the new zoning ordinance made it easier to build apartments

25. According to the above paragraph, the apartment construction boom

    A. increased the population density in the Core
    B. spurred a population shift to the suburbs
    C. did not halt the outward flow of the population from the Core
    D. was most significant in the outer areas of the Region

KEY (CORRECT ANSWERS)

1. A
2. C
3. D
4. C
5. C

6. A
7. B
8. D
9. D
10. B

11. C
12. D
13. D
14. C
15. B

16. C
17. A
18. D
19. D
20. D

21. B
22. A
23. C
24. B
25. C

TEST 2

DIRECTIONS: Each question or incomplete statement is followed by several suggested answers or completions. Select the one that BEST answers the question or completes the statement. *PRINT THE LETTER OF THE CORRECT ANSWER IN THE SPACE AT THE RIGHT.*

Questions 1-4.

DIRECTIONS: Questions 1 through 4 are to be answered SOLELY on the basis of the following paragraph.

Although the suburbs have provided housing and employment for millions of additional families since 1950, many suburban communities have maintained controls over the kinds of families who can live in them. Suburban attitudes have been formed by reaction against a perception of crowded, harassed city life and threatening alien city people. As population, taxable income, and jobs have left the cities for the suburbs, the *urban crisis* of substandard housing, declining levels of education and public services, and decreasing employment opportunities has been created. The crisis, however, is not urban at all, but national, and in part a result of the suburban policy that discourages outward movement by the urban poor.

1. According to the above paragraph, the quality of urban life

    A. is determined by public opinion in the cities
    B. has worsened in recent years
    C. is similar to rural life
    D. can be changed by political means

2. According to the above paragraph, suburban communities have

    A. tried to show that the urban crisis is really a national crisis
    B. avoided taking a position on the urban crisis
    C. been involved in causing the urban crisis
    D. been the innocent victims of the urban crisis

3. According to the above paragraph, the poor have

    A. become increasingly sophisticated in their attempts to move to the suburbs
    B. generally been excluded from the suburbs
    C. lost incentive for betterment of their living conditions
    D. sought improvement of the central cities

4. As used in the above paragraph, the word perception means MOST NEARLY

    A. development   B. impression
    C. opposition   D. uncertainty

Questions 5-8.

DIRECTIONS: Questions 5 through 8 are to be answered SOLELY on the basis of the following paragraph.

The concentration of publicly assisted housing in central cities -- because the suburbs do not want them and effectively bar them -- is usually rationalized by a solicitous regard for keeping intact the city neighborhoods cherished by low-income groups. If one accepted this as valid, the devotion of minorities to blighted city neighborhoods in preference to suburban employment and housing would be an historic first. Certainly no such devotion was visible among the millions who have deserted their city neighborhoods in the last 25 years even if it meant an arduous daily trip from the suburbs to their jobs in the cities.

5. The writer implies that MOST poor people 5.____

   A. prefer isolation
   B. fear change
   C. are angry
   D. seek betterment

6. The general tone of the paragraph is BEST characterized as 6.____

   A. uncertain   B. skeptical   C. evasive   D. indifferent

7. As used in the above paragraph, the word <u>rationalize</u> means MOST NEARLY 7.____

   A. dispute   B. justify   C. deny   D. locate

8. According to the above paragraph, publicly assisted housing is concentrated in the central cities PRIMARILY because 8.____

   A. city dwellers are unable to find satisfactory housing
   B. deterioration of older housing has increased in recent years
   C. suburbanites have opposed the movement of the poor to the suburbs
   D. employment opportunities have decreased in the suburbs

Questions 9-11.

DIRECTIONS: Questions 9 through 11 are to be answered SOLELY on the basis of the following paragraph.

In recent years, new and important emphasis has been placed upon the maximum use of conservation and rehabilitation techniques in carrying out programs of urban renewal and revitalization. In urban renewal projects where existing structures are hopelessly deteriorated or land uses are incompatible with the community's overall plans, the entire area may be acquired, cleared, and sold for redevelopment. However, where existing structures are basically sound but have deteriorated to the point where they are a <u>blighting</u> influence on the neighborhood, they may be salvaged through a program of rehabilitation and reconditioning.

9. According to the above paragraph, the one of the following which is MOST likely to cause area-wide razing of the buildings in urban renewal programs is 9.____

   A. a program of rehabilitation and reconditioning
   B. concerted insistence by landlords and tenants that certain buildings be bulldozed
   C. an inability of community groups to agree on priorities for staged clearance
   D. land use contrary to the community's general plan

10. According to the above paragraph, rehabilitation of structures may take place if 10.____

    A. new conservation and rehabilitation techniques are used
    B. salvaging all the buildings in the entire area is hopeless
    C. the community wishes to preserve historic structures
    D. the existing buildings are structurally sound

11. As used in the above paragraph, the word blighting means MOST NEARLY 11._____

    A. ruining   B. infrequent   C. recurrent   D. traditional

Questions 12-13.

DIRECTIONS: Questions 12 and 13 are to be answered SOLELY on the basis of the following paragraphs.

We must also find better ways to handle the relocation of people uprooted by projects. In the past, many renewal plans have foundered on this problem, and it is still the most difficult part of the community development. Large-scale replacement of low-income residents -- many ineligible for public housing -- has contributed to deterioration of surrounding communities. However, thanks to changes in housing authority procedures, relocation has been accomplished in a far more satisfactory fashion. The step-by-step community development projects we advocate in this plan should bring further improvement.

But additional measures will be necessary. There are going to be more people to be moved; and, with the current shortage of apartments, large ones especially, it is going to be tougher to find places to move them to. The city should have more freedom to buy or lease housing that comes on the market because of normal turnover and make it available to relocatees.

12. According to the above paragraphs, one of the reasons a neighborhood may deteriorate is that 12._____

    A. there is a scarcity of large apartments
    B. step-by-step community development projects have failed
    C. people in the given neighborhood are uprooted from their homes
    D. a nearby renewal project has an inadequate relocation plan

13. From the above paragraphs, one might conclude that the relocation phase of community renewal has been improved. 13._____

    A. by changes in housing authority procedures
    B. by development of step-by-step community development projects
    C. through expanded city powers to buy housing for relocation
    D. by the addition of huge sums of money

Questions 14-15.

DIRECTIONS: Questions 14 and 15 are to be answered SOLELY on the basis of the following paragraphs.

Provision of decent housing for the lower half of the population (by income) was thus taken on as a public responsibility. Public housing was to assist the poorest quarter of urban families while the 221(d)(3) Housing Program would assist the next quarter. But limited funds meant that the supply of subsidized housing could not stretch nearly far enough to help this half of the population. Who were to be left out in the rationing process which was accomplished by the sifting of applicants for housing on the part of public and private authorities?

Discrimination on the grounds of race or color is not allowed under Federal law. In all sections of the country, encouragingly, housing programs are found which follow this law to the letter. Yet, housing programs in some cities still suffer from the residue of racial segregation policies and attitudes that for years were condoned or even encouraged.

Some sifting in the 221(d)(3) Housing Program follows the practice of many public housing authorities, the imposition of requirements with respect to character. This is a delicate matter. To fill a project overwhelmingly with broken families, alcoholics, criminals, delinquents, and other problem tenants would hardly make it a wholesome environment. Yet the total exclusion of such families is hardly an acceptable alternative. To the extent this exclusion is practiced, the very people whose lives are described in order to persuade lawmakers and the public to instigate new programs find the door shut in their faces when such programs come into being. The proper balance is difficult to achieve, but society's neediest families surely should not be totally denied the opportunities for rejuvenation in subsidized housing.

14. From the above paragraphs, it can be assumed that the 221(d)(3) Housing Program

    A. served a population earning more than the median income
    B. served a less affluent population than is served by public housing
    C. excludes all problem families from its projects
    D. is a subsidized housing program

15. According to this text, the provision of housing for the poor

    A. has not been completely accomplished with public monies
    B. is never influenced by segregationist policies
    C. is limited to providing housing for only the neediest families
    D. is primarily the responsibility of the Federal government

16. Five hundred persons attended a public hearing at which a proposed public housing project was being considered. Less than half favored the project while the majority opposed the project.
    According to the above statement, it is REASONABLE to conclude that

    A. the proposal stimulated considerable community interest
    B. the public housing project was disapproved by the city because a majority opposed it
    C. those who opposed the project lacked sympathy for needy persons
    D. the supporters of the project were led by militants

17. A vacant lot close to a polluted creek is for sale. Two buyers compete. One owns an adjacent factory which provides 300 high paying unskilled jobs. He needs to expand or move from the city. If he expands, he will provide 300 additional jobs. The other is a community group in a changing residential area close by. They hope to stabilize the neighborhood by bringing in new housing. They would build an apartment building with 100 dwelling units on the lot.
    According to the above paragraph, it is REASONABLE to conclude that

    A. jobs are more important than housing
    B. there is conflict between the factory owners and the neighborhood group
    C. the neighborhood group will not succeed in stabilizing the area by constructing new housing
    D. the polluted creek should be cleaned up

18. The housing authority faces every problem of the private developer, and it must also assume responsibilities of which private building is free. The authority must account to the community; it must conform to federal regulations; it must provide durable buildings of good standard at low cost; it must overcome the prejudices against public operations, of contractors, bankers, and prospective tenants. These authorities are being watched by anti-housing enthusiasts for the first error of judgment or the first evidence of high costs, to be torn to bits before a Congressional committee.
On the basis of this statement, it would be MOST correct to state that

   A. private builders do not have the opposition of contractors, bankers, and prospective tenants
   B. Congressional committees impede the progress of public housing by petty investigations
   C. a housing authority must deal with all the difficulties encountered by the private builder
   D. housing authorities are no more immune from errors in judgment than private developers

19. Another factor that has considerably added to the city's housing crisis has been the great influx of low-income workers and their families seeking better employment opportunities during wartime and defense boom periods. The circumstances of these families have forced them to crowd into the worst kind of housing and have produced on a renewed scale the conditions from which slums flourish and grow.
On the basis of this statement, one would be justified in stating that

   A. the influx of low-income workers has aggravated the slum problem
   B. the city has better employment opportunities than other sections of the country
   C. the high wages paid by our defense industries have made many families ineligible for tenancy in public housing projects
   D. the families who settled in the city during wartime and the defense build-up brought with them language and social customs conducive to the growth of slums

20. Much of the city felt the effects of the general postwar increase of vandalism and street crime, and the greatly expanded public housing program was no exception. Projects built in congested slum areas with a high incidence of delinquency and crime were particularly subjected to the depredations of neighborhood gangs. The civil service watchmen who patrolled the projects, unarmed and neither trained nor expected to perform police duties, were unable to cope with the situation.
On the basis of this statement, the MOST accurate of the following statements is:

   A. Neighborhood gangs were particularly responsible for the high incidence of delinquency and crime in congested slum areas having public housing programs
   B. Civil service watchmen who patrolled housing projects failed to carry out their assigned police duties
   C. Housing projects were not spared the effects of the general postwar increase of vandalism and street crime
   D. Delinquency and crime affected housing projects in slum areas to a greater extent than other dwellings in the same area

21. Another peculiar characteristic of real estate is the absence of liquidity. Each parcel is a discrete unit as to size, location, rental, physical condition, and financing arrangements. Each property requires investigation, comparison of rents with other properties, and individualized haggling on price and terms.
On the basis of this statement, the LEAST accurate of the following statements is:

   A. Although the size, location, and rent of parcels vary, comparison with rents of other properties affords an indication of the value of a particular parcel
   B. Bargaining skill is the essential factor in determining the value of a parcel of real estate
   C. Each parcel of real estate has individual peculiarities distinguishing it from any other parcel
   D. Real estate is not easily converted to other types of assets

21.____

22. In part, at least, the charges of sameness, monotony, and institutionalism directed at public housing projects result from the degree in which they differ from the city's normal housing pattern. They seem alike because their very difference from the usual makes them stand apart.
In many respects, there is considerably more variety between public housing projects than there is between different streets of apartment houses or tenements throughout the city.
On the basis of this statement, it would be LEAST accurate to state that:

   A. There is considerably more variety between public housing projects than there is between different streets of tenements throughout the city
   B. Public housing projects differ from the city's normal housing pattern to the degree that sameness, monotony, and institutionalism are characteristic of public buildings
   C. Public housing projects seem alike because their deviation from the usual dwellings draws attention to them
   D. The variety in structure between public housing projects and other public buildings is related to the period in which they were built

22.____

23. The amount of debt that can be charged against the city for public housing is limited by law. Part of the city's restricted housing means goes for cash subsidies it may be required to contribute to state-aided projects. Under the provisions of the state law, the city must match the state's contributions in subsidies; and while the value of the partial tax exemption granted by the city is counted for this purpose, it is not always sufficient.
On the basis of this statement, it would be MOST accurate to state that:

   A. The amount of money the city may spend for public housing is limited by annual tax revenues
   B. The value of tax exemptions granted by the city to educational, religious, and charitable institutions may be added to its subsidy contributions to public housing projects
   C. The subsidy contributions for state-aided public housing projects are shared equally by the state and the city under the provisions of the state law
   D. The tax revenues of the city, unless supplemented by state aid, are insufficient to finance public housing projects

23.____

24. Maintenance costs can be minimized and the useful life of houses can be extended by building with the best and most permanent materials available. The best and most permanent materials in many cases are, however, much more expensive than materials which require more maintenance. The most economical procedure in home building has been to compromise between the capital costs of high quality and enduring materials and the maintenance costs of less desirable materials.
On the basis of this statement, one would be justified in stating that:

   A. Savings in maintenance costs make the use of less durable and less expensive building materials preferable to high quality materials that would prolong the useful life of houses constructed from them
   B. Financial advantage can be secured by the home builder if he judiciously combines costly but enduring building materials with less desirable materials which, however, require more maintenance
   C. A compromise between the capital costs of high quality materials and the maintenance costs of less desirable materials makes it easier for a home builder to estimate construction expenditures
   D. The most economical procedure in home building is to balance the capital costs of the most permanent materials against the costs of less expensive materials that are cheaper to maintain

24.____

25. Personnel selection has been a critical problem for local housing authorities. The pool of qualified workers trained in housing procedures is small, and the colleges and universities have failed to grasp the opportunity for enlarging it. While real estate experience makes a good background for management of a housing project, many real estate men are deplorably lacking in understanding of social and governmental problems. Social workers, on the other hand, are likely to be deficient in business judgment.
On the basis of this statement, it would be MOST accurate to state that:

   A. Colleges and universities have failed to train qualified workers for proficiency in housing procedures
   B. Social workers are deficient in business judgment as related to the management of a housing project
   C. Real estate experience makes a person a good manager of a housing project
   D. Local housing authorities have been critical of present methods of personnel selection

25.____

KEY (CORRECT ANSWERS)

1. B
2. C
3. B
4. B
5. D

6. B
7. B
8. D
9. D
10. D

11. A
12. D
13. A
14. D
15. A

16. A
17. B
18. C
19. A
20. C

21. B
22. B
23. C
24. B
25. A

———

EVALUATING INFORMATION AND EVIDENCE
EXAMINATION SECTION
TEST 1

DIRECTIONS: Each question or incomplete statement is followed by several suggested answers or completions. Select the one that BEST answers the question or completes the statement. *PRINT THE LETTER OF THE CORRECT ANSWER IN THE SPACE AT THE RIGHT.*

Questions 1-9

Questions 1 through 9 measure your ability to (1) determine whether statements from witnesses say essentially the same thing and (2) determine the evidence needed to make it reasonably certain that a particular conclusion is true.

1. Which of the following pairs of statements say essentially the same thing in two different ways?
    I. All Hoxie steelworkers are at least six feet tall. No steelworker is less than six feet tall.
    II. Some neutered pit bulls are not dangerous dogs. Some dangerous dogs are neutered pit bulls.

    A. I only
    B. I and II
    C. II only
    D. Neither I nor II

2. Which of the following pairs of statements say essentially the same thing in two different ways?
    I. If we are in training today, it is definitely Wednesday. Every Wednesday there is training.
    II. You may go out tonight only after you clean your room. If you clean your room, you may go out tonight.

    A. I only
    B. I and II
    C. II only
    D. Neither I nor II

3. Which of the following pairs of statements say essentially the same thing in two different ways?
    I. The case will be dismissed if either the defendant pleads guilty and agrees to perform community service, or the defendant pleads guilty and makes a full apology to the victim.
    The case will be dismissed if the defendant pleads guilty and either agrees to perform community service or makes a full apology to the victim.
    II. Long books are fun to read.
    Books that aren't fun to read aren't long.

    A. I only
    B. I and II
    C. II only
    D. Neither I nor II

117

4. Which of the following pairs of statements say essentially the same thing in two different ways?

    I. If you live in a mansion, you have a big heating bill. If you do not have a big heating bill, you do not live in a mansion.
    II. Some clerks can both type and read shorthand. Some clerks can neither type nor read shorthand.

- A. I only
- B. I and II
- C. II only
- D. Neither I nor II

5. Summary of Evidence Collected to Date:
    I. Three students - Bob, Mary and Stan - each received a grade of A, C and F on the civil service exam.
    II. Stan did not receive an F on the exam.

Prematurely Drawn Conclusion: Stan received an A.

Which of the following pieces of evidence, if any, would make it *reasonably certain* that the conclusion drawn is true?

- A. Bob received an F
- B. Mary received a C
- C. Bob did not receive an A
- D. None of these

6. Summary of Evidence Collected to Date:
    I. At Walco, all the employees who work the morning shift work the evening shift as well.
    II. Some Walco employees who work the evening shift also work the afternoon shift.

Prematurely Drawn Conclusion: If Ron, a Walco employee, works the morning shift, he does not work the afternoon shift.

Which of the following pieces of evidence, if any, would make it *reasonably certain* that the conclusion drawn is true?

- A. Ron works only two shifts
- B. Ron works the evening shift
- C. All Walco employees work at least one shift
- D. None of these

7. Summary of Evidence Collected to Date:

All the family counselors at the agency have an MTF certification and an advanced degree.

Prematurely Drawn Conclusion: Any employee of the agency who has an advanced degree is a family counselor.

Which of the following pieces of evidence, if any, would make it *reasonably certain* that the conclusion drawn is true?

A. Nobody at the agency who has an advanced degree is employed as anything other than a family counselor
B. Everyone who has an MTF certification is a family counselor
C. Each person at the agency who has an MTF certification also has an advanced degree
D. None of these

8. Summary of Evidence Collected to Date:
Margery, a worker at the elder agency, is working on recreational programs.
Prematurely Drawn Conclusion: Margery is not working on cases of elder abuse.
Which of the following pieces of evidence, if any, would make it *reasonably certain* that the conclusion drawn is true?

A. Elder abuse and recreational programs are unrelated fields
B. Nobody at the elder agency who works on cases of elder abuse works on recreation programs
C. Nobody at the elder agency who works on recreational programs works on cases of elder abuse
D. None of these

9. Summary of Evidence Collected to Date:
   I. St. Leo's Cathedral is not as tall as the FarCorp building.
   II. The FarCorp building and the Hyatt Uptown are the same height.
Prematurely Drawn Conclusion: The FarCorp building is not in Springfield.
Which of the following pieces of evidence, if any, would make it *reasonably certain* that the conclusion drawn is true?

A. No buildings in Springfield are as tall as the Hyatt Uptown
B. The Hyatt Uptown is not in Springfield
C. St. Leo's Cathedral is the oldest building in Springfield
D. None of these

Questions 10-14

Questions 10 through 14 refer to Map #1 and measure your ability to orient yourself within a given section of town, neighborhood or particular area. Each of the questions describes a starting point and a destination. Assume that you are driving a car in the area shown on the map accompanying the questions. Use the map as a basis for the shortest way to get from one point to another without breaking the law.

On the map, a street marked by arrows, or by arrows and the words "One Way," indicates one-way travel, and should be assumed to be one-way for the entire length, even when there are breaks or jogs in the street.

4 (#1)

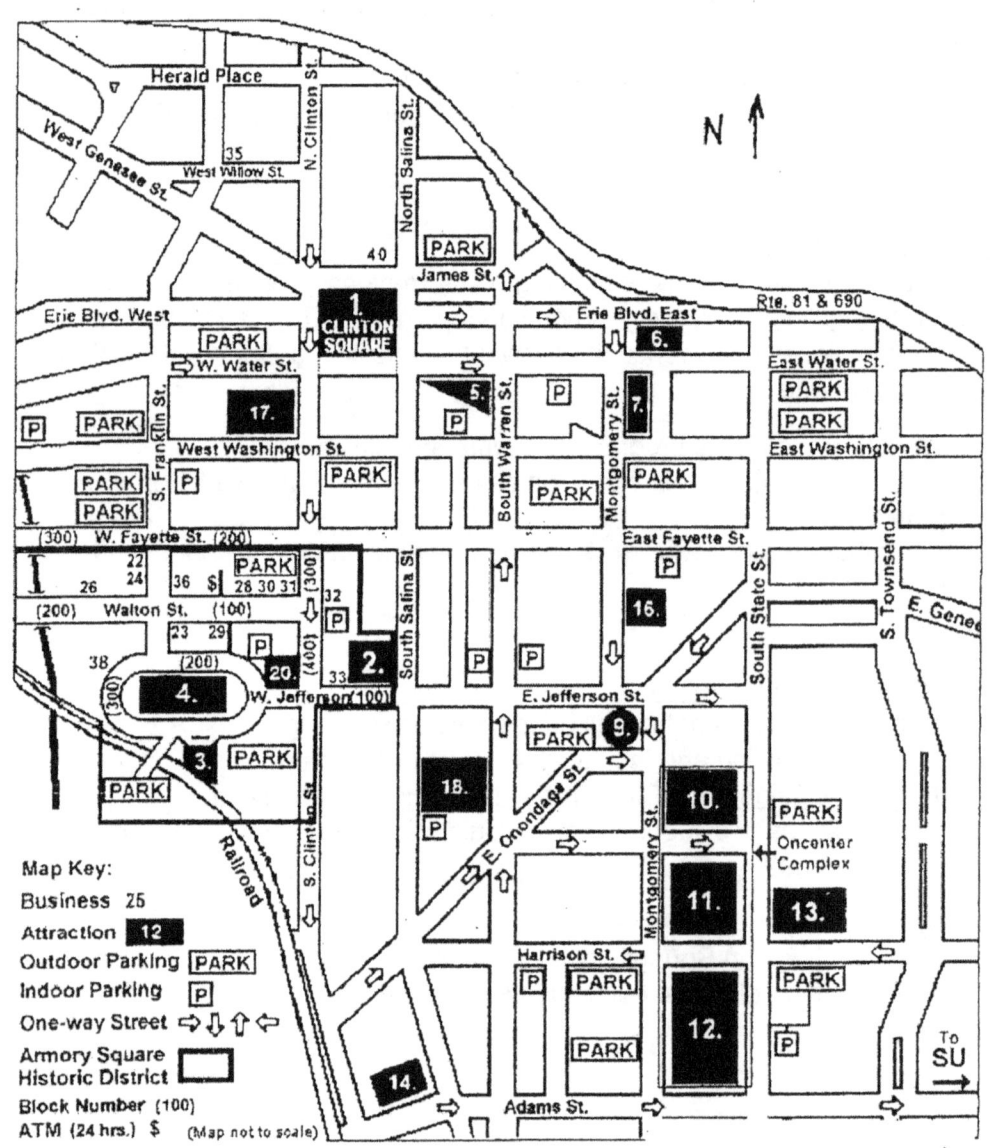

Map #1

1. Clinton Square
2. Landmark Theatre
3. OnTrack Commuter Rail Service
4. Museum of Science and Technology
5. Hanover Square
6. Erie Canal Museum
7. City Hall
9. Columbus Circle
10. Mulroy Civic Center Theaters
11. War Memorial
12. Convention Center
13. Everson Museum of Art
14. Convention and Visitors Bureau
16. Onondaga Historical Association
17. Federal Plaza
18. Galleries of Syracuse

10. The shortest legal way from Columbus Circle to Federal Plaza is 10.____

    A. west on Jefferson St., north on Salina St., west on Water St.
    B. east on Jefferson St., north on State St., west on Washington St.
    C. north on Montgomery St., west on Washington St.
    D. south on Montgomery St., west on Harrison St., north on Salina St., west on Washington St.

11. The shortest legal way from Clinton Square to the Museum of Science and Technology is 11.____

    A. south on Clinton St., west on Fayette St., south on Franklin St.
    B. west on Erie Blvd., south on Franklin St.
    C. south on Clinton St., west on Water St., south on Franklin St.
    D. south on Clinton St., west on Jefferson St.

12. The shortest legal way from Hanover Square to Landmark Theatre is 12.____

    A. west on Water St., south on Salina St.
    B. east on Water St., south on Montgomery St., west on Fayette St., south on Salina St.
    C. east on Water St., south on Montgomery St., west on Fayette St., south on Clinton St., east on Jefferson St.
    D. south on Warren St., west on Jefferson St.

13. The shortest legal way from the Convention Center to the Erie Canal Museum is 13.____

    A. north on State St., west on Washington St., north on Montgomery St.
    B. north on Montgomery St., jog west on Jefferson St., north on Montgomery St.
    C. north on State St., west on Fayette St., north on Warren St., east on Water St.
    D. north on State St., west on Water St.

14. The shortest legal way from City Hall to Clinton Square is 14.____

    A. west on Washington St., north on Salina St.
    B. south on Montgomery St., west on Fayette St., north on Salina St.
    C. north on Montgomery St., west on Erie Blvd.
    D. west on Water St.

Questions 15-19

Questions 15 through 19 refer to Figure #1, on the following page, and measure your ability to understand written descriptions of events. Each question presents a description of an accident or event and asks you which of the five drawings in Figure #1 BEST represents it.

In the drawings, the following symbols are used:

Moving vehicle: ⌂   Non-moving vehicle: ⬆

Pedestrian or bicycle: ●

The path and direction of travel of a vehicle or pedestrian is indicated by a solid line.

The path and direction of travel of each vehicle or pedestrian directly involved in a collision from the point of impact is indicated by a dotted line.

In the space at the right, print the letter of the drawing that best fits the descriptions written below:

15. A driver heading north on Elm sideswipes a parked car, veers into the oncoming lane and travels through the intersection of Elm and Main. He then sideswipes an oncoming car, veers back into the northbound lane and flees.   15.____

16. A driver heading south on Elm sideswipes a car parked in the southbound lane, then loses control and veers through the intersection of Elm and Main. The driver then collides with the rear of another parked car, which is knocked forward after the impact.   16.____

17. A driver heading north on Elm strikes the rear of a parked car, which is knocked through the intersection of Elm and Main and strikes a parked car in the southbound lane head-on.   17.____

18. A driver heading north on Elm strikes the rear of a car that is stopped at a traffic light. The car at the light is knocked through the intersection of Elm and Main and strikes a parked car in the rear.   18.____

19. A driver heading south on Elm loses control and crosses into the other lane of traffic, where he sideswipes a car parked in the northbound lane, then veers back into the southbound lane, travels through the intersection of Elm and Main and collides with the rear end of a parked car.   19.____

FIGURE #1

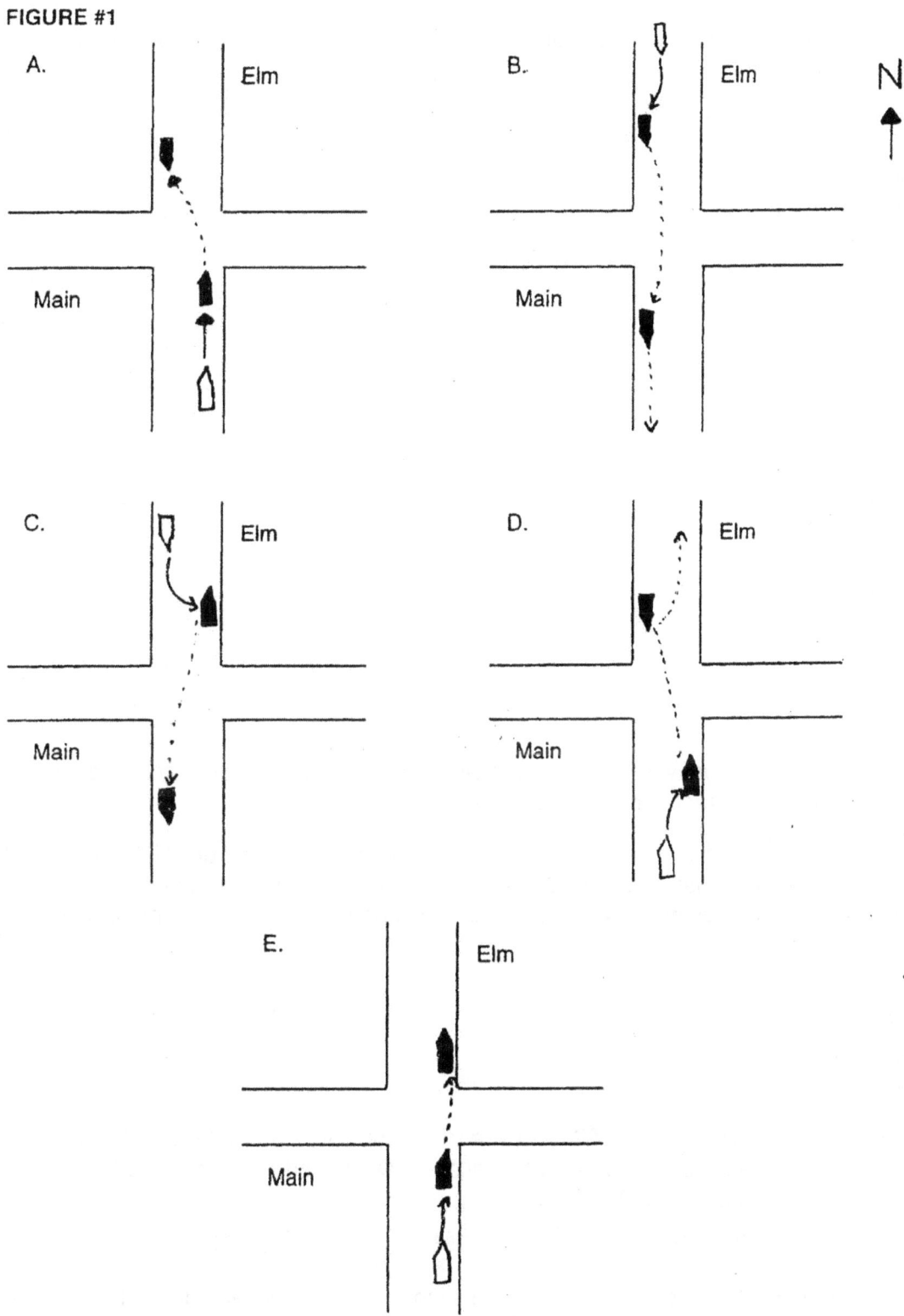

Questions 20-22

In questions 20 through 22, choose the word or phrase CLOSEST in meaning to the word or phrase printed in capital letters.

20. REDRESS

    A. suspend
    B. repeat
    C. compensate
    D. subdue

20.____

21. PRECEDENT

    A. cohort
    B. example
    C. obstruction
    D. elder

21.____

22. ADJUDICATION

    A. case
    B. judgment
    C. claim
    D. defendant

22.____

Questions 23-25

Questions 23 through 25 measure your ability to do fieldwork-related arithmetic. Each question presents a separate arithmetic problem for you to solve.

23. The Department of Sanitation purchased seven vehicles in the last year. Four of the vehicles were street sweepers that cost $95,000 each. Three were garbage compactors that cost $160,000 each. The average price of a vehicle purchased by the Department in the last year was about

    A. $98,000
    B. $108,000
    C. $122,000
    D. $145,000

23.____

24. Agent Frederick, whose car gets about 24 miles to the gallon, drives to Buffalo, 260 miles away. The average price of gasoline is $2.30 a gallon. How much did Agent Frederick spend on gas for the trip to Buffalo?

    A. $11   B. $25   C. $55   D. $113

24.____

25. Over the last four days, Precinct 11 has had 20 misdemeanor arrests each day. If the precinct records 15 misdemeanor arrests on the fifth day, what will its average daily number of misdemeanor arrests be?

    A. 16   B. 17   C. 18   D. 19

25.____

KEY (CORRECT ANSWERS)

1. D
2. C
3. A
4. A
5. B

6. A
7. A
8. C
9. A
10. B

11. A
12. B
13. C
14. A
15. D

16. B
17. A
18. E
19. C
20. C

21. B
22. B
23. C
24. B
25. D

TEST 2

DIRECTIONS: Each question or incomplete statement is followed by several suggested answers or completions. Select the one that BEST answers the question or completes the statement. *PRINT THE LETTER OF THE CORRECT ANSWER IN THE SPACE AT THE RIGHT.*

Questions 1-9

Questions 1 through 9 measure your ability to (1) determine whether statements from witnesses say essentially the same thing and (2) determine the evidence needed to make it reasonably certain that a particular conclusion is true.
To do well on this part of the test, you do NOT have to have a working knowledge of police procedures and techniques. Nor do you have to have any more familiarity with criminals and criminal behavior than that acquired from reading newspapers, listening to radio or watching TV. To do well in this part, you must read and reason carefully.

1. Which of the following pairs of statements say essentially the same thing in two different ways?
    I. All of the teachers at the school are wise, but some have proven to be bad-tempered.
       Teachers at the school are either wise or bad-tempered.
    II. If John can both type and do long division, he is qualified for this job.
        If John applies for this job, he can both type and do long division.

    A. I only
    B. I and II
    C. II only
    D. Neither I nor II

2. Which of the following pairs of statements say essentially the same thing in two different ways?
    I. If Carl rides the A train, the C train is down.
       Carl doesn't ride the A train unless the C train is down.
    II. If the three sides of a triangle are equal, the triangle is equilateral.
        A triangle is equilateral if the three sides are equal.

    A. I only
    B. I and II
    C. II only
    D. Neither I nor II

3. Which of the following pairs of statements say essentially the same thing in two different ways?
    I. If this dog has a red collar, it must be Slim.
       If this dog does not have a red collar, it can't be Slim.
    II. Dr. Slouka is not in his office during lunchtime.
        If it's not lunchtime, Dr. Slouka is in his office.

    A. I only
    B. I and II
    C. II only
    D. Neither I nor II

4. Which of the following pairs of statements say essentially the same thing in two different ways?
   I. At least one caseworker at Social Services has a degree in psychology.
   Not all the caseworkers at Social Services have a degree in psychology.
   II. If an officer doesn't pass the physical fitness test, he cannot be promoted.
   If an officer is not promoted, he hasn't passed the physical fitness test.

   A. I only
   B. I and II
   C. II only
   D. Neither I nor II

5. Summary of Evidence Collected to Date:
   I. All the Class II inspectors use multiplication when they inspect escalators.
   II. On some days, Fred, a Class II inspector, doesn't use multiplication at all.
   III. Fred's friend, Garth, uses multiplication every day.
   Prematurely Drawn Conclusion: Garth inspects escalators every day.
   Which of the following pieces of evidence, if any, would make it *reasonably certain* that the conclusion drawn is true?

   A. Garth is a Class II inspector
   B. Fred never inspects escalators
   C. Fred usually doesn't inspect escalators
   D. None of these

6. Summary of Evidence Collected to Date:
   I. Every one of the shelter's male pit bulls has been neutered.
   II. Some male pit bulls have also been muzzled.
   Prematurely Drawn Conclusion: Rex has been neutered.
   Which of the following pieces of evidence, if any, would make it *reasonably certain* that the conclusion drawn is true?

   A. Rex, a pit bull at the shelter, has been muzzled
   B. All of the pit bulls at the shelter are males
   C. Rex is one of the shelter's male pit bulls
   D. None of these

7. Summary of Evidence Collected to Date:
   I. Some of the social workers at the clinic have been welfare recipients.
   II. Some of the social workers at the clinic are college graduates.
   Prematurely Drawn Conclusion: Some of the social workers at the clinic who are college graduates have never received welfare benefits.
   Which of the following pieces of evidence, if any, would make it *reasonably certain* that the conclusion drawn is true?

   A. There are more college graduates at the clinic than those who have received welfare benefits
   B. There is an odd number of social workers at the clinic
   C. The number of college graduates and former welfare recipients at the clinic is the same
   D. None of these

8. <u>Summary of Evidence Collected to Date:</u>
Everyone who works at the library has read *War and Peace*. Most people who have read *War and Peace* have also read *Anna Karenina*.
<u>Prematurely Drawn Conclusion:</u> Marco has read *War and Peace*.
Which of the following pieces of evidence, if any, would make it *reasonably certain* that the conclusion drawn is true?

8.____

   A. Marco works at the library
   B. Marco has probably read *Anna Karenina*
   C. Everyone who has read *Anna Karenina* has read *War and Peace*
   D. None of these

9. <u>Summary of Evidence Collected to Date:</u>
Officer Skiles is working on the Martin investigation.
<u>Prematurely Drawn Conclusion:</u> Skiles is also working on the Bartlett case.
Which of the following pieces of evidence, if any, would make it *reasonably certain* that the conclusion drawn is true?

9.____

   A. Everyone who is working on the Martin investigation is also working on the Bartlett investigation
   B. Everyone who is working on the Bartlett investigation is also working on the Martin investigation
   C. The Martin investigation and Bartlett investigation are being conducted at the same time
   D. None of these

Questions 10-14

Questions 10 through 14 refer to Map #2 and measure your ability to orient yourself within a given section of town, neighborhood or particular area. Each of the questions describes a starting point and a destination. Assume that you are driving a car in the area shown on the map accompanying the questions. Use the map as a basis for the shortest way to get from one point to another without breaking the law.

On the map, a street marked by arrows, or by arrows and the words "One Way," indicates one-way travel, and should be assumed to be one-way for the entire length, even when there are breaks or jogs in the street. EXCEPTION: A street that does not have the same name over the full length.

4 (#2)

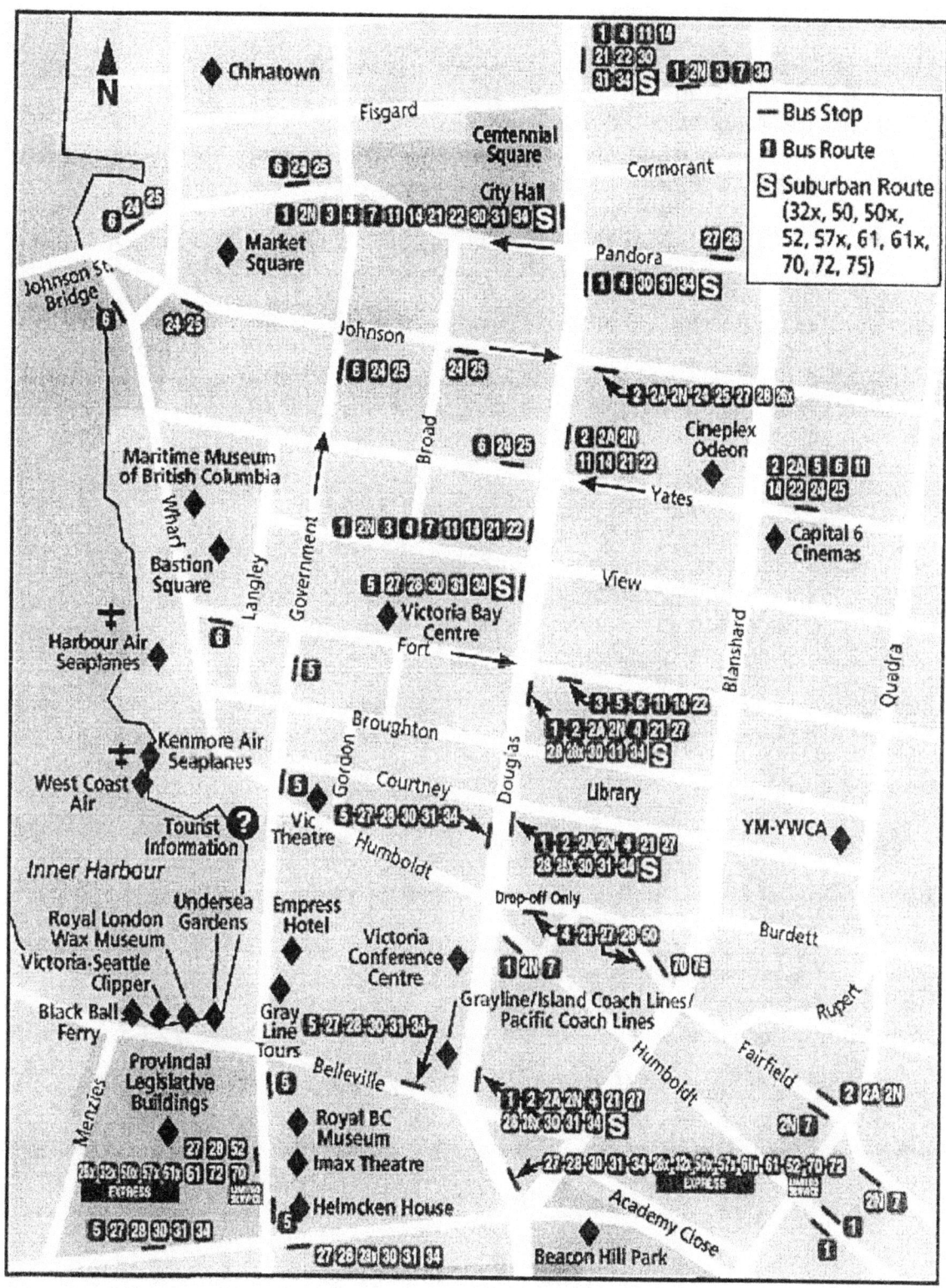

Map #2

10. The shortest legal way from the Royal London Wax Museum to the Chinatown block is   10._____

    A. east on Belleville, north on Douglas, west on Broughton, north on Government
    B. east on Belleville, north on Government
    C. east on Belleville, north on Government, west on Yates, north on Wharf
    D. east on Belleville, north on Douglas, west on Fisgard

11. The shortest legal way from the Maritime Museum of British Columbia to the Victoria   11._____
    Conference Centre is

    A. north on Wharf, east on Yates, south on Douglas
    B. south and west on Wharf, north on Government, east on Broughton, south on Douglas
    C. south on Wharf, east on Fort, south on Douglas
    D. south and west on Wharf, south on Government, east on Belleville, north on Douglas

12. The shortest legal way from Market Square to City Hall is   12._____

    A. north on Government, east on Fisgard, south on Douglas
    B. east on Pandora, north on Douglas
    C. east on Johnson, north on Blanshard, west on Pandora, north on Douglas
    D. east on Johnson, north on Douglas

13. The shortest legal way from the Victoria Bay Centre to Bastion Square is   13._____

    A. east on Fort, south on Douglas, west on Broughton, north on Wharf
    B. west on Fort, north on Government, west on Yates, south on Wharf
    C. west on Fort, north on Wharf
    D. east on Fort, north on Douglas, west on Johnson, south on Wharf

14. The shortest legal way from The Empress Hotel to the YM-YWCA is   14._____

    A. north on Government, east on Broughton
    B. north on Government, east on Courtney
    C. north on Government, southeast on Humboldt, north on Quadra
    D. north on Government, west on Courtney

Questions 15-19

Questions 15 through 19 refer to Figure #2, on the following page, and measure your ability to understand written descriptions of events. Each question presents a description of an accident or event and asks you which of the five drawings in Figure #2 BEST represents it.

In the drawings, the following symbols are used:

Moving vehicle: ◻   Non-moving vehicle: ◼

Pedestrian or bicycle: ●

The path and direction of travel of a vehicle or pedestrian is indicated by a solid line.

The path and direction of travel of each vehicle or pedestrian directly involved in a collision from the point of impact is indicated by a dotted line.

In the space at the right, print the letter of the drawing that best fits the descriptions written below:

15. A driver traveling north on Taylor strikes a parked car in the rear and knocks it forward, where it collides with a pedestrian in the crosswalk.   15._____

16. A driver headed south on Taylor strikes another car that is traveling east through the intersection of Taylor and Hayes. After the impact, the eastbound car veers to the right and strikes a pedestrian in the crosswalk on Jones.   16._____

17. A driver headed south on Taylor runs a red light and strikes another car that is headed east on Hayes. The eastbound car is knocked into a pedestrian that is using the crosswalk on Taylor   17._____

18. A driver traveling south on Taylor makes a sudden left turn onto Hayes. In the intersection, he strikes the front of an oncoming car and veers onto Hayes, where he strikes a pedestrian in the crosswalk.   18._____

19. A driver headed west on Hayes strikes a car that is traveling east through the intersection of Taylor and Hayes. After the impact, the eastbound car veers to the right and strikes a pedestrian in the crosswalk on Jones.   19._____

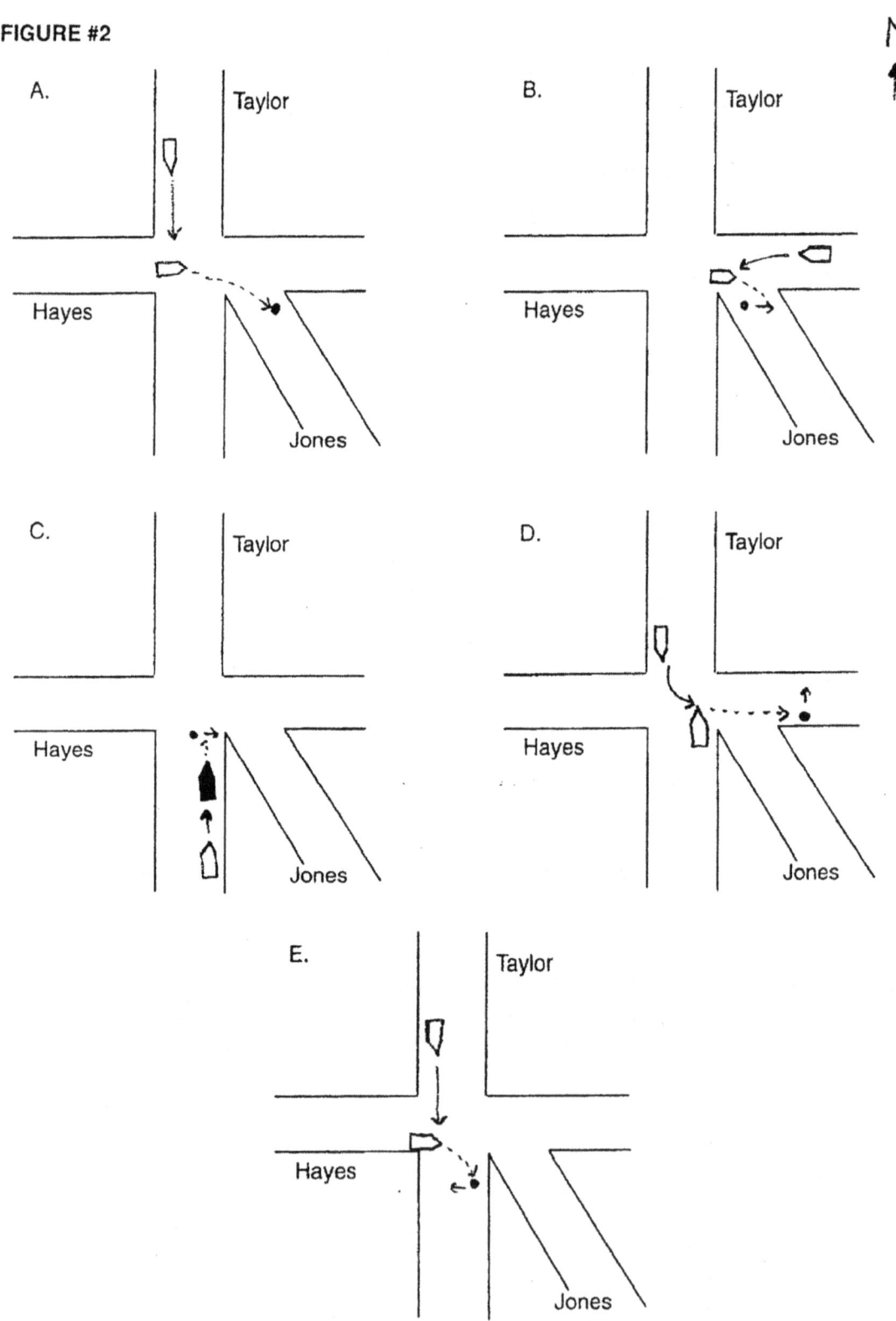

FIGURE #2

Questions 20-22

In questions 20 through 22, choose the word or phrase CLOSEST in meaning to the word or phrase printed in capital letters.

20. SEQUESTER

    A. follow
    B. separate
    C. endorse
    D. punish

20.____

21. EXECUTE

    A. carry out
    B. advance
    C. impede
    D. occur

21.____

22. SUPPRESS

    A. uphold
    B. convict
    C. forbid
    D. compensate

22.____

Questions 23-25

Questions 23 through 25 measure your ability to do fieldwork-related arithmetic. Each question presents a separate arithmetic problem for you to solve..

23. In the election for the presidency of Local Union 1134, Stan Fitz received 542 votes, Elizabeth Stuckey received 430 votes and Gene Sterner received 130 votes. Ninety percent of those eligible to vote did so. What was the number of eligible voters?

    A. 900
    B. 992
    C. 1102
    D. 1224

23.____

24. The Department of Records wants to sort its files alphabetically into boxes that hold an average of 50 files each. The Department has 1,140 records, an amount that is expected to double in the next ten years. To have enough boxes ten years from now, the Department should buy at least _____ boxes.

    A. 23   B. 38   C. 45   D. 47

24.____

25. The office's petty cash fund contains a total of $433 on Wednesday. At the beginning of the day, Arnold reimburses $270 that he had previously borrowed from the fund. Then Janet withdraws $158 for office supplies; Hank spends $87 on lunch for a committee meeting; and at the end of the day, Ernestine buys a new office calendar for $12. How much remains in the petty cash fund at the end of the day on Wednesday?

    A. $94   B. $257   C. $446   D. $527

25.____

KEY (CORRECT ANSWERS)

1.	D	11.	C
2.	B	12.	D
3.	A	13.	A
4.	D	14.	B
5.	A	15.	C
6.	C	16.	A
7.	D	17.	E
8.	A	18.	D
9.	A	19.	B
10.	B	20.	B

21.	A
22.	C
23.	D
24.	D
25.	C

PROBLEM SENSITIVITY

This section of the exam measures your ability to choose the course of action that should be taken <u>first</u> in critical situations.

Sample Questions

1. What should an officer do <u>first</u> when investigating an incident?

    A. Write a report of the incident.
    B. Inform other police officers of the incident.
    C. Proceed to the scene of the incident.
    D. Interview witnesses.

1.____

Getting the correct information to the emergency medical personnel is extremely important. It is suggested that you, the police officer, make the call if possible, or assign the task to a person who appears calm. If you are alone at the accident scene, do not leave the victim until breathing is restored, all bleeding has been stopped, the victim is no longer in danger of further injury, and all precautions have been taken against shock. When the emergency medical personnel arrive, brief them as to what happened to the victim, the type of first aid you have administered, and the physical status of the victim.

2. When the emergency medical personnel arrives at the accident scene, you <u>first</u> should tell them:

    A. how long the victim's breathing has been restored.
    B. how long the bleeding has been stopped.
    C. that the victim appeared to be going into shock.
    D. the type of first aid you administered.

2.____

KEY (CORRECT ANSWERS)

1. C
2. D

PREPARING WRITTEN MATERIAL

PARAGRAPH REARRANGEMENT
COMMENTARY

The sentences that follow are in scrambled order. You are to rearrange them in proper order and indicate the letter choice containing the correct answer at the space at the right.

Each group of sentences in this section is actually a paragraph presented in scrambled order. Each sentence in the group has a place in that paragraph; no sentence is to be left out. You are to read each group of sentences and decide upon the best order in which to put the sentences so as to form a well-organized paragraph.

The questions in this section measure the ability to solve a problem when all the facts relevant to its solution are not given.

More specifically, certain positions of responsibility and authority require the employee to discover connection between events sometimes, apparently, unrelated. In order to do this, the employee will find it necessary to correctly infer that unspecified events have probably occurred or are likely to occur. This ability becomes especially important when action must be taken on incomplete information.

Accordingly, these questions require competitors to choose among several suggested alternatives, each of which presents a different sequential arrangement of the events. Competitors must choose the MOST logical of the suggested sequences.

In order to do so, they may be required to draw on general knowledge to infer missing concepts or events that are essential to sequencing the given events. Competitors should be careful to infer only what is essential to the sequence. The plausibility of the wrong alternatives will always require the inclusion of unlikely events or of additional chains of events which are NOT essential to sequencing the given events.

It's very important to remember that you are looking for the best of the four possible choices, and that the best choice of all may not even be one of the answers you're given to choose from.

There is no one right way to solve these problems. Many people have found it helpful to first write out the order of the sentences, as they would have arranged them, on their scrap paper before looking at the possible answers. If their optimum answer is there, this can save them some time. If it isn't, this method can still give insight into solving the problem. Others find it most helpful to just go through each of the possible choices, contrasting each as they go along. You should use whatever method feels comfortable and works for you.

While most of these types of questions are not that difficult, we've added a higher percentage of the difficult type, just to give you more practice. Usually there are only one or two questions on this section that contain such subtle distinctions that you're unable to answer confidently. And you then may find yourself stuck deciding between two possible choices, neither of which you're sure about.

EXAMINATION SECTION
TEST 1

DIRECTIONS: The sentences that follow are in scrambled order. You are to rearrange them in proper order and indicate the letter choice containing the CORRECT answer. *PRINT THE LETTER OF THE CORRECT ANSWER IN THE SPACE AT THE RIGHT.*

1. Fire Marshal Adams has arrested a man for pulling a false alarm. He has recorded the following items of information about the incident in his notebook for use in his subsequent report: 1.____
    I. I was on surveillance at a frequently pulled false alarm box located at Edison Street and Harvard Road.
    II. At 1605 hours, I observed the white male, with long brown hair and a mustache, wearing black pants and a red shirt, pull the fire alarm box.
    III. I interviewed the officer of the first due ladder company, Lt. Morgan - L-37, who informed me that a search of the area disclosed no cause for an alarm to be transmitted.
    IV. A man wearing a red shirt, black pants, with long brown hair and a mustache came out of Ryan's Pub, located at Edison Street and Harvard Road, and walked directly to the alarm box.
    V. I stopped the man about five blocks away at 33rd Street and Harvard Road and asked him why he pulled the fire alarm box, and he replied, *Because I felt like it.*

    The MOST logical order for the above sentences to appear in the report is

    A. I, IV, II, III, V
    B. I, II, III, IV, V
    C. I, IV, III, II, V
    D. I, IV, V, II, III

2. A fire marshal is preparing a report regarding Tom Jones, who was a witness to an arson fire at his apartment building. Following are five sentences which will be included in the report: 2.____
    I. On July 16, I responded to the fire building, address 2020 Elm Street, to interview Tom Jones.
    II. Tom Jones described the *super* (name unknown) as a middle-aged male with beard, six feet tall, wearing a blue jumpsuit.
    III. Tom Jones stated that he saw the *super* of the building next door set the fire.
    IV. After being advised of his constitutional rights at the 44th Precinct detective's squad room, the *super* confessed.
    V. I interviewed the *super* and took him to the precinct for further investigation.

    The MOST logical order for the above sentences to appear in the report is

    A. I, II, III, V, IV
    B. I, II, III, IV, V
    C. I, III, II, IV, V
    D. I, III, II, V, IV

3. A fire marshal is preparing a report on a shooting incident which will include the following five sentences:
   I. I ran around the corner and observed a man pointing a gun at another man.
   II. I informed the man I was a police officer and that he should drop his gun.
   III. I was on the corner of 4th Avenue and 43rd Street when I heard a gunshot coming from around the corner.
   IV. The man turned around and pointed his gun at me.
   V. I fired once, shooting him in the chest and causing him to fall to the ground.
   The MOST logical order for the above sentences to appear in the report is

   A. I, III, IV, II, V
   B. IV, V, II, I, III
   C. III, I, II, IV, V
   D. III, I, V, II, IV

4. Fire Marshal Smith is writing a report. The report will include the following five sentences:
   I. I asked the woman for a description of the man and his location in the building.
   II. When I said, *Don't move, Five Marshal*, the man dropped the can containing a flammable liquid.
   III. I transmitted on my handie-talkie for fire companies to respond.
   IV. A woman approached our car and said there was a man pouring a liquid, which she thought to be gasoline, on a staircase at 123 East Street.
   V. Upon entering that location, I observed a man spilling a liquid on the floor.
   The MOST logical order for the above sentences to appear on the interview sheet is

   A. IV, I, V, II, III
   B. I, IV, III, V, II
   C. V, II, IV, I, III
   D. IV, III, I, V, II

5. Fire Marshal Fox is completing an interview report for a fire in the kitchen of an apartment at 1700 Clayton Road. The following five sentences will be included in the interview report:
   I. This is the first fire in which Mrs. Brown has ever been involved.
   II. A neighbor smelled the food burning and called the Fire Department.
   III. Mrs. Brown has been a tenant in Apt. 4C for 7 years.
   IV. Mrs. Brown was very tired and laid down to rest and fell asleep.
   V. Mrs. Brown was cooking beef stew in the kitchen after coming home from work.
   The MOST logical order for the above sentences to appear in the report is

   A. II, III, I, IV, V
   B. III, V, IV, II, I
   C. I, III, II, V, IV
   D. III, V, I, IV, II

6. A fire marshal is completing a report of an arson fire. The report will contain the following five statements made by a witness:
   I. I heard the sound of breaking glass; and when I looked out my window, I saw orange flames coming from the building across the street.
   II. I saw two young men on bicycles rapidly riding away, one with long blond hair, the other had long brown hair.
   III. He made a threat to get even when he was being evicted.
   IV. The young man with long blond hair was evicted from the fire building last week.
   V. The two young men rode in the direction of Flowers Avenue.
   The MOST logical order for the above statements to appear in the report is

A.	I, II, V, IV, III	B.	I, II, IV, V, III
C.	III, I, V, II, IV	D.	III, I, II, IV, V

7. A fire marshal is preparing a report regarding an eleven-year-old who was burned in a fire at the Midtown School for Boys. The report will include the following five sentences:
    I. The child described the fire-setter as a male with glasses, five feet tall, wearing a blue uniform.
    II. On December 12, I responded to Hill Top Hospital to interview a child who was burned in a fire at the Midtown School for Boys.
    III. The male perpetrator made a full confession in front of the Assistant District Attorney at the precinct.
    IV. I responded to the school, after interviewing the boy, and found a security guard who fit the description.
    V. I interviewed the security guard and took him to the precinct for further questioning.

    The MOST logical order for the above sentences to appear in the fire report is

    A. I, IV, V, II, III   B. IV, III, II, I, V
    C. II, I, IV, V, III   D. II, IV, I, V, III

8. A fire marshal is preparing a report concerning a fire in an auto body shop. The report will contain the following five sentences:
    I. The shop owner stated that he argued with a customer about the cost of a repair job.
    II. The shop owner will be the complainant in the arson case.
    III. While on surveillance, my partner and I saw the fire and called it in over the Department radio.
    IV. The customer paid the bill and left saying, *I'll fix you for charging so much*.
    V. According to witnesses, the customer returned to the shop and threw a Molotov cocktail on the floor.

    The MOST logical order for the above sentences to appear in the report is

    A. I, IV, V, II, III   B. III, I, IV, V, II
    C. V, I, IV, III, II   D. III, V, I, IV, II

9. Security Officer Mace is completing an entry in her memo-book. The entry has the following five sentences:
    I. I observed the defendant removing a radio from a facility vehicle.
    II. I placed the defendant under arrest and escorted him to the patrolroom.
    III. I was patrolling the facility parking lot.
    IV. I asked the defendant to show identification.
    V. I determined that the defendant was not authorized to remove the radio.

    The MOST logical order for these sentences to be entered in Officer Mace's memo-book is

    A. I, III, II, IV, V   B. II, V, IV, I, III
    C. III, I, IV, V, II   D. IV, V, II, I, III

10. Security Officer Riley is completing an entry in his memo-book. The entry has the following five sentences:
    I. Anna Jones admitted that she stole Mary Green's wallet.
    II. I approached the women and asked them who they were and why they were arguing.
    III. I arrested Anna Jones for stealing Mary Green's wallet.
    IV. They identified themselves and Mary Green accused Anna Jones of stealing her wallet.
    V. I was in the lobby area when I observed two women arguing about a wallet.

    The MOST logical order for these sentences to be entered in Officer Riley's memo-book is

    A. II, IV, I, III, V
    B. III, I, IV, V, II
    C. IV, I, V, II, III
    D. V, II, IV, I, III

11. Assume that Security Officer John Ryan is completing an entry in his memobook. The entry has the following five sentences:
    I. I then cleared the immediate area of visitors and staff.
    II. I noticed smoke coming from a broom closet outside Room A71.
    III. Sergeant Mueller arrived with other officers to assist in clearing the area.
    IV. Upon investigation, I determined the smoke was due to burning material in the broom closet.
    V. I pulled the corridor fire alarm and notified Sergeant Mueller of the fire.

    The MOST logical order for these sentences to be entered in Officer Ryan's memo-book is

    A. II, III, IV, V, I
    B. II, IV, V, I, III
    C. IV, I, II, III, V
    D. V, III, II, I, IV

12. Security Officer Hernandez is completing an entry in his memobook. The entry has the following five sentences:
    I. I asked him to leave the premises immediately.
    II. A visitor complained that there was a strange man loitering in Clinic B hallway.
    III. I went to investigate and saw a man dressed in rags sitting on the floor of the hallway.
    IV. As he walked out, he started yelling that he had no place to go.
    V. I asked to see identification, but he said that he did not have any.

    The MOST logical order for these sentences to be entered in Officer Hernandez's memobook is

    A. II, III, V, I, IV
    B. III, I, II, IV, V
    C. IV, I, V, II, III
    D. III, I, V, II, IV

13. Officer Hogan is completing an entry in his memobook. The entry has the following five sentences:
    I. When the fighting had stopped, I transmitted a message requesting medical assistance for Mr. Perkins.
    II. Special Officer Manning assisted me in stopping the fight.
    III. When I arrived at the scene, I saw a client, Adam Finley, strike a facility employee, Peter Perkins.
    IV. As I attempted to break up the fight, Special Officer Manning came on the scene.
    V. I received a radio message from Sergeant Valez to investigate a possible fight in progress in the waiting room.

    The MOST logical order for these sentences to be entered in Officer Hogan's memo-book is

    A. II, I, IV, V, III
    B. III, V, II, IV, I
    C. IV, V, III, I, II
    D. V, III, IV, II, I

14. Police Officer White is preparing a crime report concerning the burglary of Mr. Smith's home. The report will contain the following five sentences:
    I. Upon entering the house, Mr. Smith noticed that the mortgage money, which had been left on the kitchen table, had been taken.
    II. An investigation by the reporting Officer determined that the burglar had left the house through the first floor rear door.
    III. Further investigation revealed that there were no witnesses to the burglary.
    IV. In addition, several pieces of jewelry were missing from a first floor bedroom.
    V. After arriving at home, Mr. Smith discovered that someone had broken into the house by jimmying the front door.

    The MOST logical order for the above sentences to appear in the report is

    A. V, IV, II, III, I
    B. V, I, III, IV, II
    C. V, I, IV, II, III
    D. V, IV, II, I, III

15. Police Officer Jenner responds to the scene of a burglary at 2106 La Vista Boulevard. He is approached by an elderly man named Richard Jenkins, whose account of the incident includes the following five sentences:
    I. I saw that the lock on my apartment door had been smashed and the door was open.
    II. My apartment was a shambles; my belongings were everywhere and my television set was missing.
    III. As I walked down the hallway toward the bedroom, I heard someone opening a window.
    IV. I left work at 5:30 P.M. and took the bus home.
    V. At that time, I called the police.

    The MOST logical order for the above sentences to appear in the report is

    A. I, V, IV, II, III
    B. IV, I, II, III, V
    C. I, V, II, III, IV
    D. IV, III, II, V, I

16. Police Officer LaJolla is writing an Incident Report in which back-up assistance was required. The report will contain the following five sentences:
    I. The radio dispatcher asked what my location was and he then dispatched patrol cars for back-up assistance.
    II. At approximately 9:30 P.M., while I was walking my assigned footpost, a gunman fired three shots at me.
    III. I quickly turned around and saw a White male, approximately 5'10", with black hair, wearing blue jeans, a yellow T-shirt, and white sneakers, running across the avenue carrying a handgun.
    IV. When the back-up officers arrived, we searched the area but could not find the suspect.
    V. I advised the radio dispatcher that a gunman had just fired a gun at me, and then I gave the dispatcher a description of the man.

    The MOST logical order for the above sentences to appear in the report is

    A. III, V, II, IV, I
    B. II, III, V, I, IV
    C. III, II, IV, I, V
    D. II, V, I, III, IV

17. Police Officer Engle is completing a Complaint Report of a burglary which occurred at Monty's Bar. The following five sentences will be included in the Complaint Report:
    I. The owner said that approximately $600 was taken, along with eight bottles of expensive brandy.
    II. The burglar apparently gained entry to the bar through the window and exited through the front door.
    III. When Mr. Barrett returned to reopen the bar at 1:00 P.M., he found the front door open and items thrown all over the bar.
    IV. Mr. Barrett, the owner of Monty's Bar, said he closed the bar at 4:00 M. and locked all the doors.
    V. After interviewing the owner, I conducted a search of the bar and found that a window in the back of the bar was broken.

    The MOST logical order for the above sentences to appear in the report is

    A. II, IV, III, V, I
    B. IV, III, I, V, II
    C. IV, II, III, I, V
    D. II, V, IV, III, I

18. Police Officer Revson is writing a report concerning a vehicle pursuit. His report will include the following five sentences:
    I. I followed the vehicle for several blocks and then motioned to the driver to pull the car over to the curb and stop.
    II. I informed the radio dispatcher that I was in a high-speed pursuit.
    III. When the driver ignored me, I turned on my siren and the driver increased his speed.
    IV. The vehicle hit a tree, and I was able to arrest the driver.
    V. While on patrol in Car #4135, I observed a motorist driving suspiciously.

    The MOST logical order for the above sentences to appear in the report is

    A. V, I, III, II, IV
    B. II, V, III, I, IV
    C. V, I, II, IV, III
    D. II, I, V, IV, III

19. Crime Reports are completed by Police Officers. One section of a report contains the following five sentences: 19.____
    I. The man, seeing that the woman had the watch, pushed Mr. Lugano to the ground.
    II. Frank Lugano was walking into the Flame Diner on Queens Boulevard when he was jostled by a man in front of him.
    III. A few minutes later, Mr. Lugano told a police officer on foot patrol about a man and a woman taking his watch.
    IV. As soon as he was jostled, a woman reached toward Mr. Lugano's wrist and removed his expensive watch.
    V. The man and woman, after taking Mr. Lugano's watch, ran around the corner.

    The MOST logical order for the above sentences to appear in the report is

    A. II, IV, I, III, V
    B. II, IV, I, V, III
    C. IV, I, III, II, V
    D. IV, II, I, V, III

20. Detective Adams completed a Crime Report which includes the following five sentences: 20.____
    I. I arrived at the scene of the crime at 10:20 A.M. and began to question Mr. Sands about the security devices he had installed.
    II. Several clearly identifiable fingerprints were found.
    III. A Fingerprint Unit specialist arrived at the scene and immediately began to dust for fingerprints.
    IV. After questioning Mr. Sands, I called the Fingerprint Unit.
    V. On Friday morning at 10 A.M., Mr. Sands, the owner of the High Fashion Fur Store on Fifth Avenue, called the precinct to report that his safe had been broken into.

    The MOST logical order for the above sentences to appear in the Crime Report is

    A. I, V, IV, III, II
    B. I, V, III, IV, II
    C. V, I, IV, II, III
    D. V, I, IV, III, II

KEY (CORRECT ANSWERS)

1. A
2. D
3. C
4. A
5. B

6. A
7. C
8. B
9. C
10. D

11. B
12. A
13. D
14. C
15. B

16. B
17. B
18. A
19. B
20. D

TEST 2

DIRECTIONS: The sentences that follow are in scrambled order. You are to rearrange them in proper order and indicate the letter choice containing the CORRECT answer. *PRINT THE LETTER OF THE CORRECT ANSWER IN THE SPACE AT THE RIGHT.*

1. Police Officer Ling is preparing a Complaint Report of a missing person. His report will contain the following five sentences:
    I. I was greeted by Mrs. Miah Ali, who stated her daughter Lisa, age 17, did not return from school.
    II. I questioned Mrs. Ali as to what time her daughter left for school and what type of clothing she was wearing.
    III. I notified the Patrol Sergeant, searched the building and area, and prepared a Missing Person Complaint Report.
    IV. I received a call from the radio dispatcher to respond to 9 Maple Street, Apartment 1H, on a missing person complaint.
    V. Mrs. Ali informed me that Lisa was wearing a grey suit and black shoes, and departed for school at 7:30 A.M.

    The MOST logical order for the above sentences to appear in the report is

    A. IV, I, V, II, III
    B. I, IV, V, III, II
    C. IV, I, II, V, III
    D. III, I, IV, II, V

    1.____

2. Police Officer Dunn is preparing a Complaint Report which will include the following five sentences:
    I. Mrs. Field screamed and fought with the man.
    II. A man wearing a blue ski mask grabbed Mrs. Field's purse.
    III. Mrs. Field was shopping on 34th Street and Broadway at 1 o'clock in the afternoon.
    IV. The man then ran around the corner.
    V. The man was white, five feet six inches tall with a medium build.

    The MOST logical order for the above sentences to appear in the report is

    A. I, V, II, IV, III
    B. III, II, I, IV, V
    C. III, IV, V, I, II
    D. V, IV, III, I, II

    2.____

3. Police Officer Davis is preparing a written report concerning child abuse. The report will include the following five sentences:
    I. I responded to the scene and was met by an adult and a child who was approximately four years old.
    II. I was notified by an unidentified pedestrian of a possible case of child abuse at 325 Belair Terrace.
    III. The adult told me that the child fell and that the police were not needed.
    IV. I felt that this might be a case of child abuse, and I requested that a Sergeant respond to the scene.
    V. The child was bleeding from the head and had several bruises on the face.

    The MOST logical order for the above sentences to appear in the report is

    A. II, I, V, III, IV
    B. I, II, IV, III, V
    C. I, III, IV, II, V
    D. II, IV, I, V, III

    3.____

4. The following five sentences will be part of a memobook entry concerning found property:

   I. Mr. Gustav said that while cleaning the lobby he found six credit cards and a passport.
   II. The credit cards and passport were issued to Manuel Gomez.
   III. I went to the precinct to give the property to the Desk Officer.
   IV. I prepared a receipt listing the property, gave the receipt to Mr. Gustav, and had him sign my memobook.
   V. While on foot patrol, I was approached by Mr. Gustav, the superintendent of 50-12 Maiden Parkway.

   The MOST logical order for the above sentences to appear in the memobook is

   A. V, I, II, IV, III
   B. I, II, IV, III, V
   C. V, I, III, IV, II
   D. I, IV, III, II, V

5. Police Officer Thomas is making a memobook entry that will include the following five sentences:

   I. My partner obtained a brief description of the suspects and the direction they were heading when they left the store.
   II. Edward Lemkin was asked to come with us to search the immediate area.
   III. I transmitted this information over the radio.
   IV. At the corner of 72nd Street and Broadway, our patrol car was stopped by Edward Lemkin, the owner of PJ Records.
   V. He told us that a group of teenagers stole some merchandise from his record store.

   The MOST logical order for the above sentences to appear in the report is

   A. V, IV, I, III, II
   B. IV, V, I, III, II
   C. V, I, III, II, IV
   D. IV, I, III, II, V

6. Police Officer Caldwell is completing a Complaint Report. The report will include the following five sentences:

   I. When I yelled, *Don't move, Police,* the taller man dropped the bat and ran.
   II. I asked the girl for a description of the two men.
   III. I called for an ambulance.
   IV. A young girl approached me and stated that a man with a baseball bat was beating another man in front of 1700 Grande Street.
   V. Upon approaching the location, I observed the taller man hitting the other man with the bat.

   The MOST logical order for the above sentences to appear in the report is

   A. IV, V, I, II, III
   B. V, IV, II, III, I
   C. V, I, III, IV, II
   D. IV, II, V, I, III

7. Police Officer Moore is writing a memobook entry concerning a summons he issued. The entry will contain the following five sentences:
   I. As I was walking down the platform, I heard music coming from a radio that a man was holding on his shoulder.
   II. I asked the man for some identification.
   III. I was walking in the subway when a passenger complained about a man playing a radio loudly at the opposite end of the station.
   IV. I then gave the man a summons for playing the radio. V. As soon as the man saw me approaching, he turned the radio off.
   The MOST logical order for the above sentences to appear in the memobook entry is

   A. III, V, II, I, IV
   B. I, II, V, IV, III
   C. III, I, V, II, IV
   D. I, V, II, IV, III

8. Police Officer Kashawahara is completing an Incident Report regarding fleeing suspects he had pursued earlier. The report will include the following five sentences:
   I. I saw two males attempting to break into a store through the front window.
   II. On Myrtle Avenue, they ran into an alley between two abandoned buildings.
   III. I yelled to them, *Hey, what are you guys doing by that window?*
   IV. At that time, I lost sight of the suspects and I returned to the station house.
   V. They started to run south on Wycoff Avenue heading towards Myrtle Avenue.
   The MOST logical order for the above sentences to appear in the report is

   A. I, V, II, IV, III
   B. III, V, II, IV, I
   C. I, III, V, II, IV
   D. III, I, V, II, IV

9. Police Officer Bloom is completing an entry in his memo-book regarding a confession made by a perpetrator. The entry will include the following five sentences:
   I. I went towards the dresser and took $400 in cash and a jewelry box with rings, watches, and other items in it.
   II. There in the bedroom, lying on the bed, a woman was sleeping.
   III. It was about 1:00 A.M. when I entered the apartment through an opened rear window.
   IV. I spun around, punched her in the face with my free hand, and then jumped out the window into the street.
   V. I walked back to the window carrying the money and the jewelry box and was about to go out when all of a sudden I heard the woman scream.
   The MOST logical order for the above sentences to appear in the memobook entry is

   A. I, III, II, V, IV
   B. I, V, IV, III, II
   C. III, II, I, V, IV
   D. III, V, IV, I, II

10. Police Officer Webster is preparing an Arrest Report which will include the following five sentences:
    I. I noticed that the robber had a knife placed at the victim's neck.
    II. I told the robber to drop the knife.
    III. While on patrol, I observed a robbery which was in progress.
    IV. I grabbed the robber, placed him in handcuffs, and took him to the precinct.
    V. The robber dropped the knife and tried to flee.
    The MOST logical order for the above sentences to appear in the report is

    A. I, II, V, IV, III
    B. III, I, II, V, IV
    C. III, II, IV, I, V
    D. I, III, IV, V, II

11. Police Officer Lee is preparing a report regarding someone who apparently attempted to commit suicide with a gun. The report will include the following five sentences:
    I. At the location, the woman pointed to the open door of Apartment 7L.
    II. I called for an ambulance to respond.
    III. The male had a gun in his hand and a large head wound.
    IV. A call was received from the radio dispatcher regarding a woman who heard a gunshot at 936 45th Avenue.
    V. Upon entering Apartment 7L, I saw the body of a male on the kitchen floor.

    The MOST logical order for the above sentences to appear in the report is

    A. IV, I, V, III, II
    B. I, III, V, IV, II
    C. I, V, III, II, IV
    D. IV, V, III, II, I

12. Police Officer Modrak is completing a memobook entry which will include the following five sentences:
    I. The victim, a male in his thirties, told me that the robbery occurred a few minutes ago.
    II. My partner and I jumped out of the patrol car and arrested the suspect.
    III. We responded to an armed robbery in progress at Billings Avenue and 59th Street.
    IV. On Chester Avenue and 68th Street, the victim spotted and identified the suspect.
    V. I told the victim to get into the patrol car and that we would drive him around the area.

    The MOST logical order for the above sentences to appear in the memobook is

    A. III, I, V, IV, II
    B. I, III, V, II, IV
    C. I, IV, III, V, II
    D. III, V, I, II, IV

13. Police Officer Rodriguez is preparing a report concerning an incident in which she used her revolver. Her report will include the following five sentences:
    I. Upon seeing my revolver, the robber dropped his gun to the ground.
    II. At about 10:55 P.M., I was informed by a passerby that several people were being robbed at gunpoint on 174th Street and Walton Avenue.
    III. I was assigned to patrol on 174th Street and Ghent Avenue during the evening shift.
    IV. I saw a man holding a gun on three people, took out my revolver, and shouted, *Police, don't move!*
    V. After calling for assistance, I went to 174th Street and Walton Avenue and took cover behind a car.

    The MOST logical order for the above sentences to appear in the report is

    A. II, III, IV, V, I
    B. IV, V, I, III, II
    C. III, II, V, IV, I
    D. II, IV, I, V, III

14. Police Officer Davis is completing an Activity Log entry which will include the following five sentences:
    I. A radio car was dispatched and the male was taken to Greenville Hospital.
    II. Several people saw him and called the police.
    III. A naked man was running down the street waving his arms above his head and screaming, *Insects are all over me!*
    IV. I arrived on the scene and requested an ambulance.
    V. The dispatcher informed me that no ambulances were available.

    The MOST logical order for the above sentences to appear in the Activity Log is

    A. III, IV, V, I, II
    B. II, III, V, I, IV
    C. III, II, IV, V, I
    D. II, IV, III, V, I

15. Police Officer Peake is completing an entry in his Activity Log. The entry contains the following five sentences:
    I. He went to his parked car only to find he was blocked in.
    II. The owner of the vehicle refused to move the van until he had finished his lunch.
    III. Approximately 30 minutes later, I arrived on the scene and ordered the owner of the van to remove the vehicle.
    IV. Mr. O'Neil had an appointment and was in a hurry to keep it.
    V. Mr. O'Neil entered a nearby delicatessen and asked if anyone in there drove a dark blue van, license plate number BUS 265.

    The MOST logical order for the above sentences to appear in the Activity Log is

    A. II, III, I, IV, V
    B. IV, I, V, II, III
    C. V, IV, I, III, II
    D. II, I, III, IV, V

16. Police Officer Harrison is preparing a report regarding a 10-year-old who was sexually abused at school. The report will include the following five sentences:
    I. The child described the perpetrator as a white male with a mustache, six feet tall, wearing a green uniform.
    II. On September 10, I responded to General Hospital to interview a child who was sexually abused.
    III. He later confessed at the station house.
    IV. After I interviewed the child, I responded to the school and found a janitor who fit the description.
    V. I interviewed the janitor and took him to the station house for further investigation.

    The MOST logical order for the above sentences to appear in the report is

    A. II, IV, I, V, III
    B. I, IV, V, II, III
    C. II, I, IV, V, III
    D. V, III, II, I, IV

17. Police Officer Madden is completing a report of a theft. The report will include the following five sentences:
    I. I followed behind the suspect for two blocks.
    II. I saw a man pass by the radio car carrying a shopping bag.
    III. I looked back in the direction he had just come from and noticed that the top of a parking meter was missing.
    IV. As he saw me, he started to walk faster, and I noticed a red piece of metal with the word *violation* drop out of the shopping bag.
    V. When I saw a parking meter in the shopping bag, I apprehended the suspect and placed him under arrest.
    The MOST logical order for the above sentences to appear in the report is

    A. I, IV, II, III, V
    B. II, I, IV, V, III
    C. II, IV, III, I, V
    D. III, II, IV, I, V

18. Police Officer McCaslin is preparing a report of disorderly conduct which will include the following five sentences:
    I. Police Officer Kenny and I were on patrol in a radio car when we received a dispatch to go to the Hard Rock Disco on Third Avenue.
    II. We arrived at the scene and found three men arguing loudly and obviously intoxicated.
    III. The dispatcher had received a call from a bartender regarding a dispute.
    IV. Two of the men left the disco shortly before we did.
    V. We calmed the men down after managing to separate them.
    The MOST logical order for the above sentences to appear in the report is

    A. I, II, V, III, IV
    B. III, I, IV, II, V
    C. II, I, III, IV, V
    D. I, III, II, V, IV

19. Police Officer Langhorne is completing a report of a murder. The report will contain the following five statements made by a witness:
    I. The noise created by the roar of a motorcycle caused me to look out of my window.
    II. I ran out of the house and realized the man was dead, which is when I called the police.
    III. I saw a man driving at high speed down the dead-end street on a motorcycle, closely followed by a green BMW.
    IV. The motorcyclist then parked the bike and approached the car, which was occupied by two males.
    V. Two shots were fired and the cyclist fell to the ground; then the car made a u-turn and sped down the street.
    The MOST logical order for the above sentences to appear in the report is

    A. I, II, IV, III, V
    B. V, II, I, IV, III
    C. I, III, IV, V, II
    D. III, IV, I, II, V

20. Police Officer Murphy is preparing a report of a person who was assaulted. The report will include the following five sentences:
    I. I responded to the scene, but Mr. Jones had already fled.
    II. She was bleeding profusely from a cut above her right eye.
    III. Mr. and Mrs. Jones apparently were fighting in the street when Mr. Jones punched his wife in the face.
    IV. I then applied pressure to the cut to control the bleeding.
    V. I called the dispatcher on the radio to send an ambulance to respond to the scene.

    The MOST logical order for the above sentences to appear in the report is

    A. III, II, IV, I, V
    B. III, I, II, IV, V
    C. I, V, II, III, IV
    D. II, V, IV, III, I

KEY (CORRECT ANSWERS)

1.	C	11.	A
2.	B	12.	A
3.	A	13.	C
4.	A	14.	C
5.	B	15.	B
6.	D	16.	C
7.	C	17.	C
8.	C	18.	D
9.	C	19.	C
10.	B	20.	B

PREPARING WRITTEN MATERIALS
EXAMINATION SECTION
TEST 1

DIRECTIONS: Each question consists of a sentence which may be classified appropriately under one of the following four categories:
    A. Incorrect because of faulty grammar or sentence structure.
    B. Incorrect because of faulty punctuation.
    C. Incorrect because of faulty spelling or capitalization.
    D. Correct

Examine each sentence carefully. Then, in the space at the right, print the capital letter preceding the option which is the BEST of the four suggested above. All incorrect sentences contain only one type of error. Consider a sentence correct if it contains none of the types of errors mentioned, although there may be other correct ways of expressing the same thought.

1. The fire apparently started in the storeroom, which is usually locked.   1.____

2. On approaching the victim two bruises were noticed by this officer.   2.____

3. The officer, who was there examined the report with great care.   3.____

4. Each employee in the office had a separate desk.   4.____

5. The suggested procedure is similar to the one now in use.   5.____

6. No one was more pleased with the new procedure than the chauffeur.   6.____

7. He tried to pursuade her to change the procedure.   7.____

8. The total of the expenses charged to petty cash were high.   8.____

9. An understanding between him and I was finally reached.   9.____

10. It was at the supervisor's request that the clerk agreed to postpone his vacation.   10.____

11. We do not believe that it is necessary for both he and the clerk to attend the conference.   11.____

12. All employees, who display perseverance, will be given adequate recognition.   12.____

13. He regrets that some of us employees are dissatisfied with our new assignments.   13.____

14. "Do you think that the raise was merited," asked the supervisor? 14.____

15. The new manual of procedure is a valuable supplament to our rules and regulation. 15.____

16. The typist admitted that she had attempted to pursuade the other employees to assist her in her work. 16.____

17. The supervisor asked that all amendments to the regulations be handled by you and I. 17.____

18. They told both he and I that the prisoner had escaped. 18.____

19. Any superior officer, who, disregards the just complaints of his subordinates, is remiss in the performance of his duty. 19.____

20. Only those members of the national organization who resided in the Middle west attended the conference in Chicago. 20.____

21. We told him to give the investigation assignment to whoever was available. 21.____

22. Please do not disappoint and embarass us by not appearing in court. 22.____

23. Despite the efforts of the Supervising mechanic, the elevator could not be started. 23.____

24. The U.S. Weather Bureau, weather record for the accident date was checked. 24.____

KEY (CORRECT ANSWERS)

1.	D	11.	A
2.	A	12.	B
3.	B	13.	D
4.	D	14.	B
5.	D	15.	C
6.	D	16.	C
7.	C	17.	A
8.	A	18.	A
9.	A	19.	B
10.	D	20.	C

21.	D
22.	C
23.	C
24.	B

TEST 2

DIRECTIONS: Each question consists of a sentence. Some of the sentences contain errors in English grammar or usage, punctuation, spelling, or capitalization. A sentence does not contain an error simply because it could be written in a different manner. Choose answer:
- A. If the sentence contains an error in English grammar or usage.
- B. if the sentence contains an error in punctuation.
- C. If the sentence contains an error in spelling or capitalization
- D. If the sentence does not contain any errors.

1. The severity of the sentence prescribed by contemporary statutes—including both the former and the revised New York Penal Laws—do not depend on what crime was intended by the offender.

2. It is generally recognized that two defects in the early law of attempt played a part in the birth of burglary: (1) immunity from prosecution for conduct short of the last act before completion of the crime, and (2) the relatively minor penalty imposed for an attempt (it being a common law misdemeanor) vis-à-vis the completed offense.

3. The first sentence of the statute is applicable to employees who enter their place of employment, invited guests, and all other persons who have an express or implied license or privilege to enter the premises.

4. Contemporary criminal codes in the United States generally divide burglary into various degrees, differentiating the categories according to place, time and other attendent circumstances.

5. The assignment was completed in record time but the payroll for it has not yet been prepaid.

6. The operator, on the other hand, is willing to learn me how to use the mimeograph.

7. She is the prettiest of the three sisters.

8. She doesn't know; if the mail has arrived.

9. The doorknob of the office door is broke.

10. Although the department's supply of scratch pads and stationery have diminished considerably, the allotment for our division has not been reduced.

11. You have not told us whom you wish to designate as your secretary.

12. Upon reading the minutes of the last meeting, the new proposal was taken up for consideration.

13. Before beginning the discussion, we locked the door as a precautionery measure.   13._____

14. The supervisor remarked, "Only those clerks, who perform routine work, are permitted to take a rest period."   14._____

15. Not only will this duplicating machine make accurate copies, but it will also produce a quantity of work equal to fifteen transcribing typists. 15._____

16. "Mr. Jones," said the supervisor, "we regret our inability to grant you an extention of your leave of absence."   16._____

17. Although the employees find the work monotonous and fatigueing, they rarely complain.   17._____

18. We completed the tabulation of the receipts on time despite the fact that Miss Smith our fastest operator was absent for over a week. 18._____

19. The reaction of the employees who attended the meeting, as well as the reaction of those who did not attend, indicates clearly that the schedule is satisfactory to everyone concerned. 19._____

20. Of the two employees, the one in our office is the most efficient.   20._____

21. No one can apply or even understand, the new rules and regulations. 21._____

22. A large amount of supplies were stored in the empty office.   22._____

23. If an employee is occassionally asked to work overtime, he should do so willingly.   23._____

24. It is true that the new procedures are difficult to use but, we are certain that you will learn them quickly.   24._____

25. The office manager said that he did not know who would be given a large allotment under the new plan.   25._____

KEY (CORRECT ANSWERS)

1. A
2. D
3. D
4. C
5. C

6. A
7. D
8. B
9. A
10. A

11. D
12. A
13. C
14. B
15. A

16. C
17. C
18. B
19. D
20. A

21. B
22. A
23. C
24. B
25. D

TEST 3

DIRECTIONS: Each of the following sentences may be classified MOST appropriately under one of the following categories:
- A. Faulty because of incorrect grammar
- B. Faulty because of incorrect punctuation
- C. Faulty because of incorrect capitalization
- D. Correct

Examine each sentence carefully. Then, in the space at the right, print the capital letter preceding the option which is the BEST of the four suggested above. All incorrect sentence contain but one type of error. Consider a sentence correct if it contains none of the types of errors mentioned, even though there may be other correct ways of expressing the same thought.

1. The desk, as well as the chairs, were moved out of the office.   1.____

2. The clerk whose production was greatest for the month won a day's vacation as first prize.   2.____

3. Upon entering the room, the employees were found hard at work at their desks.   3.____

4. John Smith our new employee always arrives at work on time.   4.____

5. Punish whoever is guilty of stealing the money.   5.____

6. Intelligent and persistent effort lead to success no matter what the job may be.   6.____

7. The secretary asked, "can you call again at three o'clock?"   7.____

8. He told us, that if the report was not accepted at the next meeting, it would have to be rewritten.   8.____

9. He would not have sent the letter if he had known that it would cause so much excitement.   9.____

10. We all looked forward to him coming to visit us.   10.____

11. If you find that you are unable to complete the assignment please notify me as soon as possible.   11.____

12. Every girl in the office went home on time but me; there was still some work for me to finish.   12.____

13. He wanted to know who the letter was addressed to, Mr. Brown or Mr. Smith.   13.____

14. "Mr. Jones, he said, please answer this letter as soon as possible."   14.____

15. The new clerk had an unusual accent inasmuch as he was born and educated in the south. 15.____

16. Although he is younger than her, he earns a higher salary. 16.____

17. Neither of the two administrators are going to attend the conference being held in Washington, D.C. 17.____

18. Since Miss Smith and Miss Jones have more experience than us, they have been given more responsible duties. 18.____

19. Mr. Shaw the supervisor of the stock room maintains an inventory of stationery and office supplies. 19.____

20. Inasmuch as this matter affects both you and I, we should take joint action. 20.____

21. Who do you think will be able to perform this highly technical work? 21.____

22. Of the two employees, John is considered the most competent. 22.____

23. He is not coming home on tuesday; we expect him next week. 23.____

24. Stenographers, as well as typists must be able to type rapidly and accurately. 24.____

25. Having been placed in the safe we were sure that the money would not be stolen. 25.____

KEY (CORRECT ANSWERS)

1.	A	11.	B
2.	D	12.	D
3.	A	13.	A
4.	B	14.	B
5.	D	15.	C
6.	A	16.	A
7.	C	17.	A
8.	B	18.	A
9.	D	19.	B
10.	A	20.	A

21.	D
22.	A
23.	C
24.	B
25.	A

TEST 4

DIRECTIONS: Each of the following sentences consist of four sentences lettered A, B, C, and D. One of the sentences in each group contains an error in grammar or punctuation. Indicate the INCORRECT sentence in each group. *PRINT THE LETTER OF THE CORRECT ANSWER IN THE SPACE AT THE RIGHT.*

1. A. Give the message to whoever is on duty.
    B. The teacher who's pupil won first prize presented the award.
    C. Between you and me, I don't expect the program to succeed.
    D. His running to catch the bus caused the accident.

2. A. The process, which was patented only last year is already obsolete.
    B. His interest in science (which continues to the present) led him to convert his basement into a laboratory.
    C. He described the book as "verbose, repetitious, and bombastic".
    D. Our new director will need to possess three qualities: vision, patience, and fortitude.

3. A. The length of ladder trucks varies considerably.
    B. The probationary fireman reported to the officer to who he was assigned.
    C. The lecturer emphasized the need for we firemen to be punctual.
    D. Neither the officers nor the members of the company knew about the new procedure.

4. A. Ham and eggs is the specialty of the house.
    B. He is one of the students who are on probation.
    C. Do you think that either one of us have a chance to be nominated for president of the class?
    D. I assume that either he was to be in charge or you were.

5. A. Its a long road that has no turn.
    B. To run is more tiring than to walk.
    C. We have been assigned three new reports: namely, the statistical summary, the narrative summary, and the budgetary summary.
    D. Had the first payment been made in January, the second would be due in April.

6. A. Each employer has his own responsibilities.
    B. If a person speaks correctly, they make a good impression.
    C. Every one of the operators has had her vacation.
    D. Has anybody filed his report?

7. A. The manager, with all his salesmen, was obliged to go.
    B. Who besides them is to sign the agreement?
    C. One report without the others is incomplete.
    D. Several clerks, as well as the proprietor, was injured.

2 (#4)

8. A. A suspension of these activities is expected.   8._____
    B. The machine is economical because first cost and upkeep are low.
    C. A knowledge of stenography and filing are required for this position.
    D. The condition in which the goods were received shows that the packing was not done properly.

9. A. There seems to be a great many reasons for disagreement.   9._____
    B. It does not seem possible that they could have failed.
    C. Have there always been too few applicants for these positions?
    D. There is no excuse for these errors.

10. A. We shall be pleased to answer your question.   10._____
    B. Shall we plan the meeting for Saturday?
    C. I will call you promptly at seven.
    D. Can I borrow your book after you have read it?

11. A. You are as capable as I.   11._____
    B. Everyone is willing to sign but him and me.
    C. As for he and his assistant, I cannot praise them too highly.
    D. Between you and me, I think he will be dismissed.

12. A. Our competitors bid above us last week.   12._____
    B. The survey which was began last year has not yet been completed.
    C. The operators had shown that they understood their instructions.
    D. We have never ridden over worse roads.

13. A. Who did they say was responsible?   13._____
    B. Whom did you suspect?
    C. Who do you suppose it was?
    D. Whom do you mean?

14. A. Of the two propositions, this is the worse.   14._____
    B. Which report do you consider the best—the one in January or the one in July?
    C. I believe this is the most practicable of the many plans submitted.
    D. He is the youngest employee in the organization.

15. A. The firm had but three orders last week.   15._____
    B. That doesn't really seem possible.
    C. After twenty years scarcely none of the old business remains.
    D. Has he done nothing about it?

KEY (CORRECT ANSWERS)

1.	B	6.	B	11.	C
2.	A	7.	D	12.	B
3.	C	8.	C	13.	A
4.	C	9.	A	14.	B
5.	A	10.	D	15.	C

REPORT WRITING

EXAMINATION SECTION

TEST 1

DIRECTIONS: Each question or incomplete statement is followed by several suggested answers or completions. Select the one that BEST answers the question or completes the statement. *PRINT THE LETTER OF THE CORRECT ANSWER IN THE SPACE AT THE RIGHT.*

Questions 1-5.

DIRECTIONS: Questions 1 through 5 are to be answered SOLELY on the basis of the following report.

REPORT OF DEFECTIVE EQUIPMENT

DEPARTMENT: *Social Services*   REPORT NO. 3026
DIVISION: *Personnel*   DATE OF REPORT: *5/27*
ROOM: 120B

DEFECTIVE EQUIPMENT: *Six office telephones with pick-up and hold buttons*

DESCRIPTION OF DEFECT: *Marjorie Black, a Clerk, called on 5/22 to report that the button lights for the four lines on all six telephones in her office were not functioning and it was, therefore, impossible to know which lines were in use. On 5/26, Howard Perl, Admin. Asst., called in regard to the same telephones. He was annoyed because no repairs had been made and stated that all the employees in his unit were being inconvenienced. He requested prompt repair service.*

Ruth Gomez
SIGNATURE OF REPORTING EMPLOYEE
Sr. Telephone Operator
TITLE

JUDITH O'LAUGHLIN
SIGNATURE OF SUPERVISOR

TO BE COMPLETED AFTER SERVICING
DATE: 5/28
APPROVED: *Judy O'Laughlin*

---

1. The person who made a written report about the improper functioning of telephones in the Personnel division is
   A. Marjorie Black
   B. Ruth Gomez
   C. Howard Perl
   D. Judith O'Laughlin

1.____

2. How many days elapsed between the original request for telephone repair service and the completion of service?   2.____
   A. 2   B. 4   C. 5   D. 6

3. Of the following, the only information NOT given in the report is   3.____
   A. number of employees affected by the defective service
   B. number of the report
   C. number of telephones with a button defect
   D. telephone numbers of the defective phones

4. The one of the following items of information which would have been LEAST helpful to the repairman who was assigned this repair job is that   4.____
   A. the defect involved pick-up buttons for 4 serviced lines
   B. the location is Room 120B in the Department of Social Services
   C. Marjorie Black initially reported the defective equipment
   D. six telephone units need to be repaired

5. Which of the following statements is CORRECT concerning the people mentioned in the report?   5.____
   A. Ruth Gomez has a higher titled than Judith O'Laughlin
   B. Judith O'Laughlin's signature appears twice on this form
   C. Howard Perl reported on May 25 that the telephones needed adjusting
   D. Marjorie Black reported that she was disturbed that no repairs had been made

Questions 6-10.

DIRECTIONS: Questions 6 through 10 are based on the UNUSUAL OCCURRENCE REPORT given below. Five phrases in the report have been removed and are listed below the report as 1. through 5. in each of the five places where phrases of the report have been left out, the number of a question has been inserted. For each question, select the number of the missing phrase which would make the report read correctly.

UNUSUAL OCCURRENCE REPORT

POST _____
TOUR _____
DATE _____

Location of Occurrence:_____
REMARKS: While making rounds this morning, I thought that I heard some strange sounds coming from Storeroom #55. Upon investigation, I saw that <u>6</u> and that the door to the storeroom was slightly opened. At 2:45 A.M. I <u>7</u>.

Suddenly two men jumped out from <u>8</u>, dropped the tools which they were holding, and made a dash for the door. I ordered them to stop, but they just kept running.

3 (#1)

I was able to get a good look at both of them. One man was wearing a green jacket and had a full beard, and the other was short and had blond hair. Immediately, I called the police; and about two minutes later, I notified 9. I 10 the police arrived, and I gave them the complete details of the incident.

                                                Security Officer Donald Rimson   23807
                                                         Signature   Pass No.

1. the special inspection control desk
2. behind some crates
3. the lock had been tampered with
4. remained at the storeroom unit
5. entered the storeroom and began to look around

6.   A. 1   B. 3   C. 4   D. 5   6.____

7.   A. 2   B. 3   C. 4   D. 5   7.____

8.   A. 1   B. 2   C. 3   D. 4   8.____

9.   A. 1   B. 2   C. 3   D. 4   9.____

10. A. 2   B. 3   C. 4   D. 5   10.____

Questions 11-13.

DIRECTIONS: Below is a report consisting of 15 numbered sentences, some of which are not consistent with the principles of good report writing. Questions 11 through 13 are to be answered SOLELY on the basis of the information contained in the report and your knowledge of investigative principles and practices.

To: Tom Smith, Administrative Investigator
From: John Jones, Supervising Investigator

1. On January 7, I received a call from Mrs. H. Harris of 684 Sunset Street, Brooklyn.
2. Mr. Harris informed me that she wanted to report an instance of fraud relating to public assistance payments being received by her neighbor, Mrs. I Wallace.
3. I advised her that such a subject would best be discussed in person.
4. I then arranged a field visitation for January 10 at Mrs. Harris' apartment, 684 Sunset Street, Brooklyn.
5. On January 10, I discussed the basis for Mrs. Harris' charge against Mrs. Wallace at the former's apartment.
6. She stated that her neighbor is receiving Aid to Dependent Children payments for seven children, but that only three of her children are still living with her.
7. In addition, Mrs. Harris also claimed that her husband, whom she reported to the authorities as missing, usually sees her several times a week.
8. After further questioning, Mrs. Harris admitted to me that she had been quite friendly with Mrs. Wallace until they recently argued about trash left in their adjoining hall corridor.

9. However, she firmly stated that her allegations against Mrs. Wallace were valid and that she feared repercussions for her actions.
10. At the completion of the interview, I assured Mrs. Harris of the confidentiality of her statements and that an attempt would be made to verify her allegations.
11. As I was leaving Mrs. Harris' apartment, I noticed a man, aged approximately 45, walking out of Mrs. Wallace's apartment.
12. I followed him until he entered an old green Oldsmobile and sped away.
13. On January 3, I returned to 684 Sunset Court, having determined that Mrs. Wallace is receiving assistance as indicated by Mrs. Harris.
14. However, upon presentation of official identification Mrs. Wallace refused to admit me to her apartment or grant an interview.
15. I am therefore referring this matter to you for further instructions.

          John Jones
          Supervising Investigator

11. The one of the following statements that clearly lacks vital information is Statement
    A. 8   B. 10   C. 12   D. 14

12. Which of the following sentences from the report is ambiguous?
    A. 2   B. 3   C. 7   D. 10

13. Which of the following sentences contains information contradicting other data in the above report? Sentence
    A. 3   B. 8   C. 10   D. 13

Questions 14-16.

DIRECTIONS: Questions 14 through 16 are to be answered on the basis of the following report.

To: Ralph King   Date: April 3
       Senior Menagerie Keeper   Subject:

From: William Rattner
         Menagerie Keeper

This memorandum is to inform you of the disappearance of the boa constrictor from the Reptile Collection in the Main Building.

This morning upon entering the room, I realized that the snake was missing. After having asked around, I am of the opinion that the boa constrictor has been stolen. Since there are no signs of forced entry, it seems likely that whoever removed the snake from the premises entered the room through a window which had been left unlocked the previous night. I, therefore, suggest that all zoo personnel be more concerned with proper security measures in the future so that something like this does not happen again.

14. Which one of the following pieces of information has been OMITTED from the report by the Menagerie Keeper?
    A. Action taken by him after his discovery that the boa constrictor was missing
    B. The date that the disappearance of the boa constrictor was noted
    C. The time that the disappearance of the boa constrictor was noted
    D. The building in which the boa constrictor was kept

    14.____

15. Based upon information contained in the above paragraph, which of the following statements would be BEST as the subject of this report?
    A. Request for more effective security measures in the oo
    B. Vandalism in the zoo
    C. Disappearance of boa constrictor
    D. Request for replacement of boa constrictor

    15.____

16. According to the above report, which of the following statements CANNOT be considered factual?
    A. The boa constrictor was being kept in the Main Building
    B. The boa constrictor is missing
    C. All zoo personnel are careless about security measures
    D. There are no signs of forced entry

    16.____

Questions 17-19.

DIRECTIONS: Questions 17 through 19 are to be answered on the basis of the Accident Report below. Read this report carefully before answering the questions. Select your answers ONLY on the basis of this report.

ACCIDENT REPORT

February 14

On February 14 at 3:45 P.M., Mr. Warren, while on the top of a stairway at the 34th Street Station, realized the *D* train was in the station loading passengers. In this haste to catch the train, he forcefully ran down the stairs, pushing aside three other people also going down the stairs. Mr. Parker, one of the three people, lost his footing and fell to the bottom of the stairs. Working on the platform, I saw Mr. Parker lose his footing as a result of Mr. Warren's actions, and I immediately went to his aid. Assistant Station Supervisor Brown was attracted to the incident after a crowd had gathered. After 15 minutes, the injured man, Mr. Parker, got up and boarded a train that was in the station and, therefore, he was not hurt seriously.

R. Sands #3214
Conductor

17. Since accident reports should only contain facts, which of the following should NOT be put into the accident report?
    A. The incident took place at the 34th Street Station.
    B. Mr. Parker was not hurt seriously.
    C. The date that the report was written
    D. Mr. Sands went to the aid of the injured an

18. The title of the person submitting the report was
    A. Porter
    B. Assistant Station Supervisor
    C. Conductor
    D. Passenger

    18.____

19. The TOTAL number of different persons mentioned in this report is
    A. seven   B. six   C. five   D. four

    19.____

Questions 20-24.

DIRECTIONS: Questions 20 through 24 are to be answered SOLELY on the basis of the following report which is similar to those used in departments for reporting accidents,

REPORT OF ACCIDENT

Date of Accident 3/21   Tim: 3:43 P.M.   Date of Report: 3/24

Department Vehicle
Operator's Name: James Doe
Title: Motor Vehicle Operator
Vehicle Code No. 22-187
License Plate No.: 3N-1234

Damage to Vehicle: Right rear fender ripped, hubcap dented, rear bumper twisted
Place of Accident: 8th Avenue & 48th Street

Vehicle No. 2
Operator's Name: Richard Roe
Operator's Address: 841 W. 68th St.
Owner' Name: Jane Roe
Owner's Address: 2792 Beal Ave.
License Plate No. 8Y-6789
Damage to Vehicle: Grill, radiator, right side of front bumper, right-front fender and headlight crushed.

Description of Accident: I was driving east on 48th Street with the green light. I was almost across 8th Avenue when Ford panel truck started forth and crashed into my rear right fender. Denver of Ford used abusive language and accused me of rolling into his truck.

Persons Injured

Name Richard Roe   Address 841 W. 68TH Street
Name _____   Address _____
Name _____   Address _____

20. Witnesses

Name Richard Roe   Address 841 W. 68th Street
Name John Brown   Address 226 South Avenue
Name Mary Green   Address 42 East Street

Report Prepared By James Doe
Title MVO Badge No. 11346

20. According to the above description of the accident, the diagram that would BEST show how and where the vehicles crashed is

A.
B.
C.
D.

21. Of the following words used in the report, the one spelled INCORRECTLY is
A. abussive   B. accused   C. radiator   D. twisted

22. The city vehicle involved in this accident can BEST be identified
A. as a panel truck
B. the Department vehicle
C. by the Badge Number of the operator
D. by the Vehicle Code Number

23. According to the information in the report, the right-of-way belonged to
A. neither vehicle   B. the Department vehicle
C. the vehicle that took it D. Vehicle No. 2

24. An entry on the report that seems to be INCORRECT is the
A. first witness   B. second witness
C. third witness   D. owner's name

25. Assume that the following passage is taken from a report which you, a deputy chief, receive from a battalion chief under your command. The report relates to a fire for which the department received public criticism because of delay in response and extension of fire to neighboring buildings.
Alarm from box ____ was received at 5:13 P.M. on Friday, October 2. All first alarm companies departed from quarters expeditiously but progress along the vehicle-glutted arterial thoroughfare was agonizingly slow. By dint of

extraordinary effort and by virtue of great skill in maneuvering through impassable traffic, Engine Co. _____ arrived at the scene at 5:21 P.M. The sight which greeted them was a virtual Dante's INFERNO, of holocaust proportions. The hub of the conflagration was the penultimate structure of a row of houses, with extension impending to contiguous edifices. The MAIN fault with the above report is that it
  A. contains spelling and punctuation errors
  B. contains unnecessary details
  C. uses words not in accordance with dictionary definitions
  D. uses inappropriate language and style.

KEY (CORRECT ANSWERS)

1.	B		11.	C
2.	D		12.	C
3.	A		13.	D
4.	C		14.	C
5.	B		15.	C
6.	B		16.	C
7.	D		17.	B
8.	B		18.	C
9.	A		19.	B
10.	C		20.	A

21.	A
22.	D
23.	B
24.	A
25.	D

TEST 2

DIRECTIONS: Each question or incomplete statement is followed by several suggested answers or completions. Select the one that BEST answers the question or completes the statement. *PRINT THE LETTER OF THE CORRECT ANSWER IN THE SPACE AT THE RIGHT.*

Questions 1-4.

DIRECTIONS: Questions 1 through 4 are to be answered on the basis of the information in the report below.

On February 15, Mr. Smith and Mr. Brown were injured in an accident occurring in the shop at 10 Long Road. No one was in the area of the accident other than Mr. Smith and Mr. Brown. Both of these employees described the following circumstances.

1. Mr. Brown saw the largest tool on the wall begin to fall from where it was hanging and run up to push Mr. Smith out of the way and to prevent the tool from falling, if possible.
2. Mr. Smith was standing near the wall under some tools which were hanging on nails in the wall.
3. Mr. Brown was standing a few steps from the wall.
4. Mr. Brown stepped toward Mr. Smith, who was on the floor and away from the falling tool. He tripped and fell over a piece of equipment on the floor.
5. Mr. Brown pushed Mr. Smith, who slipped on some grease on the floor and fell to the side, out of the way of the falling tool.
6. Mr. Brown tried to avoid Mr. Smith as he fell. In so doing, he fell against some pipes which were leaning against the wall. The pipes fell on both Mr. Brown and Mr. Smith.

Mr. Smith and Mr. Brown were both badly bruised and shaken. They were sent to the General Hospital to determine if any bones were broken. The office was later notified that neither employee was seriously hurt.

Since the accident, matters relating to safety and accident prevention around the shop have occupied the staff. There have been a number of complaints about the location of tools and equipment. Several employees are reluctant to work in the shop unless conditions are improved. Please advise as to the best way to handle this situation.

1. The one of the following which it is MOST important to add to the above memorandum is
   A. a signature line
   B. a transmittal note
   C. the date of the memo
   D. the initials of the typist

2. The MOST logical order in which to list the circumstances relative to the accident is
   A. as shown (1, 2, 3, 4, 5, 6)
   B. 2, 3, 1, 5, 4, 6
   C. 1, 5, 4, 6, 3, 2
   D. 3, 2, 4, 6, 1, 5

3. The one of the following which does NOT properly belong with the rest of the memorandum is
   A. the first section of paragraph 1
   B. the list of circumstances
   C. paragraph 2
   D. paragraph 3

4. According to the information in the memorandum, the BEST description of the subject is:
   A. Effect of accident on work output of the division
   B. Description of accident involving Mr. Smith and Mr. Brown
   C. Recommendations on how to avoid future accidents
   D. Safety and accident control in the shop

Questions 5-10.

DIRECTIONS: A ferry terminal supervisor is asked to write a report on the incident described in the following passage. Questions 5 through 10 are to be answered on the basis of the incident and the supervisor's report. Your answers should be based on the assumption that everything described in the passage is true.

On July 27, a rainy, foggy day, Joseph Jones and Steven Smith were in the Whitehall Ferry Terminal at about 9:50 A.M. waiting for the 10:00 A.M. ferry to Staten Island. Smith, seated with his legs stretched out in the aisle, was reading the sports page of the DAILY NEWS. Jones was walking by, drinking ginger ale from a cup. Neither man paid any attention to the other until Jones tripped over Smith's foot, fell to the floor, and dropped his drink. Smith looked at Jones as he lay on the floor and burst out laughing. Jones, infuriated, got up and punched Smith in the jaw. The force of the blow drove Smith's head back against the bench on which he was sitting. Smith did not fight back; he appeared to be dazed. Bystanders called a terminal worker, who assisted in making Smith as comfortable as possible.

One of the other people in the terminal for the ferry was a nurse, who examined Smith and told the ferry terminal supervisor that Smith probably had a concussion. An ambulance was called to take Smith to the hospital. A policeman arrived on the scene.

Jones' injury consisted of a sprained ankle and some bruises, but he refused medical attention. Jones explained to the supervisor what had happened. Jones truly regretted what he had done and went to the local police station with the policeman.

5. Of the following facts about the above incident, which one would be MOST important to include in the ferry terminal supervisor's report?
   A. The time the next boat was due to arrive
   B. Jones was carrying a cup of ginger ale
   C. Smith was sitting with his legs stretched out in the aisle
   D. Why Smith and Jones were in the terminal

6. The MAIN purpose of writing a report of the above incident is to
   A. make recommendations for preventing fights in the terminal
   B. state the important facts of the incident
   C. blame Jones for not looking where he was going
   D. provide evidence that Smith was not at fault

7. An adequate report of the above incident MUST give the names of the participants, the names of witnesses, and the
    A. date, the place, the time, and the events that took place
    B. date, the events that took place, the time, and the names of the terminal personnel on duty that day
    C. place, the names of the terminal personnel on duty that day, the weather conditions, and the events which took place
    D. names of the passengers in the terminal, the time, the place, and the events which took place

8. The supervisor asked for individuals who had witnessed the entire incident to give their account of what they had seen. Thomas White, a twelve-year-old boy said that Jones fell, got up, turned, and then hit Smith.
Thomas White's description of the incident is
    A. *adequate*; it is truthful, straight-forward, and includes necessary details
    B. *adequate*; it shows that the incident was not started on purpose
    C. *inadequate*; he is too young to understand the implications of his testimony
    D. *inadequate*; it omits certain pertinent facts about the incident

9. Another witness, Mary Collins, told the ferry terminal supervisor that when she heard Jones fall, she looked in that direction and saw Jones get up and hit Smith, who was laughing. She immediately ran to find a terminal worker to prevent further fighting. When she returned, she found Smith slumped on the bench.
Mrs. Collins' report is USEFUL because
    A. it proves that Smith antagonized Jones
    B. it indicates that Jones beat Smith repeatedly
    C. she witnessed that Jones hit Smith
    D. it shows that only one punch was thrown

10. Based on the description given above, which of the following would be the MOST accurate summary for the ferry terminal supervisor to put in his report?
    A. Jones fell and Smith laughed, which caused Jones to beat him until bystanders got a terminal worker to separate them.
    B. Smith was reading a newspaper when Jones fell. Then Jones hit Smith and dazed him. Smith was examined by a nurse who said that Smith had a serious concussion.
    C. Jones tripped accidentally over Smith's legs and fell. Smith laughed at Jones, who lost his temper and hit Smith, driving Smith's head against the back of a bench.
    D. Smith antagonized Jones first, by tripping him second, by laughing at him, and third by not fighting back. Smith was aided by a nurse and went to the hospital.

Questions 11-13.

DIRECTIONS: Questions 11 through 13 are to be answered SOLELY on the basis of the following report.

To: John Greene
    General Park Foreman

Date: May 5

From: Earl Jones
       Gardener

Subject:

On May 3rd, as I was finishing a job six feet from the boat-house, I observed that the hole which had been filled in last week was now not level with the ground around it. This seems to be a hazardous condition because it might cause pedestrians to fall into it. I, therefore, suggest that this job be redone as soon as possible.

11. This report should be considered poorly written MAINLY because
    A. it does not give enough information to take appropriate action
    B. too many different tenses are used
    C. it describes no actual personal injury to anyone
    D. there is no recommendation in the report to remedy the situation

11._____

12. It is noted that the subject of the report has been left out.
Which of the following statements would be BEST as the subject of this report?
    A. Observation made by Earl Jones, Gardener
    B. Deteriorating condition of park grounds
    C. Report of dangerous condition near boathouse
    D. A dangerous walk through the park

12._____

13. In order for John Greene to take appropriate action, additional information should be added to the report giving the
    A. exact date the repair was made
    B. exact location of the hole
    C. exact time the observation was made
    D. names of the crew who previously filled in the hole

13._____

Questions 14-18.

DIRECTIONS: Questions 14 through 18 consist of sets of four sentences lettered A, B, C, and D. For each question, choose the sentence which is grammatically and stylistically MOST appropriate for use in a formal written report.

14. A. It is recommended, therefore, that the impasse panel hearings are to be convened on September 30.
    B. It is therefore recommended that the impasse panel hearings be convened on September 30.
    C. Therefore, it is recommended to convene the impasse panel hearings on September 30.
    D. It is recommended that the impasse panel hearings therefore should be convened on September 30.

14._____

15. A. Penalties have been assessed for violating the Taylor Law by several unions.
    B. When they violated provisions of the Taylor Law, several unions were later penalized.
    C. Several unions have been penalized for violating provisions of the Taylor Law.
    D. Several unions' violating provisions of the Taylor Law resulted in them being penalized.

15.____

16. A. The number of disputes settled through mediation has increased significantly over the past two years.
    B. The number of disputes settled through mediation are increasing significantly over two-year periods.
    C. Over the past two years, through mediation, the number of disputes settled increased significantly.
    D. There is a significant increase over the past two years of the number of disputes settled through mediation.

16.____

17. A. The union members will vote to determine if the contract is to be approved.
    B. It is not yet known whether the union members will ratify the proposed contract.
    C. When the union members vote, that will determine the new contract.
    D. Whether the union members will ratify the proposed contract, it is not yet known.

17.____

18. A. The parties agreed to an increase in fringe benefits in return for greater worker productivity.
    B. Greater productivity was agreed to be provided in return for increased fringe benefits.
    C. Productivity and fringe benefits are interrelated; the higher the former, the more the latter grows.
    D. The contract now provides that the amount of fringe benefits will depend upon the level of output by the workers.

18.____

19. Of the following excerpts, selected from letters, the one which is considered by modern letter writing experts to be the BEST is:
    A. Attached please find the application form to be filled out by you. Return the form to this office at the above address.
    B. Forward to this office your check accompanied by the application form enclosed with this letter.
    C. If you wish to apply, please complete and return the enclosed form with your check.
    D. In reply to your letter of December _____, enclosed herewith please find the application form you requested.

19.____

20. A city employee who writes a letter requesting information from a businessman should realize that, of the following, it is MOST important to
    A. end the letter with a polite closing
    B. make the letter short enough to fit on one page
    C. use a form, such as a questionnaire, to save the businessman's time
    D. use a courteous tone that will get the desired cooperation

20.____

Questions 21-22.

DIRECTIONS: Questions 21 and 22 consist of four sentences. Choose the one sentence in each set of four that would be BEST for a formal letter or report. Consider grammar and appropriate usage.

21. A. Most all the work he completed before he become ill.
    B. He completed most of the work before becoming ill.
    C. Prior to him becoming ill, his work was mostly completed.
    D. Before he became ill most of the work he had completed.

21.____

22. A. Being that the report lacked a clearly worded recommendation, it did not matter that it contained enough information.
    B. There was enough information in the report, although it, including the recommendation, were not clearly worded.
    C. Although the report contained enough information, it did not have a clearly worded recommendation.
    D. Though the report did not have a recommendation that was clearly worded, and the information therein contained was enough.

22.____

Questions 23-25.

DIRECTIONS: In Questions 23 through 25, choose the sentence which is BEST from the point of view of English usage suitable for a business letter or report.

23. A. Answering of veterans' inquiries, together with the receipt of fees, have been handled by the Bursar's Office since the new President came.
    B. Since the new President's arrival, the handling of all veteran's inquiries has been turned over to the Bursar's Office.
    C. In addition to the receipt of fees, the Bursar's Office has been handling veterans' inquiries since the new President came.
    D. The principle change in the work of the Bursar's Office since the new President came is that it now handles veterans' inquiries as well as the receipt of fees.

23.____

24. A. The current unrest about education undoubtedly stems in part from the fact that the people fear the basic purposes of the schools are being neglected or supplanted by spurious ones.
    B. The fears of people that the basic purposes of the schools are being neglected or supplanted by spurious ones contributes to the current unrest about education.

24.____

C. Undoubtedly some responsibility for the current unrest about education must be assigned to peoples' fears that the purpose and base of the school system is being neglected or supplanted.
D. From the fears of people that the basic purposes of the schools are being neglected or supplanted by spurious ones undoubtedly stem in part the current unrest about education.

25. A. The existence of administrative phenomena are clearly established, but their characteristics, relations and laws are obscure.
B. The obscurity of the characteristics, relations and laws of administrative phenomena do not preclude their existence.
C. Administrative phenomena clearly exists in spite of the obscurity of their characteristics, relations and laws.
D. The characteristics, relations and laws of administrative phenomena are obscure but the existence of the phenomena is clear.

25.____

KEY (CORRECT ANSWERS)

1.	C	11.	A
2.	B	12.	C
3.	D	13.	B
4.	B	14.	B
5.	C	15.	C
6.	B	16.	A
7.	A	17.	B
8.	D	18.	A
9.	C	19.	C
10.	C	20.	D

21. B
22. C
23. C
24. A
25. D

TEST 3

DIRECTIONS: Each question or incomplete statement is followed by several suggested answers or completions. Select the one that BEST answers the question or completes the statement. *PRINT THE LETTER OF THE CORRECT ANSWER IN THE SPACE AT THE RIGHT.*

1. Of the following, the BEST statement concerning the placement of *Conclusions and Recommendations* in a management report is:
   A. Recommendations should always be included in a report unless the report presents the results of an investigation.
   B. If a report presents conclusions, it must present recommendations.
   C. Every statement that is a conclusion should grow out of facts given elsewhere in the report.
   D. Conclusions and recommendations should always conclude the report because they depend on its contents.

1.____

2. Assume you are preparing a systematic analysis of our agency's pest control program and its effect on eliminating rodent infestation of premises in a specific region. To omit from your report important facts which you originally received from the person to whom you are recording is GENERALLY considered to be
   A. *desirable*; anyone who is likely to read the report can consult his files for extra information
   B. *undesirable*; the report should include major facts that are obtained as a result of your efforts
   C. *desirable*; the person you are reporting to does not pass the report on to others who lack his own familiarity with the subject
   D. *undesirable*; the report should include all of the facts that are obtained as a result of your efforts

2.____

3. Of all the non-verbal devices used in report writing, tables are used most frequently to enable a reader to compare statistical information more easily. Hence, it is important that an analyst know when to use tables.
   Which one of the following statements that relate to tables is generally considered to be LEAST valid?
   A. A table from an outside source must be acknowledged by the report writer.
   B. A table should be placed far in advance of the point where it is referred to or discussed in the report.
   C. The notes applying to a table are placed at the bottom of the table, rather than at the bottom of the page on which the table is found.
   D. A table should indicate the major factors that effect the data it contains.

3.____

4. Assume that an analyst writes reports which contain more detail than might be needed to serve their purpose. Such a practice is GENERALLY considered to be
   A. *desirable*; this additional detail permits maximized machine utilization
   B. *undesirable*; if specifications of reports are defined when they are first set up, loss of flexibility will follow

4.____

C. *desirable*; everything ought to be recorded so it will be there if it is ever needed
D. *undesirable*; recipients of these reports are likely to discredit them entirely

Questions 5-6.

DIRECTIONS: Questions 5 and 6 consist of sentences lettered A, B, C, and D. For each question, choose the sentence which is stylistically and grammatically MOST appropriate for a management report.

5. A. For too long, the citizen has been forced to rely for his productivity information on the whims, impressions, and uninformed opinion of public spokesmen.
   B. For too long, the citizen has been forced to base his information about productivity on the whims, impressions and uninformed opinion of public spokesmen.
   C. The citizen has been forced do base his information about productivity on the whims, impressions and uninformed opinion of public spokesmen for too long.
   D. The citizen has been forced for too long to rely for his productivity information on the whims, impressions and uninformed opinion of public spokesmen.

5.____

6. A. More competition means lower costs to the city, thereby helping to compensate for inflation.
   B. More competition, helping to compensate for inflation, means lower costs to the city.
   C. Inflation may be compensated for by more competition, which will reduce the city's costs.
   D. The costs to the city will be lessened by more competition, helping to compensate for inflation.

6.____

Questions 7-11.

DIRECTIONS: In Questions 7 through 11, choose the sentence which is BEST from the point of view of English usage suitable for a business letter or report.

7. A. It is the opinion of the Commissioners that programs which include the construction of cut-rate municipal garages in the central business district is inadvisable.
   B. Having reviewed the material submitted, the program for putting up cut-rate garages in the central business district seemed likely to cause traffic congestion.
   C. The Commissioners believe that putting up cut-rate municipal garages in the central business district is inadvisable.
   D. Making an effort to facilitate the cleaning of streets in the central business district, the building of cut-rate municipal garages presents the problem that it would encourage more motorists to come into the central city.

7.____

8.
- A. This letter, together with the reports, are to be sent to the principal.
- B. The reports, together with this letter, is to be sent to the principal.
- C. The reports and this letter is to be sent to the principal.
- D. This letter, together with the reports, is to be sent to the principal.

8.____

9.
- A. Each employee has to decide for themselves whether to take the examination.
- B. Each of the employees has to decide or himself whether to take the examination.
- C. Each of the employees has to decide for themselves whether to take the examination.
- D. Each of the employees have to decide for himself whether to take the examination.

9.____

10.
- A. The reason a new schedule is being prepared is that there has been a change in priorities.
- B. Because there has been a change in priorities is the reason why a new schedule is being made up.
- C. The reason why a new schedule is being made up is because there been a change in priorities.
- D. Because of a change in priorities is the reason why a new schedule is being prepared.

10.____

11.
- A. The changes in procedure had an unfavorable affect upon the output of the unit.
- B. The increased output of the unit was largely due to the affect of the procedural changes.
- C. The changes in procedure had the effect of increasing the output of the unit.
- D. The increased output of the unit from the procedural changes were the effect.

11.____

Questions 12-19.

DIRECTIONS: Questions 12 through 19 each consist of four sentences. Choose the one sentence in each set of four that would be BEST for a formal letter or report. Consider grammar and appropriate usage.

12.
- A. These statements can be depended on, for their truth has been guaranteed by reliable employees.
- B. Reliable city employees guarantee the facts with regards to the truth of these statements.
- C. Most all these statements have been supported by city employees who are reliable and can be depended upon.
- D. The city employees which have guaranteed these statements are reliable.

12.____

13.
- A. I believe the letter was addressed to either my associate or I.
- B. If properly addressed, the letter will reach my associate and I.
- C. My associate's name, as well as mine, was on the letter.
- D. The letter had been addressed to myself and my associate.

13.____

14.
- A. The secretary would have corrected the errors if she knew that the supervisor would see the report.
- B. The supervisor reprimanded the secretary, whom she believed had made careless errors.
- C. Many errors were found in the report which she typed and could not disregard.
- D. The errors in the typed report were so numerous that they could hardly be overlooked.

14.____

15.
- A. His consultant was as pleased as he with the success of the project.
- B. The success of the project pleased both his consultant and he.
- C. He and also his consultant was pleased with the success of the project.
- D. Both his consultant and he was pleased with the success of the project.

15.____

16.
- A. Since the letter did not contain the needed information, he could not use it.
- B. Being that the letter lacked the needed information, he could not use it.
- C. Since the letter lacked the needed information, it was of no use to him.
- D. This letter was useless to him because there was no needed information in it.

16.____

17.
- A. Scarcely had the real estate tax increase been declared than the notices were sent out.
- B. They had no sooner declared the real estate tax increases when they sent the notices to the owners.
- C. The city had hardly declared the real estate tax increase till the notices were prepared for mailing.
- D. No sooner had the real estate tax increase been declared than the notices were sent out

17.____

18.
- A. Though deeply effected by the setback, the advice given by the admissions office began to seem more reasonable.
- B. Although he was deeply effected by the setback, the advice given by the admissions office began to seem more reasonable.
- C. Though the setback had affected him deeply, the advise given by the admissions office began to see more reasonable.
- D. Although he was deeply affected by the setback, the advice given by the admissions office began to seem more reasonable.

18.____

19.
- A. Returning to the administration building after attendance at a meeting, the door was locked despite an agreement that it would be left open.
- B. When he returned to the administration building after attending a meeting, he found the door locked, despite an agreement that it would be left open.
- C. After attending a meeting, the door to the administration building was locked, despite an agreement that it would be left open.
- D. When he returned to the administration building after attendance at a meeting, he found the door locked, despite an agreement that it would be left open.

19.____

5 (#3)

20. A. A formal business report may consist of many parts, including the following:
    1. Table of Contents
    2. List of references
    3. Preface
    4. Index
    5. List of Tables
    6. Conclusions or recommendations

    Of the following, in setting up a formal report, the PROPER order of the six parts listed is:
    A. 1, 3, 6, 5, 2, 4
    B. 4, 3, 2, 5, 6 1
    C. 3, 1, 5, 6, 2, 4
    D. 2, 5, 3, 1, 4, 6

    20.____

21. Suppose you are writing a report on an interview you have just completed with a particularly hostile applicant for public assistance.
    Which of the following BEST describes what you should include in this report?
    A. What you think caused the applicant's hostile attitude during the interview
    B. Specific examples of the applicant's hostile remarks and behavior
    C. The relevant information uncovered during the interview
    D. A recommendation that the applicant's request be denied because of his hostility.

    21.____

22. When including recommendations in a report to your supervisor, which of the following is MOST important for you to do?
    A. Provide several alternative courses of action for each recommendation.
    B. First present the supporting evidence, then the recommendations.
    C. First present the recommendations, then the supporting evidence.
    D. Make sure the recommendations arise logically out of the information in the report.

    22.____

23. It is often necessary that the writer of a report present facts and sufficient arguments to gain acceptance of the points, conclusions, or recommendations set forth in the report.
    Of the following, the LEAST advisable step to take in organizing a report, when such argumentation is the important factor, is a(n)
    A. elaborate expression of personal belief
    B. businesslike discussion of the problem as a whole
    C, orderly arrangement of convincing data
    D. reasonable explanation of the primary issues

    23.____

24. Assume that a clerk is asked to prepare a special report which he has not prepared before. He decides to make a written outline of the report before writing it in full. This decision by the clerk is
    A. *good*, mainly because it helps the writer to organize his thoughts and decide what will go into the report
    B. *good*, mainly because it clearly shows the number of topics, number of '

    24.____

184

C. *poor*, mainly because it wastes the time of the writer since he will have to write the full report anyway.
D. *poor*, mainly because it confines the writer to those areas listed in the outline

25. Assume that a clerk in the water resources central shop is asked to prepare an important report, giving the location and condition of various fire hydrants in the city. One of the hydrants in question is broken and is spewing rusty water in the street, creating a flooded condition in the area. The clerk reports that the hydrant is broken but does not report the escaping water or the flood.
Of the following, the BEST evaluation of the clerk's decision about what to report is that it is basically
    A. *correct*; chiefly because a lengthy report would contain irrelevant information
    B. *correct*; chiefly because a more detailed description of a hydrant should be made by a fireman, not a clerk
    C. *incorrect*; chiefly because the clerk's assignment was to describe the condition of the hydrant and he should give a full explanation
    D. *incorrect*; chiefly because the clerk should include as much information as possible in his report whether or not it is relevant

25.____

KEY (CORRECT ANSWERS)

1.	C		11.	C
2.	B		12.	A
3.	B		13.	C
4.	D		14.	D
5.	B		15.	A
6.	A		16.	C
7.	C		17.	D
8.	D		18.	D
9.	B		19.	B
10.	A		20.	C

21.	C
22.	D
23.	A
24.	A
25.	C

ENGLISH EXPRESSION
EXAMINATION SECTION
TEST 1

DIRECTIONS: Each question or incomplete statement is followed by several suggested answers or completions. Select the one that BEST answers the question or completes the statement. *PRINT THE LETTER OF THE CORRECT ANSWER IN THE SPACE AT THE RIGHT.*

Questions 1-9.

DIRECTIONS: The following sentences contain problems in grammar, usage diction (choice of words), and idiom. Some sentences are correct. No sentence contains more than one error. You will find that the error, if there is one, is underlined and lettered. Assume that all other elements of the sentence are correct and cannot be changed. In choosing answers, follow the requirements of standard written English. If there is an error, select the *one underlined* part that must be changed in order to make the sentence correct. If there is no error, mark E.

1. <u>In planning</u> your future, <u>one must be</u> as honest with yourself as possible, make careful   1.____
       A   B
   decisions about the best course <u>to follow to achieve</u> a particular purpose, and, above all,
                                           C
   have the courage <u>to stand by those</u> decisions. <u>No error</u>
                         D   E

2. <u>Even though</u> history does not actually repeat itself, knowledge <u>of</u> history <u>can give</u>   2.____
       A   B   C
   current problems a familiar, <u>less</u> formidable look. <u>No error</u>
                                 D   E

3. The Curies <u>had almost exhausted</u> their resources, and <u>for a time it seemed</u>   3.____
                          A   B
   <u>unlikely that they ever</u> would find the <u>solvent to their financial problems</u>. <u>No error</u>
          C   D   E

4. <u>If the rumors are</u> correct, Deane <u>will not be convicted</u>, for each of the officers   4.____
           A   B
   on the court realizes that Colson and Holdman may be <u>the real culprit and</u> that
                                                                             C
   <u>their</u> testimony is not completely trustworthy. <u>No error</u>
     D   E

5. The citizens of Washington, <u>like Los Angeles</u>, prefer to commute by automobile,
                                     A
   even though motor vehicles contribute <u>nearly as many</u> contaminants to the air
                                                 B
   <u>as do all other</u> sources <u>combined</u>. <u>No error</u>
        C   D   E

   5._____

6. <u>By the time Robert Vasco completes</u> his testimony, every major executive of our
                     A
   company but Ray Ashurst <u>and I</u> <u>will have been</u> <u>accused of</u> complicity in the stock
                           B   C   D
   swindle. <u>No error</u>
            E

   6._____

7. <u>Within six months</u> the store was operating <u>profitably and efficient</u>; shelves
        A   B
   <u>were well stocked</u>, goods were selling rapidly, and the cash register
        C
   <u>was ringing constantly</u>. <u>No error</u>
       D   E

   7._____

8. Shakespeare's comedies have an advantage <u>over Shaw</u> <u>in that Shakespeare's</u> were
                                             A   B
   <u>written primarily</u> to entertain and <u>not to</u> argue for a cause. <u>No error</u>
       C   D   E

   8._____

9. Any true insomniac <u>is well aware of</u> the futility of <u>such measures as</u> drinking
                             A   B
   hot milk, <u>regular hours, deep breathing</u>, counting sheep, and <u>concentrating on</u>
                   C   D
   black velvet. <u>No error</u>
                  E

   9._____

Questions 10-15.

DIRECTIONS: In each of the following sentences, some part of the sentence or the entire sentence is underlined. Beneath each sentence you will find five ways of phrasing the underlined part. The first of these repeats the original; the other four are different. If you think the original is better than any of the alternatives, choose answer A; otherwise choose one of the others. In choosing answers, follow the requirements of standard written English; that is, pay attention to grammar, choice of words, sentence construction, and punctuation. Choose the answer that produces the most effective sentence—clear and exact, without awkwardness or ambiguity. Do not make a choice that changes the meaning of the original sentence.

10. The tribe of warriors believed that boys and girls should be <u>reared separate, and, as soon as he was weaned, the boys were taken from their mothers.</u>
    A. reared separate, and, as soon as he was weaned, the boys were taken from their mothers

    10._____

B. reared separate, and, as soon as he was weaned, a boy was taken from his mother
C. reared separate, and, as soon as he was weaned, the boys were taken from their mothers
D. reared separately, and, as soon as a boy was weaned, they were taken from their mothers
E. reared separately, and, as soon as a boy was weaned, he was taken from his mother

11. Despite Vesta being only the third largest, it is by far the brightest of the known asteroids.
    A. Despite Vesta being only the third largest, it is by far the brightest of the known asteroids.
    B. Vesta, though only the third largest asteroid, is by far the brightest of the known ones.
    C. Being only the third largest, yet Vesta is by far the brightest of the known asteroids.
    D. Vesta, though only the third largest of the known asteroids, is by far the brightest.
    E. Vesta is only the third largest of the asteroids, it being, however, the brightest one.

12. As a result of the discovery of the Dead Sea Scrolls, our understanding of the roots of Christianity has had to be revised considerably.
    A. has had to be revised considerably
    B. have had to be revised considerably
    C. has had to undergo revision to a considerable degree
    D. have had to be subjected to considerable revision
    E. has had to be revised in a considerable way

13. Because it is imminently suitable to dry climates, adobe has been a traditional building material throughout the southwestern states.
    A. it is imminently suitable to
    B. it is eminently suitable for
    C. It is eminently suitable when in
    D. of its eminent suitability with
    E. of being imminently suitable in

14. Martell is more concerned with demonstrating that racial prejudice exists than preventing it from doing harm, which explains why his work is not always highly regarded.
    A. Martell is more concerned with demonstrating that racial prejudice exists than preventing it from doing harm, which explains
    B. Martell is more concerned with demonstrating that racial prejudice exists than with preventing it from doing harm, and this explains
    C. Martell is more concerned with demonstrating that racial prejudice exists than with preventing it from doing harm, an explanation of
    D. Martell's greater concern for demonstrating that racial prejudice exists than preventing it from doing harm—this explains
    E. Martell's greater concern for demonstrating that racial prejudice exists than for preventing it from doing harm explains

15. Throughout this history of the American West there runs a steady commentary on the deception and mistreatment of the Indians.   15._____
    A. Throughout this history of the American West there runs a steady commentary on the deception and mistreatment of the Indians.
    B. There is a steady commentary provided on the deception and mistreatment of the Indians and it runs throughout this history of the American West.
    C. The deception and mistreatment of the Indians provide a steady comment that runs throughout this history of the American West.
    D. Comment on the deception and mistreatment of the Indians is steadily provided and runs throughout this history of the American West.
    E. Running throughout this history of the American West is a steady commentary that is provided on the deception and mistreatment of the Indians.

Questions 16-20.

DIRECTIONS: In each of the following questions you are given a complete sentence to be rephrased according to the directions which follow it. You should rephrase the sentence mentally to save time, although you may make notes in your test book if you wish. Below each sentence and its directions are listed words or phrases that may occur in your revised sentence. When you have thought out a good sentence, look in the choices A through E for the word or entire phrase that is included in your revised sentence, and print the letter of the correct answer in the space at the right. The word or phrase you choose should be the most accurate and most nearly complete of all the choices given, and should be part of a sentence that meets the requirements of standard written English. Of course, a number of different sentences can be obtained if the sentence is revised according to directions, and not all of these possibilities can be included in only five choices. If you should find that you have thought of a sentence that contains none of the words or phrases listed in the choices, you should attempt to rephrase the sentence again so that it includes a word or phrase that is listed. Although the directions may at times require you to change the relationship between parts of the sentence or to make slight changes in meaning in other ways, make only those changes that the directions require; that is, keep the meaning the same, or as nearly the same as the directions permit. If you think that more than one good sentence can be made according to the directions, select the sentence that is most exact, effective, and natural in phrasing and construction.

EXAMPLES

I. Sentence: Coming to the city as a young man, he found a job as a newspaper reporter.
   Directions: Substitute He came for Coming.
   A. and so he found   B. and found
   C. and there he had found   D. and then finding
   E. and had found

5 (#1)

Your rephrased sentence will probably read: "He came to the city as a young man and found a job as a newspaper reporter." This sentence contains the correct answer: B. and found. A sentence which used one of the alternate phrases would change the meaning or intention of the original sentence, would be a poorly written sentence, or would be less effective than another possible revision.

II. Sentence: Owing to her wealth, Sarah had many suitors.
Directions: Begin with Many men courted.
A. so   B. while   C. although   D. because   E. and

Your rephrased sentence will probably read: "Many men courted Sarah because she was wealthy." This new sentence contains only choice D, which is the correct answer. None of the other choices will fit into an effective, correct sentence that retains the original meaning.

16. The archaeologists could only mark out the burial site, for then winter came.
Begin with Winter came before.
 A. could do nothing more
 B. could not do anything
 C. could only do
 D. could do something
 E. could do anything more

17. The white reader often receives some insight into the reasons why black men are angry from descriptions by a black writer of the injustice they encounter in a white society.
Begin with A black writer often gives.
 A. when describing
 B. by describing
 C. he has described
 D. in the descriptions
 E. because of describing

18. The agreement between the university officials and the dissident students provides for student representation on every university committee and on the board of trustees.
Substitute provides that for provides for.
 A. be
 B. are
 C. would have
 D. would be
 E. is to be

19. English Romanticism had its roots in German idealist philosophy, first described in England by Samuel Coleridge.
Begin with Samuel Coleridge was the first in.
 A. in which English
 B. and from it English
 C. where English
 D. the source of English
 E. the birth of English

20. Four months have passed since his dismissal, during which time Alan has looked for work daily.
Begin with Each day.
 A. will have passed
 B. that have passed
 C. that passed
 D. were to pass
 E. had passed

KEY (CORRECT ANSWERS)

1.	B	11.	D
2.	E	12.	A
3.	D	13.	B
4.	C	14.	E
5.	A	15.	A
6.	B	16.	E
7.	B	17.	B
8.	A	18.	A
9.	C	19.	D
10.	E	20.	B

STANDPIPE SYSTEMS

This study material contains the information you will need to prepare for the examination for the Certificate of Fitness for Standpipe Systems. The study material includes information taken from relevant sections of the Fire Prevention Code and the Building Code of New York.

All questions on the Certificate of Fitness examination are multiple choice, with four alternative answers to each question. Only one answer is correct for each question. If you do not answer a question, or if you mark more than one alternative, your answer will be scored as incorrect. A score of 70% correct is required on the examination in order to qualify for the Certificate of Fitness. Read each question carefully before marking your answer. There is no penalty for guessing.

Sample Questions

1. A standpipe system is primarily used for
    A. draining water from low level areas
    B. firefighting operations
    C. washing down the floors in a building
    D. draining water from kitchen areas in the building

    The CORRECT answer is B.

2. When a gravity tank is required in a yard system, the tank should be
    A. underground
    B. on the ground level
    C. elevated above ground level
    D. filled with compressed foam

    The CORRECT answer is C.

INTRODUCTION AND OVERVIEW OF STANDPIPE SYSTEMS

Standpipe systems are an important part of the fire protection system in a building. The standpipe system provides water that firefighters can manually discharge through hoses onto a fire. Water is fed into a piping system. The piping runs vertically (up and down) and horizontally (side to side) throughout the building. The piping running vertically are usually called riders. The risers are usually located in the staircase enclosures or in the hallways in the building. This piping system supplies water to every floor in the building. When a standpipe system is installed and properly maintained, it is a very effective means for extinguishing fires. A typical standpipe system is shown below in the illustration below.

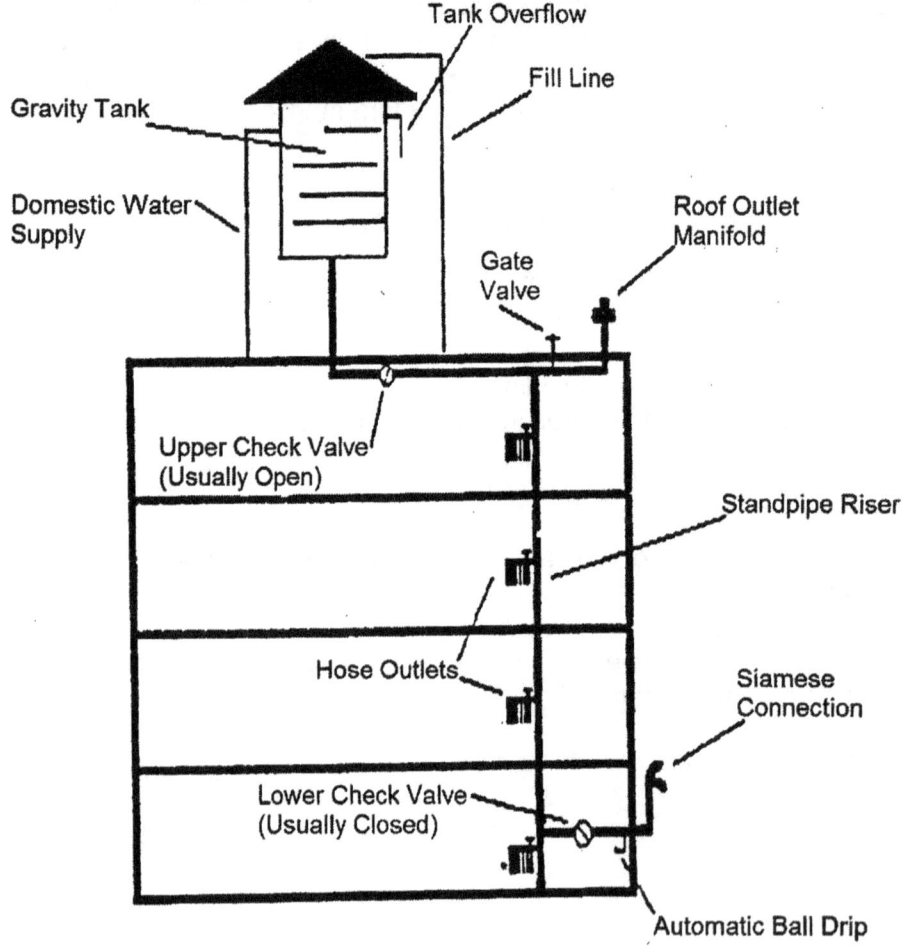

A Typical Standpipe System

STANDPIPE DESIGN

Standpipe systems are used in buildings where it may be difficult for the fire department to pump water on the fire. For example, standpipe systems are required in buildings that are over 75 feet in height. A standpipe system may be combined with an automatic fire protection system. For example, a standpipe system and a sprinkler system may be installed in the same building. The standpipe and the sprinkler systems may even share the same water supply and riser piping. The top of the standpipe riser extends up onto the roof. Three hose connections are attached to the top of the standpipe riser. These three connections make up the roof manifold. The roof manifold is used when extinguishing fires on the roof. It is also used when testing the water flow in the standpipe. An example of a typical roof manifold is shown in the picture below.

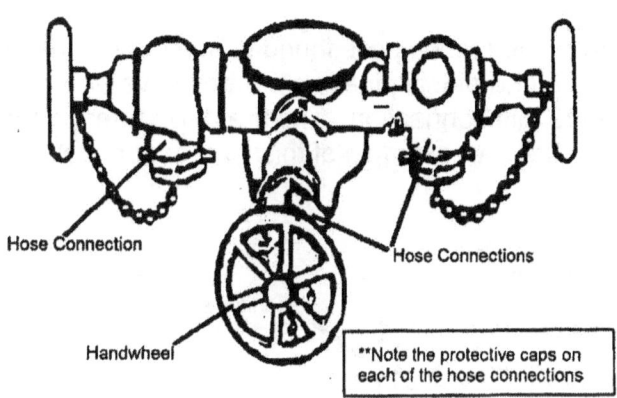

A Typical Roof Manifold

At selected locations in the building, the piping is connected to a hose. These connections are controlled by gate valves. No water is allowed into the hose until the valve is opened. The gate valve must be manually opened by the firefighter. The hose is usually stored on a quick release rack. An example of a typical quick release rack is shown below.

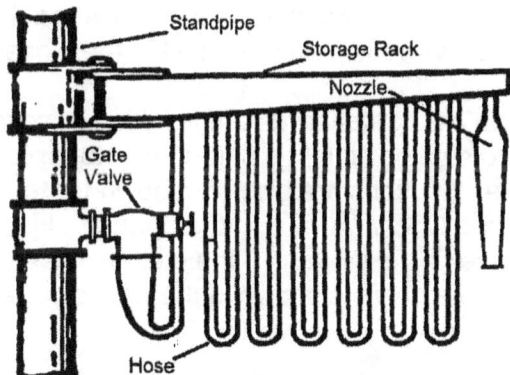

A Typical Fire Hose Outlet and Release Rack

A nozzle is attached at the end of the hose. The nozzle is used to direct the stream of water from the hose. An example of a typical nozzle is shown in the picture below.

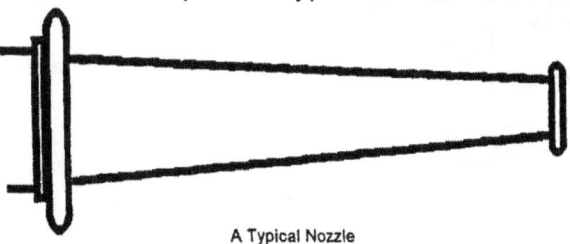

A Typical Nozzle

The hose and nozzle must be easy to reach at all times. The hose outlets are located so that every part of the building may be reached with a hose stream. The maximum length of a single hose line is 125 feet. Sometimes the hoses are installed n cabinets. If the hoses are installed in cabinets, each cabinet should be labeled "FIRE HOSE". When the hose outlets are not easy to see, signs should be posted telling where the hose outlet is located.

A pressure reducing device should be installed in the piping at each hose outlet. An occupant of the building may be injured if a hose is used when the pressure reducing device is not installed. The pressure reducing device may be adjusted or removed by fire department personnel during an emergency.

Another kind of connection to the standpipe is found in some systems. A short length of piping is welded to the riser. At the end of this pipe is a control valve and a 2½ inch hose connection. No hose is installed to this connection. The fire department attaches its own hose to this connection when fighting a fire. An example of this kind of connection is shown in the picture below.

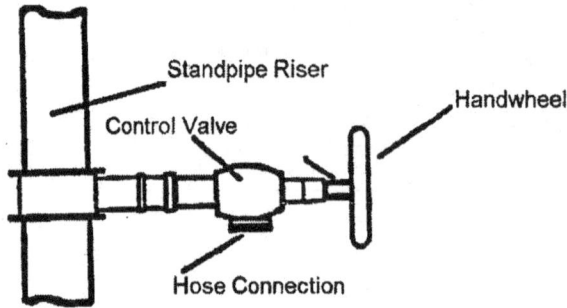

Fire Department Connection to a Standpipe Riser

Each standpipe system is also fitted with a drain valve. The drain valve is located at the lowest point on the standpipe system. The drain valve is used when the standpipe system is being tested or repaired. The drain valve is usually sealed in the closed position.

OS&Y (Outside Screw and Yoke) gate valves are installed at several places in the system. The OS&Y valves can be used to shut down just a part of the standpipe system. Sections may be shut down when fighting a fire. Sections are also shut down for testing, repairs or maintenance. It is easy to tell if the OS&Y valve is in the open or closed position. If the stem is raised above the control wheel, the valve is open. If the stem is flush with the control wheel, the valve is closed. A typical OS&Y gate valve is shown in the next picture. The valve in the picture is open.

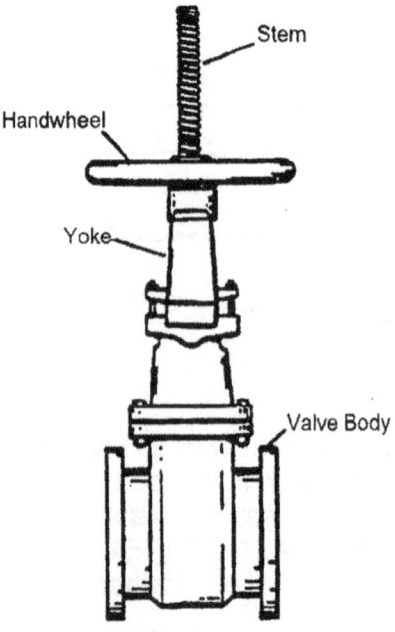

Typical OS&Y Gate Valve

TYPES OF STANDPIPE SYSTEMS

Wet Standpipe: This system always has water in the standpipe. The water in the system is always under pressure. In some cases, a fire pump may be used to increase the water pressure. The wet pipe system is the most commonly used standpipe system. It is used in heating buildings where there is no danger of the water in the piping freezing. Any part of the standpipe system that is exposed to freezing temperatures should be insulated. It is very important that the water in the piping does not freeze. Frozen water may prevent the standpipe system from working.

Dry Standpipe With an Automatic Dry Pipe Valve: This system is usually supplied by a public water main. Under normal conditions, there is no water in the standpipe. Instead, there is air under pressure in the standpipe. A dry pipe valve is installed to prevent water from entering the standpipe. The dry pipe valve is designed to open when there is drop of air pressure in the standpipe. When a hose is opened, it causes a drop in air pressure in the standpipe system. Then the dry pipe valve automatically lets water flow into the standpipe. A control valve is installed at the automatic water supply connection. This valve should be kept open at all times to supply the standpipe system. This system is usually installed in a building that is not heated.

Dry Standpipe With a Manual Control Valve: This system is supplied by a public water main. Under normal conditions, this system has no water in the piping. The water is not allowed into the standpipe until a control valve is manually operated. The control valve remains closed until a fire occurs. This system is usually used in a building that is not heated.

Dry Standpipe with No Permanent Water Supply: Under normal conditions, this system has no water in the standpipe. Water is pumped into the standpipe system by the fire department. The water is pumped in through the Siamese connection. This system cannot be used unless water is supplied by the fire department. A sign must be attached to each of the hose outlets. It should read "Dry Standpipe for Fire Department Use Only". This system is usually used in a building that is not heated.

CLASSES OF STANDPIPE SYSTEMS

Standpipe systems are classified depending on who is expected to use the system. The three classes are briefly described below.

Class I: This system is designed to be used by professional firefighters. For example, the system is used by Fire Department and Fire Brigade personnel. The fire hoses in these systems are 2½ inches in diameter. The large hose diameter makes it difficult to control the stream of water from the hose.

Class II: This system is designed to be used by the occupants of a building. The hose and nozzle are connected to the standpipe. They are ready to be used by occupants in case of a fire. The hose is 1½ inches in diameter. The hose stream is easier to control than the Class I hose.

Class III: This system may be used by either professional firefighters or by occupants of the building. The hosing may be adjusted to either 1½ or 2½ inches in diameter. This is done by attaching special reducing valves to the hose line.

WATER SUPPLIES

Acceptable water supplies for the standpipe system include connection to public or private water mains, connection to fire pumps, pressure tanks, and gravity tanks. These sources may be also used in combination to supply a standpipe system. At least one of the water sources should be able to supply the standpipe system automatically. This supply must have the needed water volume and water pressure for the entire system. The public water works system is the most commonly used water supply source. In tall buildings the connection to the public water system may not have enough water pressure to supply the upper floors. In this situation, a second supply source is often required to increase the water pressure. For example, a fire pump may be installed in a building that is more than 10 stories high. The higher the building, the greater the water pressure needed to supply the standpipe system.

Connections to Public Water Works System: Connection to a reliable public water works system is the preferred primary water supply. A check valve is installed next to the connection. This valve makes sure that the standpipe system does not backflow into the public water supply.

Fire Pumps: The fire pump is designed to draw water from a supply source. The water is then pumped into the standpipe under high pressure. A fire pump with both a reliable source of power and a reliable water supply is a desirable piece of equipment. A suction water supply is simply a source of water that the pump can draw water from. With a good water supply, a fire pump can pump water into a standpipe system for a long time. Sometimes more than one fire pump is installed in high rise buildings. The extra fire pumps are needed to maintain the desired water pressure levels at the top floors of the buildings.

Automatic fire pumps are usually installed where a high water demand may occur immediately. Automatic fire pups are activated as soon as a drop of air or water pressure is noticed in the standpipe. The drop in pressure occurs when a hose line is opened. The automatic fire pump is also used when someone is not always present to activate a manual pump. Automatic fire pumps are usually needed where a high water demand may occur immediately.

Manually started pumps may be used as a secondary supply source. They are used if the primary water supply will last long enough to allow the pump to be started.

Gravity Tanks: Gravity tanks of adequate capacity and elevation area good water supply source. They are acceptable as a primary supply. A gravity tank is usually located on the top of a building or on a tall tower. The water in the tank is distributed throughout the standpipe system because of the pull of gravity.

Pressure Tanks: Pressure tanks are used in automatic standpipe protection. The tank is normally kept two-thirds full of water and one-third full of air. The air pressure in the tank should be kept above 75 psi. Air for the pressure tank is supplied by air compressors. Because the water is always under pressure, it can be forcefully distributed throughout the standpipe system. The pressure tank is limited by the small amount of water that can be stored in the tank. If a small pressure tank is used as the water supply, the system is called a Limited Supply System. Pressure tanks are often used where there is enough water from a supply but the water pressure is too low. Pressure tanks are often used in tall buildings that need extra water pressure to supply the highest lines of hoses.

Siamese Connections for Fire Department Use: Normally, a standpipe system is connected to an automatic water supply source. Other sources of water are supplied through fire department siamese connections at the building. At least one siamese connection must be installed in all standpipe systems. When responding to an alarm, most fire departments supply water to the standpipe system first. The standpipe system then supplies water to the fire hoses in the building. There may be a siamese connection for a standpipe system and for a sprinkler system in the same building. The exact purpose of each siamese connection should be shown nearby or on the siamese connection itself. The New York Building Code requires siamese connections to be color coded. The siamese connections to a standpipe system should be painted red. Two examples of typical standpipe siamese connections are shown in the pictures below.

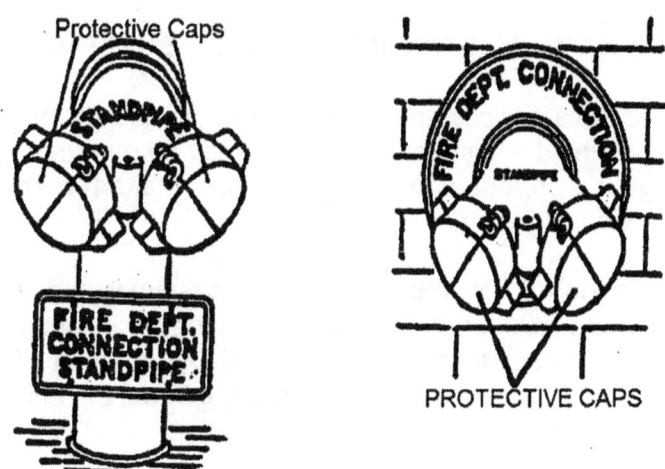

Typical Siamese Connections

Fire department siamese connections must always be accessible. Each connection should be fitted with a check valve, but not with a gate valve. The check valve prevents the backflow of the private water supply into the public water supply. An automatic drip device between the check valve and the outside hose coupling prevents water from building up in the piping. The drip device makes sure that the fire department connection is not blocked by water which has frozen in the piping. If water freezes in the piping, the fire department will not be able to pump water into the system. Under normal conditions, the automatic drip should be dry. A wet drip device indicates that the check valve may be defective. If the check valve is defective, it should be replaced immediately. Many standpipe systems use the fire department siamese connection as the second water supply for the standpipe system. The figure below shows the main features of a fire department siamese connection.

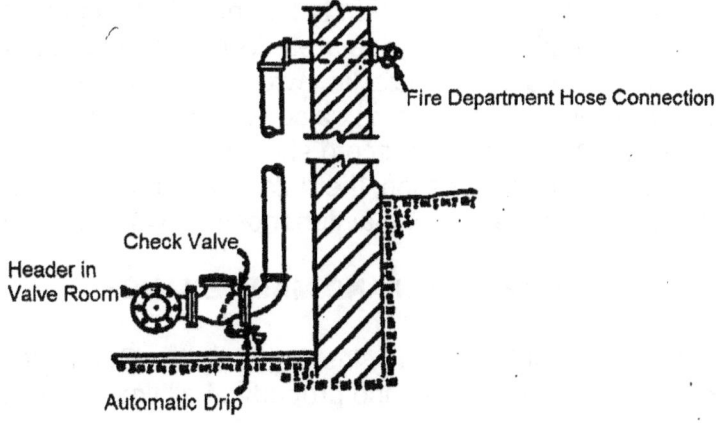

Fire Department Connection

COMBINATION STANDPIPE AND SPRINKLER SYSTEM

A building may have both a standpipe and a sprinkler system installed. Each system may have its own water supply source. For example, the standpipe system may be supplied by a gravity tank and the sprinkler system supplied by a pressure tank.

It is quite common for the two systems to share the same water supply source. For example, both systems may use the same gravity tank as a water supply source. The gravity tank is a limited water supply. The amount of water that is allocated to each system is regulated by local building laws.

WATERFLOW ALARMS AD STANDPIPE SYSTEM SUPERVISION

Standpipe systems should have devices and equipment for signaling when water flows through the risers or mains supplying the system. Water flow may be due to fire, leakage, or accidental rupture of the piping. It is important that prompt action is taken when water flow is noticed or signaled by these devices.

Functions of Alarms and Supervisory Signals: A standpipe system with a water flow alarm serves two functions: (a) It is an effective fire extinguishing system; (b) It is an automatic fire alarm. An alarm is signaled as soon as a hose line has opened. As soon as a fire is discovered, the Certificate of Fitness holder should immediately contact the local fire department.

Supervisory devices are often connected to a central station which monitors the standpipe system for problems with equipment and when the hoses are opened.

The central station and the fire department should be notified when any control valves are closed for maintenance or repair. This reduces the number of false alarms.

Devices and Equipment Supervised: Standpipe system supervision is commonly provided for several purposes. These purposes include: (a) water supply control valves, (b) low water level in water supply tanks, (c) low temperature in water supply tanks or ground level reservoirs, (d) high or low water level in pressure tanks, (e) high or low air pressure in pressure tanks, (f) high or low air pressure in dry pipe standpipe systems, (g) failure of electric power to fire pumps, (h) automatic operation of electric fire pumps.

Gate Valves: Gate valves of the non-indicating type are provided in water distribution systems. Gate valves allow parts of the standpipe system to be shut off for repairs or maintenance. This is done without reducing protection over a wide area. Such valves are normally a non-rising stem type. They are operated using a special key wrench. A valve box is located over the valve to keep dirt from the valve. The valve box also provides a convenient access point for the valve wrench to the valve nut. A complete record should be made for each valve in the system. This record should include the exact location, the date it was installed, the make, the direction of opening, number of turns to open, and any maintenance that was performed.

INSPECTION AND MAINTENANCE

The standpipe system must be regularly inspected by the Certificate of Fitness holder. This is to make sure that the system is working properly at all times. All parts of the standpipe system should be visibly checked monthly. This visual inspection should make sure that the system is free from corrosion. The inspection should also make sure that there is no physical damage to the system. Special attention should be paid to any evidence of tampering with the standpipe system. Any part of the system that is damaged or missing should be repaired or replaced immediately.

All valves and connections to the automatic water supply sources should be inspected weekly. The valves should be checked to make sure that they are in the correct position. The valves should also be labeled to show their correct position and purpose. The hose outlets should be checked to make sure that the pressure reducing devices are present. The fire department should be notified when any part of the system is shut down for maintenance or repairs. A sign should be posted indicating that the section is shut down. All fire department connections must be tested at least once every 5 years.

All major defects in the system should be immediately reported to the local fire department. The owner of the building and the Bureau of Fire Prevention should also be notified. Major defects include: an empty tank, a break or a leak in the system water piping, an inoperative or shut water supply valve and a defective siamese connection. The defects should be corrected as soon as possible. A complete or partial shutdown of the standpipe system for repairs or any other reason must also be reported.

Minor defects should be reported to the owner of the building. The defects should be repaired within 30 days. If the defects are not corrected within 30 days, they must be reported to the Bureau of Fire Prevention.

The date of all inspections, maintenance, and repairs made on the system must be recorded on the inspection record card. The record should also include the Certificate of Fitness number and the signature of the Certificate of Fitness holder. This record must be posted near the main control valve. All records must be kept for a period of at least one year. They should be made available to any representative of the fire department.

GRAVITY TANKS

Gravity tanks are used for water storage. They are made of wood, steel, or concrete. Gravity tanks are used as a primary or secondary water supply source for standpipe systems. A gravity tank system delivers water from the tank through the standpipe system without the use of pumping equipment.

A gravity tank should be at least 25 feet above the highest standpipe hose outlet that it supplies. Tanks may be located on the tops of buildings or raised on tall supporting towers. An example of a typical gravity tank is shown on the next page.

The water pressure in a gravity tank system depends on the elevation of the tank. This is its main advantage over other kinds of systems. Every 1 foot the tank is above the discharge outlet generates 0.434 psi (pounds per square inch) of water pressure. So in other words, the higher the tank is elevated, the greater the water pressure. The gravity tank is extremely reliable. It does not depend on the operation of mechanical equipment to supply the standpipe system.

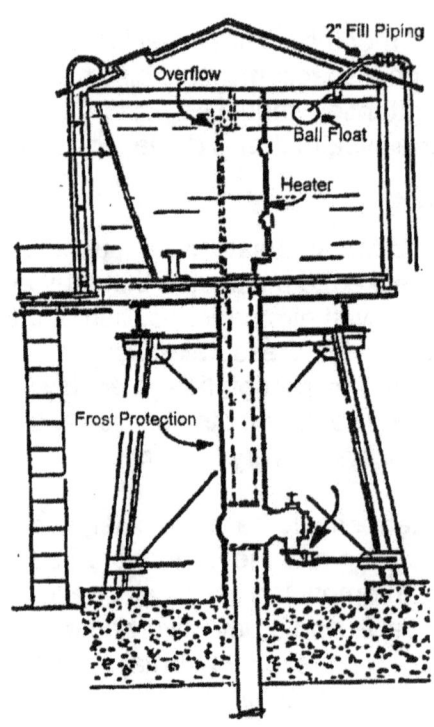

Automatic fill pumps supply the water to most gravity tanks. The pumps fill the tank at a rate of 65 gpm (gallons per minute) or more. Two floats control the amount of water in the tank. The floats turn on the fill pump when the water in the tank is too low. The floats shut off the pump when the desired water level is reached. The floats make sure the gravity tank always has the right amount of water to supply the standpipe system. All gravity tanks have an overflow pipe that drains off too much water in the tank. This happens if the floats do not turn off the fill pump. A fill pump is not necessary if the water pressure in the city water main is able to keep the tank filled with the right amount of water.

Gravity tanks are exposed to very low temperatures. All parts of the gravity tank must be insulated or heated to keep the water from freezing. Several methods are used to heat the tank and the pipe that supplies the water. (1) Hot water is circulated by gravity. (2) Steam is discharged directly into the tank. (3) Steam coils are placed inside the tanks. (4) Heat from the sun is used. The Certificate of Fitness holder can find out the temperature of the water by looking at a thermometer. The thermometer is located near the heating device. The tank can be severely damaged if the water inside freezes. During freezing weather, the temperature of the water inside the tank and the riser must be checked daily. The temperature of the water should always be at least 40 degrees Fahrenheit.

Ice should not be allowed to build up on the gravity tank. The extra weight of the ice might weaken the supports of the tank and cause the tank to collapse. Falling icicles may also cause damage or injury. It is essential to be sure that the tank is properly heated, insulated, and carefully maintained.

The water level in the gravity tank should be inspected each month. The gravity tank should always have a full supply of water. A full tank of water is needed to be sure the standpipe system works properly during a fire. Keeping the tank full of water also prevents wooden tanks from shrinking. A full tank of water helps keep steel tanks from rusting.

Gravity Tank Supervision

The gravity tank must be constantly monitored to be sure that the tank and its parts are working. Electrical supervision devices monitor the water temperature and the water level in the gravity tank. These devices send signals to a central station about the water level and water temperature. The central station notifies the Certificate of Fitness holder when a problem with the gravity tank is detected. The Certificate of Fitness holder should correct the problem as soon as possible. The supervisory devices are sometimes called high and low alarms since they also send audible signals to alert the Certificate of Fitness holder when there is a problem.

Failure of a standpipe system supplied by a gravity tank during a fire is usually caused by not enough water in the tank. The standpipe system cannot be supplied if there is not enough water in the tank. Too much water in the tank can also cause the system to fail. Too much water in the tank may cause damage due to the weight of the extra water. This could cause the gravity tank to collapse.

Inspection and Maintenance of the Gravity Tank

The gravity tank should be regularly inspected and maintained. Maintenance is needed to be sure that the tank functions correctly. For example, the tank may need to be painted regularly to prevent rusting. Before the inside of a gravity tank is repainted, the surface should be thoroughly dried. All loose paint, rust, scale, and other surface contamination should be removed. The outside of the gravity tank will require local patching. A complete finish coat of paint is needed when the paint has weathered thin. A new coat of paint also improves the appearance of the tank after it has been patched.

Painters must be careful that scrapings or other foreign materials do not fall down the outlet into the riser piping. The discharge outlet may be covered for protection during repairs. Only a few sheets of paper or a paper bag tied over the end of the settling basin stub should be used. The paper should be removed upon immediately after the job is finished.

It is best if gravity tanks are used only for fire protection and for no other purpose. Tanks used for other purposes need to be refilled more often. The tanks become settling basins for sediment mixed in with the water. This sediment is then drawn into the piping. This may cause the standpipe system to become clogged and not work properly.

The local fire department should always be notified when a tank cannot be used for any reason.

Combination Gravity Tank and Pressure Tank Installation

Pressure tanks may be used in combination with gravity tanks to supply a standpipe system. Both systems may be used to make sure that an adequate water supply is available. The pressure tanks also provide added water pressure to the standpipe system. An example of a combined installation is shown on the next page.

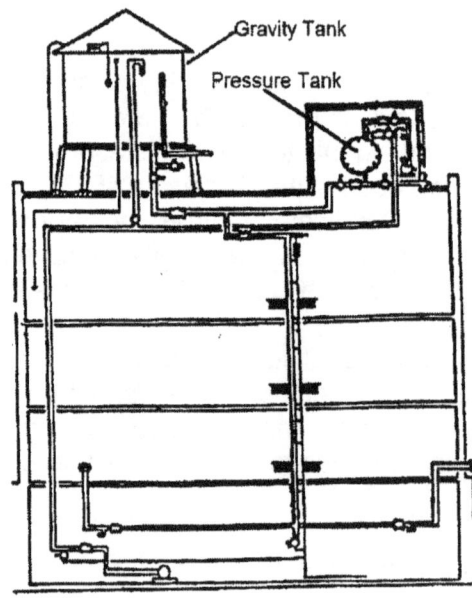

FIRE PUMPS

A fire pump can be used as a primary water supply source for a standpipe system. The fire pump is usually connected to the public water main for most of its water supply. Water tanks and the fire department siamese connection may also be connected to the fire pump. Fire pumps are designed to take the water from a supply source and then discharge the water into the standpipe system under pressure. The pressure with which the water is discharged from the pump is called the total head. The total head is usually measured in pounds per square inch (psi). The higher the psi rating of the pump, the greater the pressure with which the water can be discharged.

The Centrifugal Pump

The centrifugal fire pump is the standard pump used in most fire protection systems. This is the preferred pump because it is reliable, compact, and requires little maintenance. The centrifugal pump can be powered by a variety of drivers. Acceptable drivers include electric motors, internal combustion engines, and steam turbines.

Principle of Operation

The water available to the centrifugal pump must always be under pressure. The fire pump cannot draw water by itself from the supply source. A water tank can be used if the tank uses gravity to supply the pump. In other words, the weight of the water forces the water to flow into the pump. This type of water tank is called a suction tank. The water flows from the tank through the supply inlet into the pump. As the water passes to the center of the pump, it reaches a rotating impeller. The impeller "grabs" the water on the inlet side of the pump. Then the impeller discharges the water under increased pressure into the standpipe system.

There are several kinds and models of centrifugal pumps. Some centrifugal pumps can discharge water from 250 gpm (gallons per minute) up to 5,000 gpm. Most centrifugal pumps have a single impeller and are, therefore, commonly called single stage fire pumps. A typical centrifugal pump is shown in the picture below.

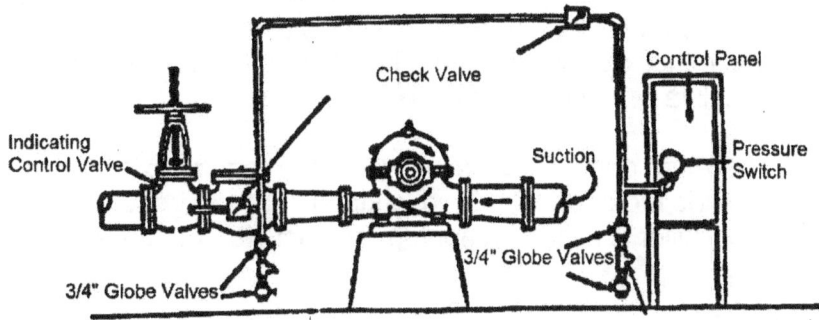

The Vertical Turbine Pump

The vertical turbine pump is really a modified centrifugal pump. The vertical turbine pump is able to draw water from streams, ponds, wells, etc. The vertical turbine pump does not need the suction supply to be under pressure. Instead, it draws the water into the pump by suction. The water is drawn from the tank into the pump. As the water passes to the center of the pump, it reaches a rotating impeller. The impeller "grabs" the water on the inlet side of the pump. Then the impeller discharges the water under increased pressure into the standpipe system.

The vertical turbine pump is able to draw water from wells. However, it is recommended not to use a well as the main water supply source. A well may dry up without warning. If the well dried up, it would make the fire pump useless. It is better to draw water from the well and to fill a water storage tank. The fire pump should then be attached to the storage tank as it is a more reliable supply source.

It is important to inspect the water intake hose, foot valve, and the strainer regularly. Mud, gravel, leaves, or other materials could cause damage to the pump or obstruct the system's piping. A vertical fire pump arrangement using a water reservoir is shown in the picture below.

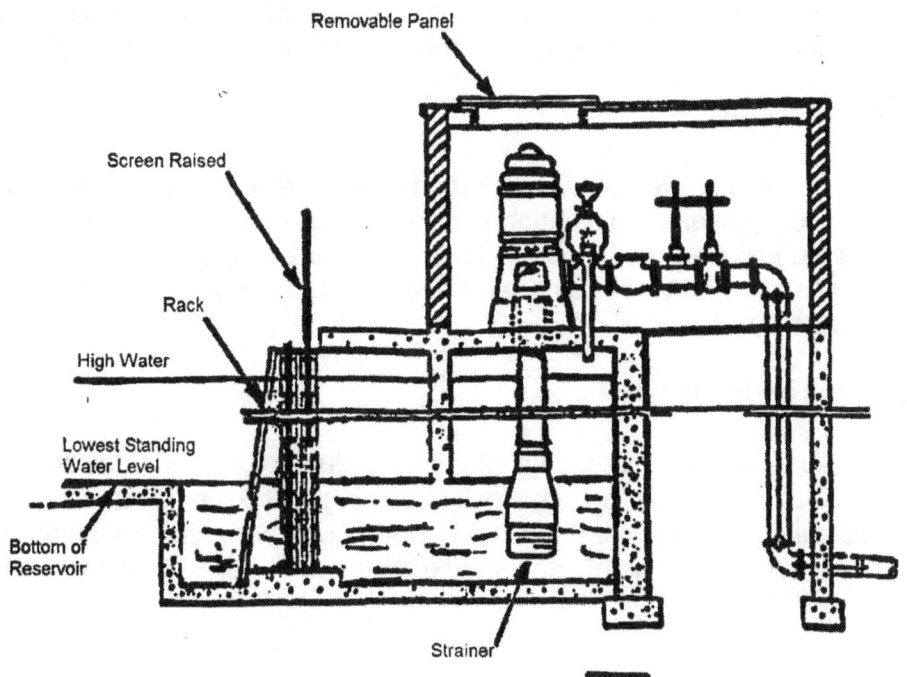

Pump Activation

A fire pump can be started automatically or manually. An automatic pump is started by an electric controller. Controllers activate the pump when there is a drop in water pressure. The controllers also activate the pump when there is water flow in the standpipe system. The controllers are set so that minor changes in water flow do not activate the pumps. This could happen if there was a small leak in the system.

The controllers for the fire pumps are expensive. They require extensive maintenance and periodic testing. If an electric motor drive is used, a standby power generator is sometimes required. If an engine controller is used, the appropriate fuel storage tanks should be filled and checked regularly.

Manually activated pumps are usually used in combination with a gravity tank or a pressure tank. These tanks are designed to operate when there is a pressure drop in the standpipe system. For example, the opening of a hose outlet will cause a pressure drop. The operation of the gravity tank and its alarms alert the Certificate of Fitness holder to start the fire pump. Manually operated fire pumps are often found in industrial and manufacturing occupancies that have personnel on the premises at all times.

Sometimes remote pushbuttons are used to activate the pump. These remote pushbuttons are designed to start the pump but not to stop the pump. Pumps also have a timer installed that keeps the pump running for a predetermined period of time after it is started. This timer is designed to reduce the wear and tear on the pump and its parts due to excessive starting and stopping.

Fire Pump Location

The fire pump should be housed in a room that is fire-resistant or made of noncombustible material. The pump room should be located as close as possible to the standpipe system. The pump room should always be kept clean and accessible. The fire pump, driver, and controller should be protected against possible interruption of service. The temperature inside the pump room should always be maintained above 40 degrees Fahrenheit. This will prevent freezing of the water in the system. The pump room should only be used for fire protection functions.

Operation and Supervision

When fire pumps are activated by electric automatic controllers, they must be constantly monitored. The electrical power should supply the pump at all times. For this reason, supervisory devices are installed on the pumps to provide a signal when there is an electrical power failure. Similar supervisory devices are installed where steam turbines or internal combustion engines are used.

Pump Inspection and Maintenance

Regular inspections and maintenance should be conducted by the Certificate of Fitness holder. The pump should be activated each week according to the manufacturer's specifications. This will make sure that the pump is working properly. When the pump is in operation, a small water leak is desirable and should not be considered a malfunction.

If an automatic controller operates the fire pump, the pump should be activated by reducing the water pressure in the system. This can be done by opening the test drain or initiating a large water flow from the system. Starting the fire pump this way helps determine if the automatic controller is working properly. Care should be taken to make sure that the pump does not overheat.

The centrifugal pump relies on the water supply for cooling and lubrication. The pump should never be operated without the pump being supplied with water.

A visual inspection of all parts of the pump and the controlling equipment should also be conducted each week. This inspection should include the condition and reliability of the power supply. If any problems are discovered with the equipment, immediate action should be taken to correct the problem.

Fire pumps should be fully tested annually to make sure that the pump, driver, power supply, and all other parts are working properly.

DRY STANDPIPE SYSTEMS

Dry pipe standpipe systems are installed where a wet pipe system cannot be heated to prevent freezing. Under normal conditions, there is no water in the piping. Instead, the piping in the piping is filled with air under pressure. The air pressure in the system is controlled automatically by an air maintenance device. The system uses standard standpipe hoses and nozzles. When one of the nozzles is manually opened, the air pressure is reduced in the piping. The drop in air pressure causes a special dry pipe valve to open. Then water flows into the piping and out of the hose. This water flow activates an alarm to alert the people in the building that there is a fire. The water flow also activates a supervisory device which sends a signal to a central monitoring station. This station will then notify the fire department that there is a fire. In buildings where life hazard is very high (e.g., schools, hospitals), the alarm is transmitted directly to the fire department. Sometimes a combination of a wet pipe and a dry pipe system may be used when only part of the building cannot be heated.

Dry Pipe Valve Designs: These valves prevent water from entering the standpipe until a nozzle has opened. A clapper is installed in the dry pipe valve to prevent the water from flowing. Under normal conditions, this clapper is kept closed by the air pressure on the standpipe side of the valve. When the nozzle is opened, it causes a drop of pressure in the piping. This causes the clapper to open and allow water into the standpipe piping. Most dry pipe valves are designed so that a moderate air pressure in a dry standpipe will hold back a much greater water pressure. When the clapper has opened, the valve is said to have tripped. A picture of a typical dry pipe valve is shown below.

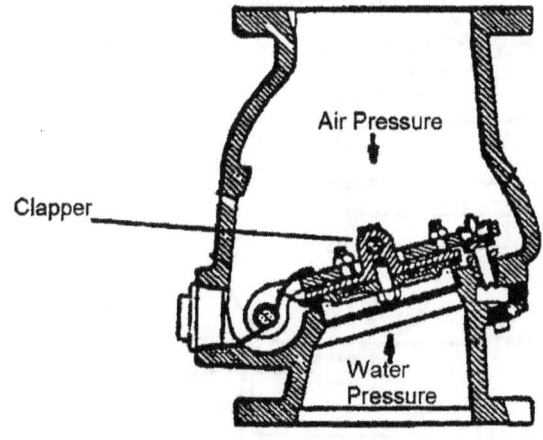

A typical clapper type dry valve

Higher than normal water pressure or a water hammer may cause the dry valve to trip by accident. Water hammer is caused by a sudden flow of water or a sudden change of water pressure in the system. To reduce this danger, air pressure is usually kept well above the normal trip point of the dry pipe valve. The air pressure is usually set at 15 to 20 psi (pounds per square inch) above the normal trip level. Some valves are specially designed for low pressures. In this case, the manufacturer's instructions regarding pressures should be followed.

Quick Opening Devices: In a dry pipe system, there is a delay between the opening of a nozzle and the discharge of water. The delay is due to the time required for the air to leave the standpipe. This delay may be reduced by installing quick opening devices in the standpipe system.

The air pressure is monitored by a sensor device that will automatically activate the quick opening devices. The quick opening devices are automatically activated when a drop of 2 psi in air pressure is noticed in the standpipe system. The quick opening devices change the water and air pressure balance in the system. This change trips the dry pipe valve, allowing the water to force its way through the standpipe in less time. The failure of the quick opening device to operate does not prevent the pipe valve from tripping normally.

Special care must be taken when using a dry standpipe system. The nozzle must never be pointed at the fire until all of the air has been drained from the system. Otherwise, pressurized air would be discharged onto the fire. This would cause the fire to burn more intensely.

PRESSURE TANKS

Pressure tanks are enclosed water tanks of limited size. Air pressure in the tank permits forceful discharge of water in the tank into the standpipe system. A pressure tank may be used as a primary or secondary water supply for a standpipe system. A pressure tank is usually housed in an enclosed structure. The temperature in the enclosure is kept at 40 degrees Fahrenheit or above. The heated structure may be located anywhere in the building or even outside the building.

Pressure tanks are usually kept approximately two-thirds full of water and one-third full of pressurized air. The minimum acceptable air pressure inside the tank is 75 psi (pounds per square inch). The air pressure in the tank is automatically maintained by an air compressor. The maximum capacity of pressure tanks is typically 9,000 gallons. Some standpipe systems require more than 9,000 gallons of water. If necessary, several pressure tanks can be used in combination to supply the system. A standard pressure tank is shown in the following diagram

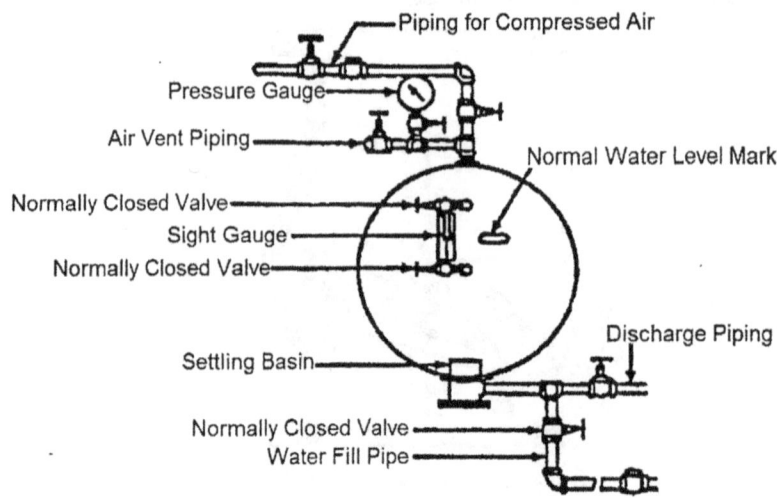

Pressure Tank Alarms

All pressure tanks used to provide the required primary water supply of a standpipe system should be equipped with two high and low alarm systems. One system monitors the high and low air pressure. The other system monitors the high and low water levels. The alarm system automatically controls the air-to-water ratio which should always be 1 (air) to 2 (water). An alarm signals the Certificate of Fitness holder when the water level or the air pressure fall is too low. When this happens, the pressure tank should be adjusted or repaired immediately.

Supervision of the Pressure Tank

The pressure tank may also be supervised by a central station which monitors the entire standpipe system. Supervisory devices are installed in the pressure tank. These devices alert the central station when there is a problem with the tank's water level, air pressure, water temperature. The devices also alert the central station when water has been discharged from the tank. When water has been discharged through a hose outlet, the local fire department is notified.

The central station notifies the Certificate of Fitness holder when a problem is caused by equipment failure. Repairs and adjustments should be made quickly. It is important that the pressure tank is returned to good working order as soon as possible.

Inspection and Maintenance of Pressure Tanks

The water level and air pressure in pressure tanks should be inspected monthly. The water level and air pressure must provide an adequate water supply to the standpipe system.

The water gauge valve must be opened to examine the water level as shown in the diagram below.

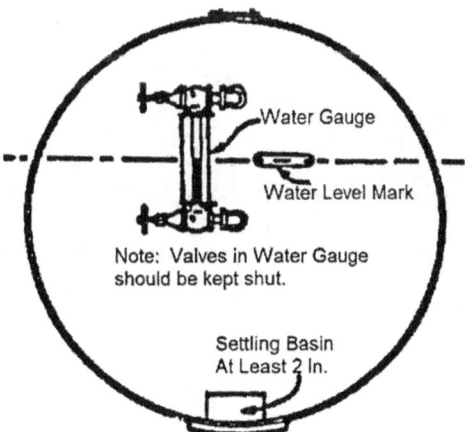

When the valve is opened, the water will flow into the gauge. This allows the Certificate of Fitness holder to compare the water level in the tank to the desired water level mark. Adjustments to the water level should be made as needed. After visually inspecting the water gauge valve, the valve should be closed. When the valve is closed, the water and air in the tank are isolated from the sight glass. If the gauge glass breaks, the volume of water and the air pressure are not affected.

The inside of pressure tanks should be inspected carefully every three years. Rusting in the tank may require repainting or other repairs. The inside of the tank should be thoroughly scraped, wire brushed, and repainted. No foreign materials should be allowed to fall into the standpipe system.

The temperature inside the structure housing the pressure tank should be checked daily during cold weather to make sure that the temperature is at least 40 degrees Fahrenheit at all times.

YARD SYSTEMS

A yard hydrant system is most often used in large private manufacturing plants or storage buildings. The yard system is often needed because the public water supply does not meet the needs of the fire protection system. The yard system usually has several private water sources supplying the total fire protection system. The total system may have a sprinkler system, hydrants, and a standpipe and hose system installed.

The water supply sources are all connected together in the yard system. This allows the water to be directly supplied to any part of the system when needed. Water can be supplied even when one of the supply sources is not working. The combined sources of water keep the water pressure in the system at a high level. The picture below shows a detailed yard fire protection system.

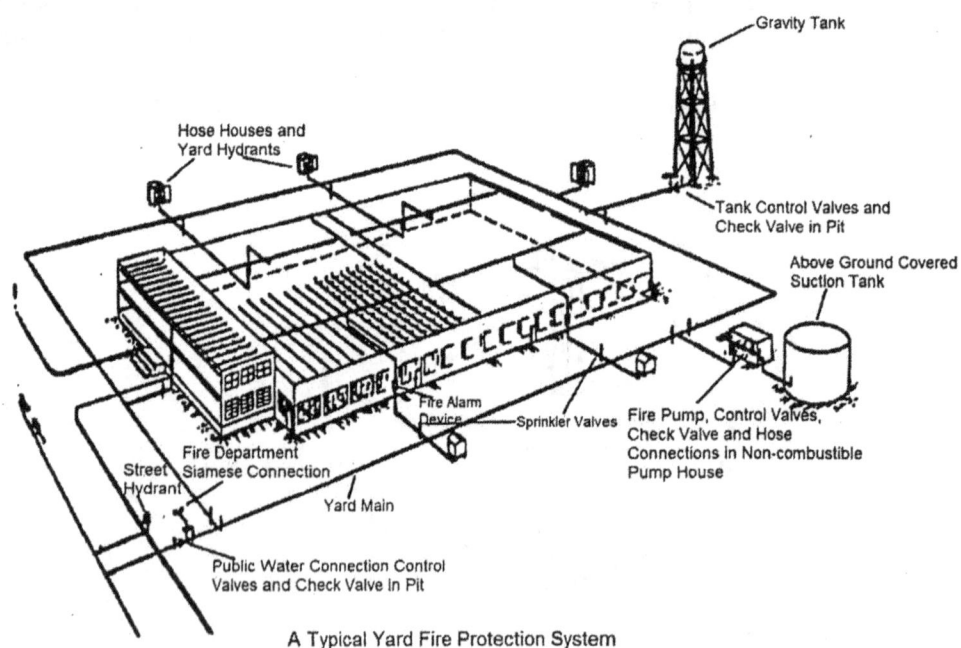

A Typical Yard Fire Protection System

The water supply sources are all connected to a main water supply grid. This supply grid surrounds the entire building. Control valves are installed at various locations on the system. These valves are called post indicator valves (PIV). As the name suggests, they indicate the position of the valve. The valves are manually operated. Each valve has two positions, opened and closed. Under normal conditions, the PIV valves are sealed open.

The PIV valves allow the fire department to shut down only part of the system. The PIV valves are also used to shut down parts of the system when conducting repairs and maintenance. A typical PIV valve is shown below.

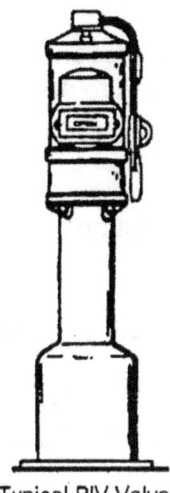

Typical PIV Valve

The water in the yard system is not allowed to flow into the public water system. It is prevented from doing so by a check valve.

Several supervisory and alarm devices are usually installed in the yard system. They indicate when there is a problem with equipment. They also indicate when water flows through the yard system. These devices are needed to make sure that the system will work properly in case of a fire. The supervisory devices may be connected to a central station. The central station is automatically signaled when there is any problem with the yard system. It will then notify the fire department.

Several different water supply sources may be used in a yard system.

Gravity Tank: The gravity tank supplies water using the force of gravity.

Fire Pump: The fire pump draws water from a suction tank and pumps it into the system when needed.

Public Waterworks Connection: The street main supplies water using the water pressure in the public water works system. Sometimes a street main may not be connected to the system if it is located too far away from the building.

Hose Houses: Hose houses may be installed on the system. The hose house must be painted red. The house is usually located outside the main water supply grid. The house must be accessible at all times. Hoses, nozzles, and other fire protection tools are kept in the hose house. Standpipe connections are located in the hose house. These connections allow the firefighters to connect directly into the yard system. They are very helpful when the street mains are located too far away from the building. The connections save a lot of time when fighting a fire.

Pressure Tank: This tank may supply water to the yard system under pressure. The tank is filled with water and air. The air forces the water out under pressure when part of the fire protection system is activated.

Fire Department Siamese Connection: A siamese connection is always installed on the system. The siamese connection is used by the fire department to pump water into the system.

Hydrants: Hydrants may be installed in some systems. They allow the fire department to run hoses from the public water mains. The location of the hydrants will depend on the layout of the public water supply system.

INSPECTION AND MAINTENANCE OF YARD SYSTEM

The Certificate of Fitness holder should conduct regular inspections of the entire yard system. A record of all inspections should be made. The Certificate of Fitness holder should sign and date all records. These records should be kept for at least one year. They should be made available to any representative of the fire department.

The Certificate of Fitness holder should make sure that the hose houses are in good working order. All equipment inside should be inspected. The hose house should be accessible at all times. The hose house should be painted red at regular intervals. Care should be taken to make sure that the area inside the house is kept clean and dry.

All valves should be checked to make sure that they are in the correct position.

Any problems with the equipment in the yard system should be noted. Major defects should be reported to the Fire Department and the owner of the building or location immediately. Minor defects should be reported to the owner. In all cases, the defects in the system should be repaired immediately.

SPRINKLER SYSTEMS

This study material contains the information you will need to prepare for the examination for the Certificate of Fitness for Sprinkler Systems. The study material includes information taken from relevant sections of the Fire Prevention Code and the Building Code of New York. Other information describes different kinds of sprinkler systems and when they are used.

All questions on the Certificate of Fitness examination are multiple choice, with four alternatives answers to each question. Only one answer is correct for each question. If you do not answer a question or mark more than one alternative your answer will be scored as incorrect. A score of 70% correct is required on the examination in order to qualify for the Certificate of Fitness. Read each question carefully before marking your answer. There is no penalty for guessing.

Sample questions

1. The minimum water pressure at the level of the highest sprinkler head should be:
    a. 15 psi
    b. 25 psi
    c. 50 psi
    d. 100 psi

The correct answer is "a". You would mark "a" on your answer sheet.

2. A supply of extra sprinkler heads:
    a. is not required to be kept
    b. may be obtained from the Bureau of Fire Prevention
    c. may be obtained from the nearest Fire Company
    d. are required to be kept on the building premises

The correct answer is "d". You would mark "d" on your answer sheet.

PROVISIONS OF THE FIRE PREVENTION CODE OF NEW YORK

All multiple dwellings, factories, office buildings, warehouses, stores and offices, theaters and music halls, and all hospitals and asylums, and all public schools and other public buildings, churches and other places where large numbers of persons are congregated for purposes of worship, instruction or amusement, and piers, bulkheads, wharves, pier sheds, bulkhead sheds or other waterfront structures shall provide such fire hose, fire extinguishers, buckets, axes, fire hooks, fire doors and other means of preventing and extinguishing fires as the commissioner may direct.

Sprinkler systems in garment factories and factories using flammable oil for processing:

A one source automatic wet pipe sprinkler system shall be provided in every non-fireproof building in which there is a garment factory or a factory engaged in the processing of combustible fabrics with a flammable oil, and which exceeds three stories in height, and in which more than fifty persons are employed above the street floor. A flammable oil is defined as an oil which emits a flammable vapor below one hundred twenty-five degrees Fahrenheit. An automatic dry pipe sprinkler system is acceptable in place of an automatic wet pipe sprinkler system where low temperatures or other conditions would prevent the installation of a wet pipe system. The sprinkler systems shall be provided in all parts of such buildings.

Sprinkler and/or standpipe system maintenance and inspections:

1. Automatic and non-automatic sprinkler systems shall be inspected at least once a month by a competent person holding a certificate of fitness, employed by the owner, to see that all parts of the system are in perfect working order, and that the fire department connection or connections, if any, are ready for immediate use by the fire department. A detailed record of each inspection shall be kept for examination by a representative of the fire department.

2. A supply of at least six extra sprinkler heads shall be kept available on the premises, to replace promptly any fused or damaged sprinklers. Any head which has opened or has been damaged shall be replaced immediately with a good sprinkler head. One or more employees instructed in the maintenance of sprinkler systems.

3. At least once in five years, the fire department connection or connections, if any, for a sprinkler and/or standpipe system shall be subjected to a hydrostatic pressure test and the standpipe system shall also be subjected to a flow and pressure test to demonstrate its suitability for fire department use. The test shall be conducted by the owner's representative before a representative of the fire department,

Maintenance and inspections of standpipe and sprinkler pumps and accessories:

Valves, hose, tools and other accessory fire fighting appliances shall be kept readily available and in good working order. Fire pumps shall be operated at least once in thirty days in a manner which will subject the standpipe system to a hydrostatic pressure of at least 50 pounds per square inch at the top story hose outlet. The qualified operator shall maintain a suitable record of his or her compliance with this requirement for inspection by the fire department. The installation of fire and booster pumps shall be subject to inspection and/or test in the presence of an inspector from the bureau of fire prevention.

PROVISIONS OF BUREAU OF FIRE PREVENTION FIRE DIRECTIVE 4-82

Record keeping

The Certificate of Fitness Holder shall maintain a detailed record of all inspections. A record card with the date of each inspection, the Certificate of Fitness number, and the signature of the Certificate of Fitness holder shall be posted near the main control valve.

The detailed inspection report shall include information relative to conditions of water supply, gravity and pressure tanks and levels therein, valves, risers, piping, sprinkler heads, hose valves, hoses and nozzles, siamese connections, alarms, fire pumps, obstructions, and conditions of all other system equipment and appurtenances. All defects of violations shall be noted on the report. Records should be kept for one year and be made available to any representative of the Fire Department.

Reporting of defects or violations

The Certificate of Fitness holder should report all major defects immediately to:
- the local Fire Company
- the owner or manager of the building
- the Bureau of Fire Prevention

Major defects or violations include: empty tank, break or major leak in system water piping, inoperative or shut water supply valves; or complete or partial shutdown of sprinkler and/or standpipe systems for repairs or other reason, and defective siamese connections.

Other defects or violations which are minor should be reported to the owner or manager of the building. If the defects are not corrected within 30 days, the defects should be reported in writing to the Bureau of Fire Prevention.

Failure to make inspections, maintain records, and report defects or violations may be cause for revocation of the Certificate of Fitness and court enforcement proceedings.

PROVISIONS OF BUREAU OF FIRE PREVENTION FIRE DIRECTIVE 1-68

Color code requirements for fire extinguishing systems in bulk oil storage and similar plants.

Automatic sprinkler systems (wet or dry):
- Piping and valve bodies and handles shall be painted red with contrasting bright green bands
- Fire Department connections shall be painted red with green caps

Non-automatic sprinkler systems (including fog spray systems):
- Piping and valve bodies and handles shall be painted red with contrasting aluminum bands

- Fire Department connections shall be painted aluminum

PROVISIONS OF THE NEW YORK BUILDING CODE

Sources of water supply for sprinkler systems:

Automatic sources of water supply for sprinkler systems include a gravity tank, pressure tank, automatic fire pump, or direct connection to the public water system. Auxiliary sources of water supply for sprinkler systems include manually activated fire pumps or siamese connections. Tanks used to provide the required primary water supply to a standpipe system may also be used as a supply for a non-automatic sprinkler system. Non-automatic sources of supply for sprinkler systems shall include siamese connections. Where siamese connections are installed, metal signs shall be fastened to or above the siamese connection indicating the area protected. Where the building has two or more frontages, additional metal signs shall be installed indicating the location of the siamese connection. The installation and construction of siamese connections shall be the same as required for fire standpipe systems, except that the caps of each automatic sprinkler siamese connection should be painted green. The entire siamese connection of a non-automatic sprinkler system shall be painted aluminum. The caps of each siamese connection used for combination standpipe and sprinkler system shall be painted yellow and signs shall be provided.

At least one automatic source of water supply shall be provided for sprinkles installed in all occupancy groups, except that:

- Two automatic sources of water supply shall be provided for sprinklers in:
    - Buildings classified in occupancy group A
    - Buildings classified in occupancy group C when the area on one floor exceeds twenty thousand square feet
    - Buildings classified in occupancy group F-1 when open heads are required for stages of unlimited size

- The domestic water supply may be used to supply a sprinkler system when installed in buildings classified in occupancy groups E, G, H and J. The domestic water supply may be used to supply sprinklers if all of the following conditions are met:
    - The domestic water supply line from the tank or street has the required pressure (as described below)
    - An O.S. & Y. valve or an approved valve having visual indication, sealed open, is installed in the sprinkler supply branch
    - The number of heads in each fire section does not exceed twenty, and no more than ten heads are supplied from any one domestic water riser
    - The connection is made at the supply or riser side of any domestic branch control valves

Direct connection of sprinklers to the public water system:

Direct connection of sprinklers to a city water main is acceptable as an automatic water supply provided the main is capable of maintaining a pressure of at least fifteen psig at the top of the highest sprinkler riser, with five hundred gpm of water flowing from a two and one-half inch hydrant outlet located at the street level within 250 feet of the building. The site of each connection shall be as large as that of the main riser and, except in sprinkler systems in multiple dwellings, shall be at least three inches and shall be controlled by an accessible shutoff valve.

Each service shall be equipped, under the sidewalk, with a control valve in a flush sidewalk box located within two feet of the front wall of the building or street line as required by the department of environmental protection. The location of the control valve shall be indicated by a sign place on the structure directly opposite the sidewalk flush box, and shall have a white background with one inch red letters reading: "Automatic Sprinkler Shutoff Valve ... Feet Opposite This Sign." Brass, bronze, or other metal signs with one-inch letters, raised or counter-sunk one-eighth of an inch may also be used.

Sprinkler booster pumps:

Where the pressure from the city water main is less than 15 psig as described above but is sufficient to give at least five psig at the highest line of sprinklers as determined by test, an automatic, electrically driven pump installed for the purpose of boosting or increasing the city water pressure in the sprinkler system may be accepted subject to the fallowing requirements:

- Pumps shall be of approved centrifugal type, capable of delivering at least 200 gpm, and shall be capable of supplying 25 percent of the heads, in the largest area supplied, at 20 gpm, at a pressure of at least 25 psig at the top of the highest sprinkler riser
- Pumps shall be maintained under approved automatic control with closed circuit supervisory attachment. The supervisory attachments shall be directly connected to an office where maintenance personnel are in attendance 24 hours a day; or, in lieu thereof, the supervisory attachment may be directly connected to the central station of an approved operating fire alarm company. The supervisory alarm services shall be arranged so as to provide positive indication at an approved central office or sprinkler alarm panel board that the pump has operated or that the source of electrical supply has failed.

When sprinklers are not directly connected to the public water system and a sprinkler booster pump is not present, a pressure or gravity tank shall be used.

Protection of sprinkler system:

All parts of an automatic system exposed to freezing temperatures shall be protected from freezing or in lieu thereof, an automatic dry pipe system or a system filled with a nonfreezing, noncombustible solution shall be used. When a system filled with nonfreezing solution is used and the system is connected to a potable water supply, it shall be subject to the requirements of the health department and the bureau of water supply of the department of environmental protection. Sprinkler heads subject to damage shall be protected.

Inspection and tests:
- Automatic wet and dry systems: Automatic wet and dry sprinkler systems shall be subjected to a hydrostatic pressure test for a period of one hour at a pressure of at least one hundred psig at the top-most sprinkler head and at least two hundred psig at the lowest cross connection to the siamese connections.

- Automatic dry pipe systems: In addition to the hydrostatic test the automatic dry pipe systems shall also be tested to 40 psig air pressure for a 24-hour period with the pressure loss not to exceed one and one-half psig.
- Non-automatic sprinkler systems: Non-automatic sprinkler systems shall be subjected to a hydrostatic pressure test of 50 psig at the top-most sprinkler head, with the test pressure maintained for a period of at least one hour.
- Pressure tanks: Pressure tanks shall be hydrostatically tested to a pressure of at least one and one-half times the working pressure for a period of one hour.
- Sprinkler branches and heads supplied from domestic water: Sprinkler branches and heads shall be tested at the pressure required by this section or at the pressure of the domestic water supply, whichever is greater.

PROVISIONS OF REFERENCE STANDARD RS 17-2
Chapter 2 - Water Supplies

Pumps

In light hazard occupancies with only limited ordinary hazard areas, an automatic fire pump serving the lower 300 feet of the standpipe system may be used as the primary supply to the sprinkler system, if a secondary automatic switching power supply is available to drive the pump. In hydraulically designed sprinkler systems supplied from a gravity tank, the pressure may be increased by means of an automatic, special service fire pump. The pump shall be arranged in a bypass to permit the portion of the system so supplied to be served by the system's siamese connections. If the pump is not supplied from the street side of the building service switch, the electrical service and pump operation shall be fully supervised; provided that a secondary automatic switching power supply is available to drive the pumps.

Pressure Tanks

A pressure tank in accordance is an acceptable water supply source. The total available quantity of water in pressure tanks need not exceed 15,000 gallons when there is a secondary source of water supply available from a gravity tank or a street connection acceptable to the Commissioner of Buildings. The maximum gross capacity of a single pressure tank shall be 9,000 gallons.

Each tank shall be kept at a maximum of 2/3 full of water and a minimum of 1/3 full of air maintained under a minimum pressure of 75 psig. The water-to-air ratio shall be so proportioned and the tank so located that a minimum pressure of 15 psig will be available on the highest line of sprinklers below the main roof when all the water is being discharged from the tank. The tanks shall be supplied with water through a fixed pipe, independent of the sprinkler piping, and at least 2 inches in size. The water supply and connection shall be capable of supplying the tank at a the rate of at least 65 gpm without reducing the pressure in the tank. The tank shall have a fixed water level plate on the end of the tank opposite the gauge glass, or equivalent devices, to indicate the level of the water in the tank.

The air compressor shall be provided with automatic controls for maintaining the air pressure. The capacity of the compressor shall be sufficient to build up the tank pressure to 75 psig within 3 hours or less. Pressure tanks shall be provided with approved closed circuit high and low water and high low air alarms. Pressure tanks shall be located at or above the top level of sprinklers.

AUTOMATIC SPRINKLER SYSTEMS

Automatic sprinkler systems are designed to automatically distribute water on a fire. The sprinkler system is designed to extinguish the fire entirely, or to prevent the spread of the fire. An automatic sprinkler system consists of a series of pipes at or near the ceiling in a building. The sprinkler system is fitted with automatic devices designed to release water on a fire. These devices are called sprinkler heads. The sprinkler heads are normally closed by a disk or cap. This cap is held in place by a heat-sensitive releasing element. A rise in temperature to a predetermined heat causes the sprinkler head to open. Water is then discharged in the form of spray. When the sprinkler heads open they are said to have fused. The sprinkler heads are fitted at standard intervals on the piping. If more than one head opens, the area sprayed by each overlaps that of the sprinkler head next to it.

Sprinkler systems are required by law in various occupancies. They also may be installed voluntarily by the owner of the building. The sprinklers are installed to protect the building and its residents. The installation of sprinklers has a major effect in reducing fire losses. About 96 percent of the fires are extinguished or controlled when sprinklers are installed. The 4 percent failure was due to a variety of causes including burst piping, closed supply valves, frozen water lines, etc.

Automatic sprinklers are very effective for life safety. They signal the existence of a fire. At the same time they discharge water to the burning area. When sprinklers are installed there are rarely problems getting to the seat of the fire. They also reduce interference with visibility for firefighting due to smoke. The downward force of the water sprayed from sprinklers lowers the smoke level in the room. The sprinklers also serve to cool the smoke. This makes it possible for persons to remain in the area much longer than they could if the room were without sprinklers.

Most standard sprinkler systems have devices that automatically give an alarm when a sprinkler discharges water. This alarm is usually an audible signal in the building. In many cases they also give an alarm at a remote location, such as the local fire department or a central station. The central station monitors the entire fire protection system for water discharge and problems with the equipment. When water discharge or equipment problems are identified, the local fire department is immediately notified. This allows the fire department to gain control of a fire as quickly as possible. Water is rarely discharged accidentally from sprinkler heads.

SPRINKLER HEADS

Sprinkler heads are made of metal. They are screwed into the piping at standard intervals. The water is prevented from leaving the sprinkler head by an arrangement of levers and links. The levers and links are soldered together on the sprinkler head. The solder is a metal alloy with a fixed melting point. Other types of sprinkler heads use a quartz bulb which expands and breaks under heat. Still another type uses a solid chemical held in a cylinder which is broken by heat action. The sprinkler head is designed to withstand at least 500 psi without injury or leakage. If properly installed, there is little danger of the sprinkler breaking apart unless it is damaged.

The latest type of sprinkler head is called the "cycling sprinkler." This sprinkler cycles water on and off depending on the temperature. When the disk reaches a temperature of 165°F, the valve opens, permitting water to flow. When the disk temperature cools the valve closes to shut off the water.

Care must be taken to make certain that no part of a sprinkler head is covered with paint when the piping is being painted! Such a coating may interfere with the free movement of parts and delay its opening, or make it inoperative. When painting the piping or nearby areas, the heads should be protected by covering them with paper bags. These bags should be removed as soon as the painting is finished.

Some sprinkler heads are designed to be used in special situations. Sprinkler heads exposed to corrosive conditions are often covered with a protective coat of wax, or lead. Corrosive vapors are likely to make automatic sprinklers inoperative or slow down the speed of operation. They can also seriously block the spray nozzles in the sprinkler heads. They can damage, weaken or destroy the delicate parts of the sprinkler heads. In most cases such corrosive action takes place over a long time. For this reason the sprinkler heads must be carefully watched for signs of corrosion. Care should be taken to make sure that the protective coating is not damaged when handling or replacing the heads.

A typical fusible link-type sprinkler head is shown in the picture below:

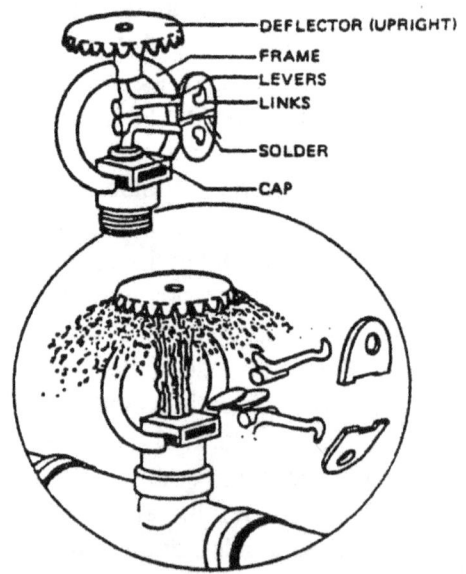

Spray Pattern of Sprinklers: The best way to put out a fire is to spray the water from the sprinkler head downward and horizontally. The spray pattern will also prevent the spread of the fire. The force of the water against the deflector creates a heavy spray which is directed outward and downward. The shape of the deflector determines the spray pattern of the water discharged from the sprinkler head. Usually, this is an umbrella-shaped spray pattern. At a distance of 4 feet below the deflector, the spray covers a circular area having a diameter of approximately 16 feet when the sprinkler is discharging 15 gpm. The newest kinds of sprinkler heads allow the sprinklers to be placed farther apart and need lower flow rates to give coverage to an area. These new heads offer more effective fire protection and are less likely to cause water damage than the old sprinkler heads.

Systems Using Large Drop Sprinklers: Large drop sprinklers are special sprinklers designed to discharge large drops of water from the head. These sprinklers are used to break through the strong updrafts of high challenge fires.

Temperature Ratings of Sprinkler Heads: Automatic sprinkler heads have various temperature ratings which state the temperatures at which they will fuse. The temperature rating of all solder type automatic sprinklers is stamped on the soldered link. For other heat sensitive units, the temperature rating is stamped on one of the releasing parts. The temperature ratings of sprinkler heads are also indicated by a color-coding system.

In places where the temperature is normally high (e.g. boilers, ovens and drying rooms) a sprinkler head with a higher temperature rating must be used. This is to make sure that the sprinkler head does not discharge water at the wrong time. If heads with a high temperature rating are used in ordinary rooms (e.g., an office, an apartment, or a store) the value of the sprinkler protection is greatly reduced. This is because the temperature will have to Increase much higher for the sprinkler head to open.

Sprinkler systems are excellent for controlling fires. However, they can cause water damage if they are not shut down soon after the fire has been extinguished. No control valve on the system should be closed except on the order of the fire officer in charge. Sometimes the fire department has a difficult time finding the control valve to shut down the system. This problem can be prevented by keeping a small sketch of the sprinkler system and the position of the control valves. This sketch should always be readily available. A sketch is very helpful to the firefighters when they have to work with the sprinkler system.

Buildup of Foreign Material on Sprinklers: Sometimes conditions exist which cause a build up of foreign material on sprinkler heads. This may prevent the sprinkler head from working properly. This buildup is commonly called loading. The buildup of foreign material insulates the sprinkler head. This prevents the sprinkler from opening at the temperature it is designed to open.

If the buildup is hard, it may prevent the sprinkler from opening. The best practice is to replace loaded sprinklers with new sprinklers rather than to attempt to clean them. If the deposits are hard, attempts to clean the heads are likely to damage the sprinkler. This damage may prevent the sprinkler from working properly. The damage may also cause the sprinkler head to leak.

Deposits of light dust are less serious than hard deposits. Dust buildup may delay the operation of sprinkler heads, however, it will not prevent the eventual discharge of water. Dust deposits can be blown or brushed off. If a brush is used, it should be soft to avoid possible injury to sprinkler parts. Scouring or acidic liquids should are likely to damage the sprinklers and should not be used for cleaning. Hot solutions of any kind should never be used to clean the sprinklers.

Sometimes sprinklers need to be protected when ceilings or piping are being painted. Usually a small lightweight paper bag or a sheet of lightweight paper is placed over the heads until the painting is completed. The bag or the sheet of paper should be secured with a rubber band. The bags are likely to delay the operation of the sprinklers and should be removed immediately after the painting is completed. There is no known method to safely remove paint from under the water cap or on the fusible link. Sprinklers that have been painted other than by the manufacturer must be replaced with new units.

A supply of at least six extra sprinklers should always be kept in a sprinkler cabinet. This extra supply should be used to promptly replace any sprinklers that have opened or have been damaged. The extra supply of sprinklers should be exactly the same as the sprinklers already installed in the system. It is very important that the replacement sprinkler heads have the same temperature rating as those installed in the system.

WET PIPE SPRINKLER SYSTEMS

Wet pipe systems have water in the piping at all times. This type of system is used where there is no danger of the water supply freezing. A picture of a typical wet pipe system is shown in the picture below:

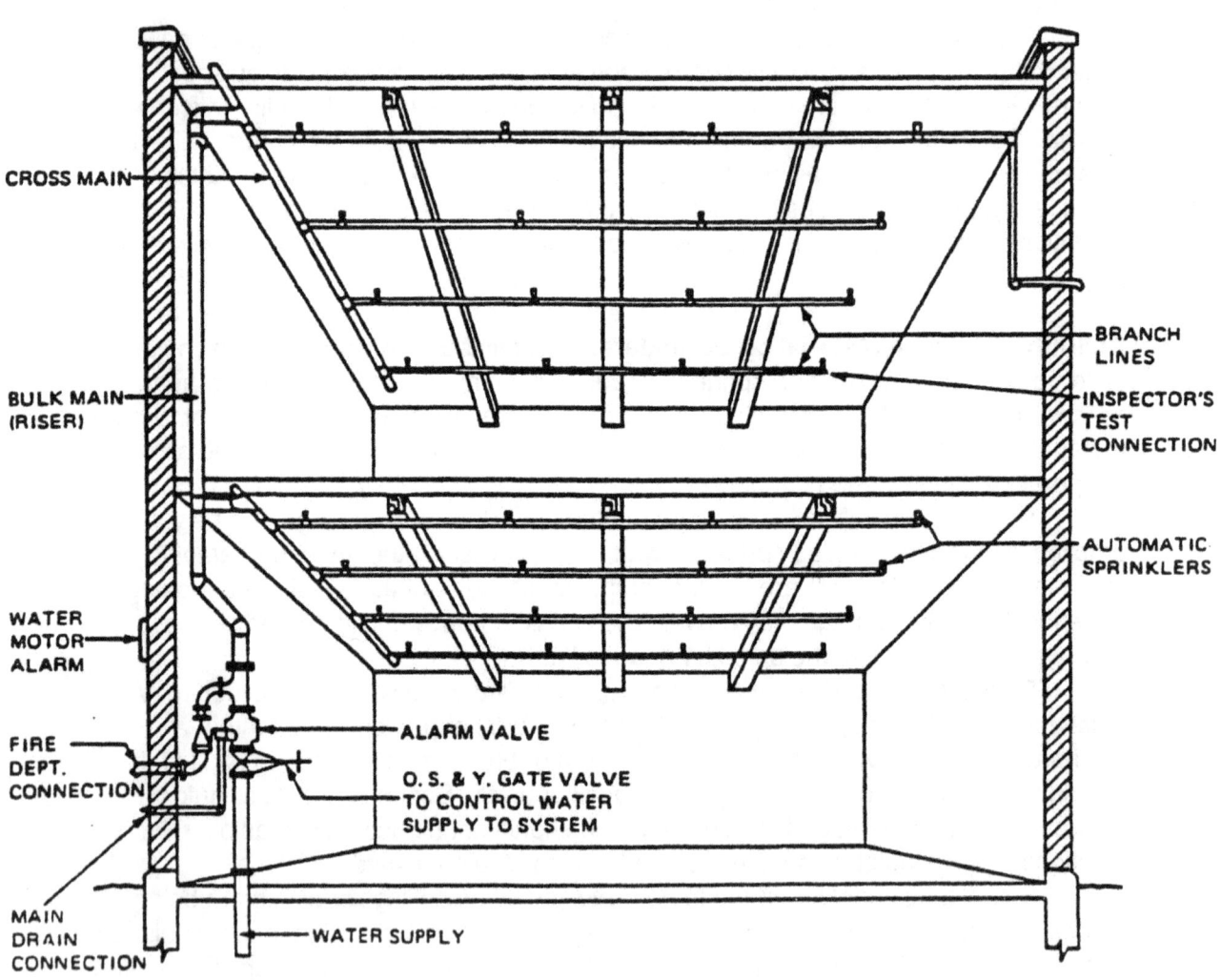

A wet pipe sprinkler valve is shown in the next picture below:

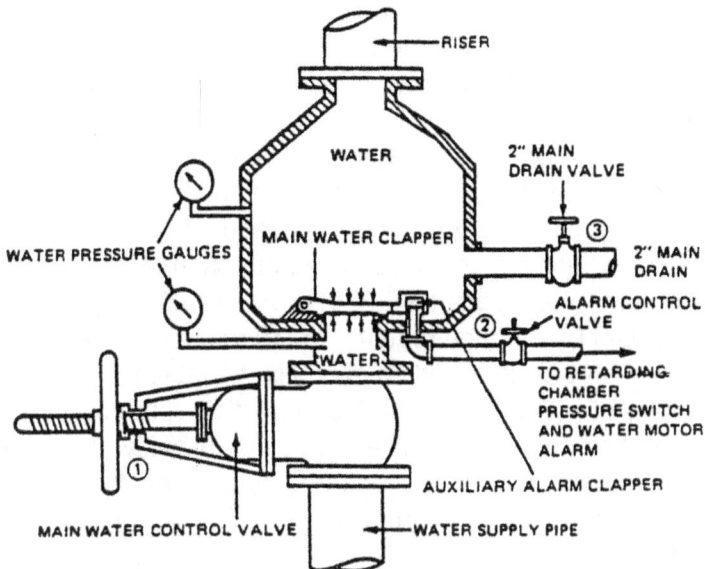

Where temperatures drop below freezing the ordinary wet pipe system cannot be used. There are two methods for using automatic sprinklers in places exposed to freezing conditions. One method is to design a system where water enters the sprinkler piping only after a control valve is opened. These are dry pipe systems, deluge systems, or preaction systems. The other method adds an antifreeze solution to the water in the wet pipe system. This solution is a mixture of chemicals designed to prevent the water from freezing.

Antifreeze Solutions: Antifreeze is added to the water in piping exposed to freezing conditions. When the sprinkler heads fuse the system works in the same way as a wet pipe system. Antifreeze solutions are costly and may be difficult to maintain. Antifreeze is usually used for small unheated areas. Solutions may be used only in accordance with applicable local health regulations.

Cold Weather Valves: An automatic sprinkler system should not be shut off and drained to avoid freezing during cold weather. However, parts of the sprinkler system may be shut down. Permission must be obtained from the local fire department and may be given to shut off a maximum of ten sprinklers in a wet pipe system. These shutoff valves are commonly referred to as cold weather valves.

WATER SUPPLIES FOR SPRINKLER SYSTEMS

The methods used to supply water to sprinkler systems are the same as those for standpipe systems. Sprinklers may be supplied from one or a combination of sources. For example, they may be supplied by public mains, gravity tanks, pressure tanks, fire pumps, reservoirs, rivers, or lakes. A single water supply would appear to be all that is needed to supply a sprinkler protection. This assumes that there is enough water at an acceptable pressure. However, a single supply may be out of service (for maintenance or repair) during a fire emergency. It may be disabled during fire or before the fire is fully extinguished. The water supply may fall below normal pressure or volume during an emergency. These are just a few reasons why it is good to have a second water supply.

In some cases it is required by law to have a second water supply source. Whether a second source is needed depends on several factors. These factors include the strength and reliability of the primary supply, the value of the property, the height, area and design of the building.

When a sprinkler system is supplied from a public water main, the entire system may be shut down by closing a control valve. This valve is located between the building and the water main in a box that is recessed into the sidewalk. The location of the box is found by reading a sign on a building or post nearby. The sign will read "Shutoff for Sprinkler System Located 6 Feet From This Sign, or it will have similar instructions. A special key may be required to operate this valve.

The control valve for the building may also be attached to an upright post, known as a post indicator valve (PIV). The building or section of the building controlled by the valve is usually marked on the post. The position of this valve (open or closed) is shown through a telltale opening in the post. On some posts, a padlock must first be opened or forced to release the operating wrench. On others, an iron strap must first be released by cutting a riveted leather section.

The main water supply for sprinklers may also be controlled by an OS&Y valve (Outside Screw and Yolk valve). The OS&Y valves are found just inside the building wall on the main riser, or outside in protected pits. It is easy to tell at a glance if the valve is open or shut. When the stem is all the way out the valve is open. When the stem is all the way in the valve is closed. Some OS&Y valves may be used to control the water supply for individual floors in a building. The OS&Y valves are also installed to shut off certain sections of an individual floor. Being able to shut off parts of a building allows the fire department to have greater control over the sprinkler system. When a fire is under control in an area the OS&Y valve can be closed to prevent any further water damage.

Sometimes repairs must be made to the sprinkler system. When this happens the OS&Y valves are used to close the water supply to only those sections being repaired. This is good because the rest of the sprinkler system does not have to be shut down.

Siamese Connections for Fire Department Use: Normally a sprinkler system is connected to an automatic water supply source. Auxiliary sources of water are supplied through Fire Department siamese connections at the building. Siamese connections are a standard part of all sprinkler systems. When responding to an alarm most fire departments supply water to the standpipe system first. The standpipe system supplies water to the fire hoses in the building. Water is then supplied to the sprinkler system through its own siamese connection. Care should be taken that standpipe and the sprinkler connections are properly marked because the connections look the same. The exact purpose of each siamese connection should be shown nearby or on the siamese connection itself. The siamese connection to an automatic sprinkler system should be painted green, and the siamese connection to a nonautomatic sprinkler system should be painted aluminum. The siamese connection to a standpipe should be painted red.

Fire department connections must always be accessible. Each connection should be fitted with a check valve, but not with a gate valve. The check valve prevents the backflow of the private water supply into the public water supply. The figure below shows the main features of a fire department siamese connection:

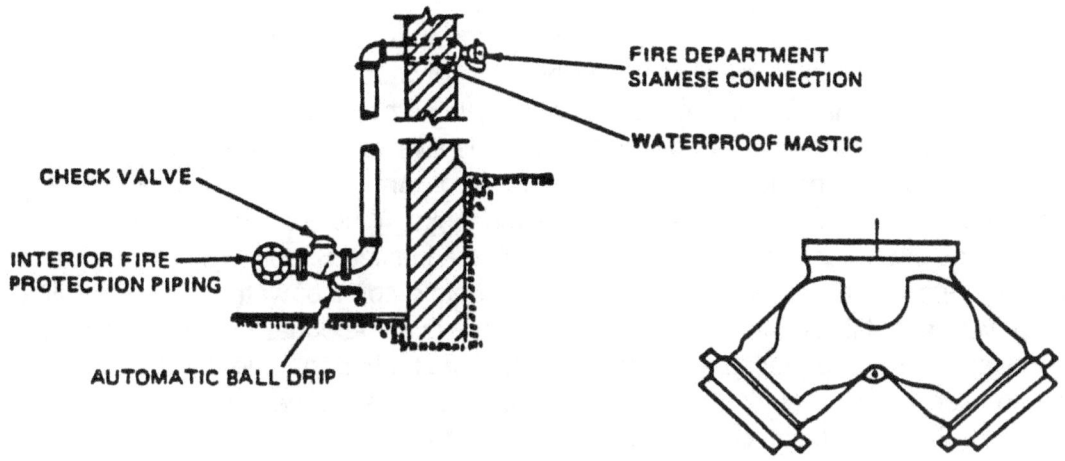

The automatic drip device between the check valve and the outside hose coupling prevents water from building up in the piping. This drip device makes sure that the fire department connection is not blocked by water that has frozen in the piping. If water freezes in the piping, the fire department will not be able to pump water into the system.

Connections to Public Water Works System: A connection from a reliable public water works tern of adequate capacity and water pressure is the preferred primary supply for automatic sprinkler systems.

Fire Pumps: A fire pump having both a reliable source of power and a reliable suction water supply is a desirable piece of equipment. A suction water supply is simply a body of water that the pump can draw water form. Fire pumps are commonly used because they can pump water into the sprinkler system under high pressure. With a good water supply a fire pump can pump water into a sprinkler system for a long time.

Manually started pumps may be used as a secondary supply source if the water supply will last long enough to allow the pump to be started. This kind of system must give an automatic waterflow signal to the Certificate of Fitness holder when the pump must be started.

Automatic fire pumps are usually needed where a high water demand may occur immediately. This demand may occur in a deluge system. The automatic fire pump is also used when someone is not always present to activate a manual pump. Automatic fire pumps must have their suction under a positive head to avoid the delays of drawing water from a supply source. Under positive head simply that the water supplying the pump must be fed into the fire pump under pressure. This can be achieved by connecting the fire pump to a suction tank. Water is forced into the pump because of gravity.

Gravity Tanks: Gravity tanks of adequate capacity and elevation make a good primary supply and may be acceptable as a single supply. A gravity tank may be located on top of a building or on a tall tower. The water in the tank is distributed throughout the sprinkler system because of the pull of gravity.

Pressure Tanks: Pressure tanks have several possible uses in automatic sprinkler protection. The tank is normally kept two-thirds full of water and one-third full of air. The air pressure in the tank should be maintained above 75 psi. Air for pressure tanks is supplied by air compressors. Because the water is always under pressure it can be forcefully distributed throughout the sprinkler system. Am important limitation is the small amount of water that can be stored in such tanks. Where a small pressure tank is accepted as the water supply, the system is called a Limited Supply System. Pressure tanks are often used in situations where an adequate amount of water can be supplied by a private or public source but the water pressure is not adequate. The pressure tank gives a strong starting pressure for the first sprinklers that open. The flow from the tank may be used while the automatic fire pumps begin to increase the water supply pressure. Pressure tanks are often used in tall buildings that need extra water pressure to supply the highest line of sprinklers. The tank supplies these sprinklers until the fire department begins pumping water into the sprinkler system.

WATERFLOW ALARMS AND SPRINKLER SYSTEM SUPERVISION

Sprinkler systems should have devices and equipment for signaling when water flows through risers or mains supplying the systems. The flow may be due to fire, leakage, or accidental rupture of the piping. It is important that prompt action is taken when waterflow is signaled by these devices.

Functions of Alarms and Supervisory Signals: A sprinkler system with a waterflow alarm serves two functions: (1) It is an effective fire extinguishing system; (2) It is an automatic fire alarm. An alarm is signaled as soon as a sprinkler has opened. This is important since it allows the occupants time to leave the building. It also signals that the fire department should be summoned.

Supervisory devices are often connected to a central station that monitors the system for problems with equipment and when sprinkler heads are opened. The station should be notified when any control valves are closed for maintenance or repair. This reduces the number of false alarms.

Waterflow and fire alarms give warning of the actual occurrence of a fire. They also signal when water flows through the system due to broken pipes. Alarms alert occupants and summon the fire department. Any signal, whether waterflow or supervisory, may be used to give an audible local sprinkler alarm. It may also send a signal to the central station, which will then contact the local fire department.

Sprinkler systems are required to have an approved water motor gong or an electric bell, horn or siren on the outside of the building. An electric bell or other audible signal device may also be located inside the building. Water operated devices must be located near the alarm valve, dry pipe valve, or other water control valves in order to avoid long runs of connecting pipe.

Devices and Equipment Supervised: Sprinkler system supervision is commonly provided for several purposes: (1) water supply control valves, (2) low water level in water supply tanks, (3) low temperature in water supply tanks or ground level reservoirs, (4) high or low water level in pressure tanks, (5) high or low air pressure in pressure tanks, (6) high or low air pressure in dry pipe sprinkler systems, (7) failure of electric power supply to fire pumps, and (8) automatic operation of electric fire pumps.

Waterflow Alarm Valves: The basic design of most waterflow alarm valves is that of a check valve which lifts from its seat when water flows into a sprinkler system. This alarm then starts an audible signal to alert the people in the building that the sprinkler system has been activated.

Alarm Retarding Devices: An alarm check valve exposed to changing water supply pressure needs an alarm retarding device. This is required to prevent fake alarms when the check valve clapper is lifted from its seat by a temporary pressure surge.

Gate Valves: Gate valves of the non-indicating are provided in water distribution systems. Gate valves allow parts of the sprinkler system to be shut off for repairs or maintenance. This is done without reducing protection over a wide area. Such valves are normally a nonrising stem type. They are operated using a special key wrench. A valve box is located over the valve to keep dirt from the valve. The valve box also provides a convenient access point for the valve wrench to the valve nut. A complete record should be made for each valve in the system. This record should include the exact location, the date it was installed, the make, the direction of opening, number of turns to open, and any maintenance that was performed.

PRESSURE TANKS

Pressure tanks are closed water tanks of limited size. Air pressure in the tank permits forceful discharge of the water in the tank into the sprinkler system. A pressure tank may be used as a primary or secondary water supply for a sprinkler system. A pressure tank is usually housed in an enclosed structure. The temperature in the enclosure is kept at 40 degrees Fahrenheit or above. The heated structure may be located anywhere in the building or even outside the building.

Pressure tanks are usually kept approximately two-thirds full of water and one-third full of pressurized air. The minimum acceptable air pressure inside the tank is 75 psi (pounds per square inch). The air pressure in the tank is automatically maintained by an air compressor. The maximum capacity of pressure tanks is typically 9,000 gallons. Some sprinkler systems require more than 9,000 gallons of water. When this happens, several pressure tanks are used in combination to supply the system. A standard pressure tank is shown in the diagram below.

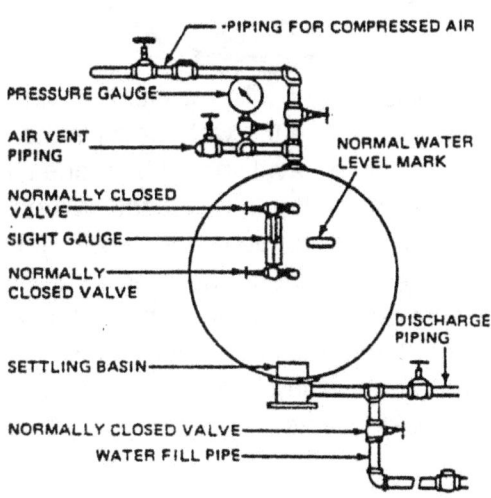

Pressure Tank Alarms

All pressure tanks used to provide the required primary water supply of a sprinkler system should be equipped with two high and low alarm systems. One system monitors high and low air pressure. The other system monitors high and low water levels. The alarm system automatically controls the air-to-water ratio, which should always be 1 to 2. An alarm signals the Certificate of Fitness holder when the water level or the air pressure is too low. When this happens the pressure tank should be adjusted or repaired immediately.

Supervision of the Pressure Tank

The pressure tank may also be supervised by a central station which monitors the entire sprinkler system. Supervisory devices are installed in the pressure tank. These devices alert the central station when there is a problem with the tank's water level, air pressure, or water temperature. The devices also alert the central station when water has been discharged from the tank. When sprinkler heads have fused and water has been discharged from the tank the local fire department is notified.

The central station notifies the Certificate of Fitness holder when a problem is caused by equipment failure. Repairs and adjustments should be made quickly to return the pressure tank to good working order.

Inspection and Maintenance of Pressure Tanks

The water level and air pressure in pressure tanks should be inspected monthly, and must provide an adequate water supply to the sprinkler system. The water gage valve must be opened to examine the water level as shown in the diagram below:

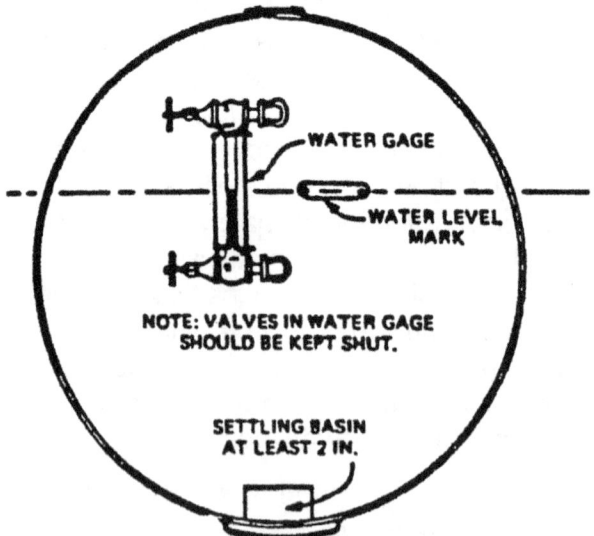

When the valve is opened water will flow into the gage. This allows the Certificate of Fitness holder to compare the water level in the tank to the desired water level mark. Adjustments to the water level should be made if needed. After visually inspecting the water gage, the valve should be closed. When the valve is closed, the water and air in the tank are isolated from the sight glass. If the gage glass breaks, the volume of water and the air pressure are not affected.

The inside of pressure tanks should be inspected carefully every three years. Rusting in the tank may require repainting or other repair. The inside of the tank should be thoroughly scraped, and wire brushed before painting. No foreign materials should be allowed to fall into the sprinkler system.

The temperature inside the structure housing the pressure tank should be checked daily during cold weather. The temperature should be at least 40 degrees Fahrenheit at all times.

GRAVITY TANKS

Gravity tanks are used for water storage. They are made of wood, steel or concrete. Gravity tanks are used as a primary or secondary water supply source for sprinkler systems. A gravity tank system delivers water from the tank through the sprinkler system without the use of pumping equipment.

A gravity tank should be at least 25 feet above the highest line of sprinkler heads that it supplies. Tanks may be located on the tops of buildings or raised on tall supporting towers. An example of a typical gravity tank is shown below:

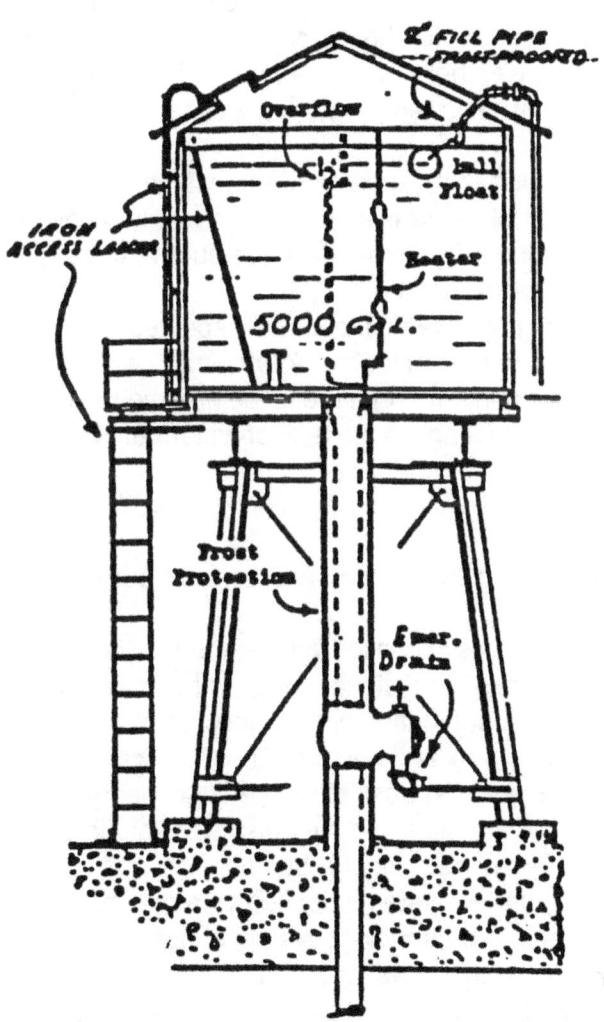

The water pressure in a gravity tank system depends on the elevation of the tank. This is a main advantage over other kinds of systems. Every foot the tank is above the discharge outlet generates 0.434 psi (pounds per square inch) of water pressure. So in other words, the higher the tank is elevated the greater the water pressure. The gravity tank is extremely reliable. It does not depend on the operation of mechanical equipment to supply the sprinkler system.

Automatic fill pumps supply the water to most gravity tanks. The pumps fill the tank at a rate of 65 gpm (gallons per minute) or more. Two floats control the amount of water in the tank. The floats turn on the fill pump when the water in the tank is too low. The floats shut off the pump when the desired water level is reached. The floats make sure the gravity tank always has the right amount of water to supply the sprinkler system. All gravity tanks have an overflow pipe that drains off too much water in the tank. This happens if the floats do not turn off the fill pump. A fill pump is not necessary if the water pressure in the city water main is able to keep the tank filled with the right amount of water.

Gravity tanks are exposed to very low temperatures. All parts of the gravity tank must be insulated or heated to keep the water from freezing. Several methods are used to heat the tank and the pipe that supplies the water. (1) Hot water is circulated by gravity; (2) Steam is discharged directly into the tank; (3) Steam coils are placed inside the tanks; (4) Heat from the sun is used. The Certificate of Fitness holder can find out the temperature of the water by looking at a thermometer located near the heating device. Severe damage can happen to the piping and the tank if the water inside the tank freezes. During freezing weather, the temperature of the water inside the tank and the riser must be checked daily. The temperature should always be at least 40 degrees Fahrenheit.

Ice should not be allowed to build up on the gravity tank. The extra weight of the ice might weaken the supports of the tank and cause the tank to collapse. Falling icicles may also cause damage or injury. It is essential to be sure that the tank is properly heated, insulated and carefully maintained.

The water level in the gravity tank should be inspected each month. The gravity tank should always have a full supply of water. A full tank of water is needed to be sure the sprinkler system works properly during a fire. Keeping the tank full of water also prevents wooden tanks from shrinking. A full tank of water helps keep steel tanks from rusting.

Gravity Tank Supervision

The gravity tank must be constantly monitored to be sure that the tank and its parts are working.

Electrical supervision devices monitor the water temperature and the water level in the gravity tank. These devices send signals to a central station about the water level and water temperature. The central station notifies the Certificate of Fitness holder when a problem with the gravity tank is detected. The Certificate of Fitness holder should correct the problem as soon as possible. The supervisory devices are sometimes called high and low alarms since they also send audible signals to alert the Certificate of Fitness holder when there is a problem.

The main reason a sprinkler system supplied by a gravity tank fails during a fire is not enough water in the tank. The sprinkler system cannot be supplied if there is not enough water in the tank. Too much water in the tank can also cause the system to fail, and may cause damage due to the weight of the extra water. This could cause the gravity tank to collapse.

Inspection and Maintenance of the Gravity Tank

The gravity tank should be regularly inspected and maintained. Maintenance is needed to be sure that the tank functions correctly. For example, the tank may need to be painted regularly to prevent rusting. Before the inside of a gravity tank is repainted the surface should be thoroughly dried. All loose paint, rust, scale, and other surface contamination should be removed. The outside of the gravity tank will require local patching. A complete finish coat of paint is needed when the paint has weathered thin. A new coat of paint also improves the appearance of the tank after it has been patched.

Painters must be careful that scrapings or other foreign materials do not fall down the outlet into the sprinkler piping. The discharge outlet may be covered for protection during repairs. Only a few sheets of paper or a paper bag tied over the end of the settling basin stub should be used. The paper should be removed immediately after finishing the job.

It is best if gravity tanks are used only for fire protection and for no other purpose. Tanks used for other purposes need to be refilled more often. The tanks become settling basins for sediment mixed in with the water. This sediment is then drawn into the piping. This may cause the sprinkler system to become clogged and not work properly.

The local fire department should always be notified when a tank cannot be used for any reason.

Combination Gravity Tank and Pressure Tank Installation

Pressure tanks may be used in combination with gravity tanks to supply a sprinkler system. Both systems may be used to make sure that an adequate water supply is available. The pressure tanks also provide added water pressure to the sprinkler system. An example of a combined installation is shown in the picture below:

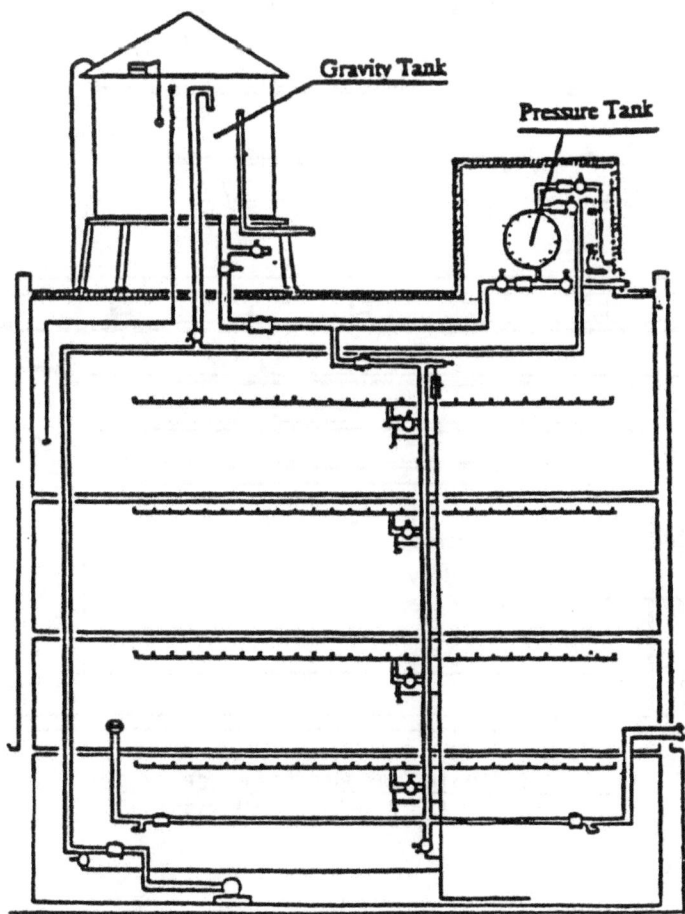

AUTO-DRY SPRINKLER SYSTEMS

Dry Pipe Sprinkler Systems are installed where a wet pipe system cannot be heated to prevent freezing. Under normal conditions there is no water in the piping. Instead the piping is filled with air under pressure. The air pressure in the system is controlled automatically by an air maintenance device and uses standard sprinkler heads. When a sprinkler head is opened by the heat from a fire, the air pressure is reduced in the piping. The drop in air pressure causes a special dry pipe valve to open. A supervisory device signals when the valve is opened, then water flows into the piping and out of the opened sprinklers. This water flow also sounds a local alarm to alert the people in the building of the fire. The alarm may also be transmitted to a central station, which then notify the fire department that there is a fire. In buildings where life hazard is very high (e.g., schools, hospitals) the alarm is transmitted directly to the fire department. Sometimes a combination of a wet pipe and a dry pipe system may be used when part of the building cannot be heated. A typical dry pipe system is shown in the picture below:

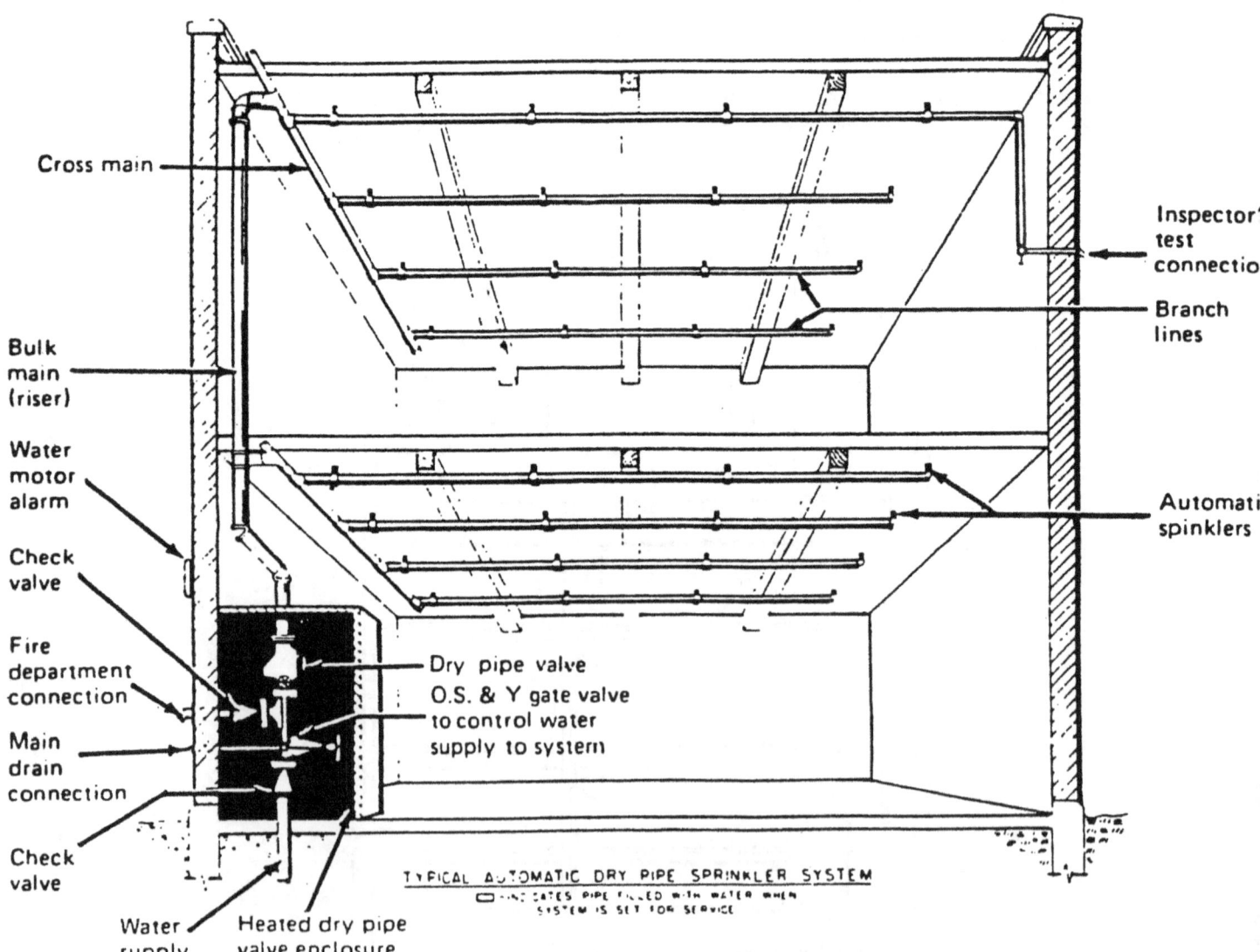

Dry Pipe Valve Designs: These valves prevent water from flowing into the piping until a sprinkler head has opened. The air pressure in the system keeps the clapper closed. This clapper prevents the water from flowing into the system. When the sprinkler head opens it causes a drop of pressure in the piping, which causes the valve to open and allows water into the system. Most dry pipe valves are designed so that a moderate air pressure in a dry pipe system will hold back a much greater water pressure. When the clapper has opened the valve is said to have tripped.

A picture of a typical dry pipe valve is shown below:

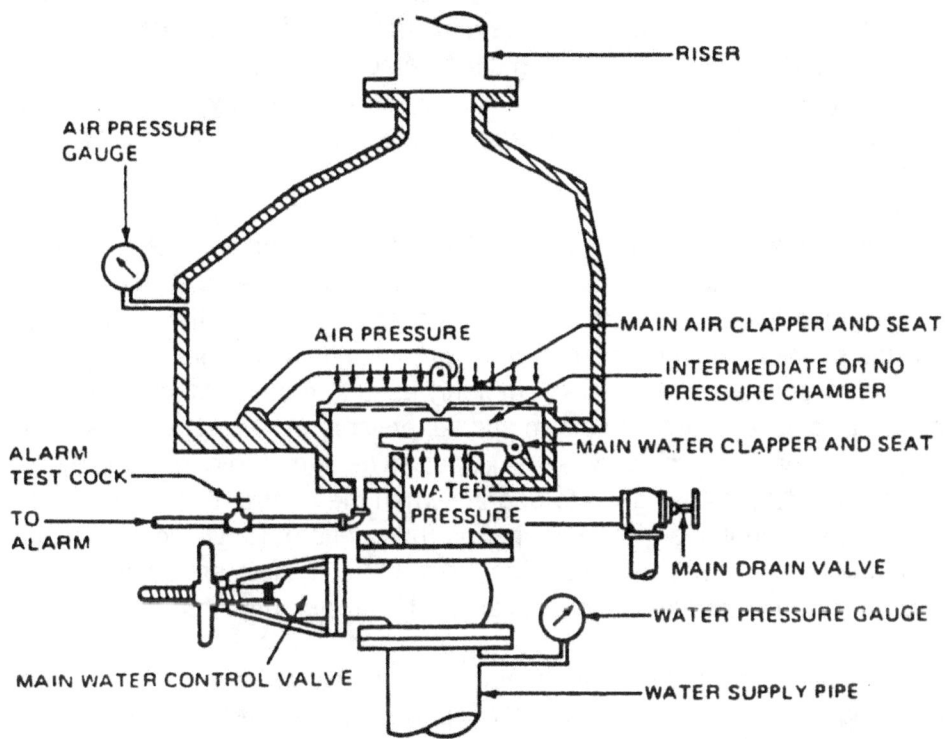

Higher than normal water pressure or a water hammer may cause the dry valve to trip by accident. Water hammer is caused by a sudden flow of water or a sudden change of water pressure in the system. To reduce this danger air pressure is usually kept well above the normal trip point. The air pressure is usually set at 15 to 20 psi (pounds per square inch) above the normal trip level. Some valves are specially designed for low pressures. In this case the manufacturer's instructions regarding pressures should be followed.

Quick Opening Devices: In a dry pipe system there is a delay between the opening of a sprinkler and the discharge of water. This delay may allow the fire to spread and more sprinklers to open. The delay is due to the time required for the air leave the sprinkler piping. This difficulty may be partly overcome by the installation of quick opening devices.

Two devices are used to reduce the time needed to open the clapper and allow water into the system. These devices are an accelerator and an exhauster. They are both automatically activated when a drop of two psi in air pressure is noticed in the system. They quickly change the water and air pressure balance in the system. This change trips the dry pipe valve allowing the water to force its way through the sprinkler piping in less time. The failure of an accelerator or exhauster to operate does not prevent normal tripping of a dry pipe valve.

The following sprinkler systems are similar to the basic design of the dry pipe sprinkler system. These are called Preaction, Deluge and Non-automatic sprinkler systems. Unlike the dry pipe system they do have pressurized air in the piping.

PREACTION SPRINKLER SYSTEMS

Preaction systems are designed for situations where there is danger of serious water damage. Water damage is usually caused by damaged sprinklers or broken piping. There is no water in the piping under normal conditions. The air in the piping is not under pressure. A preaction valve prevents the water from entering the system. The valve is automatically opened when a fire detection system discovers that there is a fire. This valve is tripped by the fire detection system before any of the sprinkler heads open. A supervisory device signals when the valve is opened. The preaction valve can also be operated manually.

The preaction system has several advantages over a dry pipe system. The preaction valve opens sooner because the fire detectors react to heat changes faster than sprinkler heads. Fire and water damage is decreased because water is sprayed on the fire more quickly and the alarm is given as soon as the preaction valve is opened. Because the sprinkler piping is normally dry, preaction systems are nonfreezing.

Heat responsive devices are commonly used to trip preaction valves. These devices are also used to activate alarm and supervisory systems. There are three main devices used to trip preaction valves – (1) Devices designed to operate at a fixed temperature; (2) devices designed to operate when the temperature in the room increases a set amount in a given time period (rate of rise); (3) Devices combining fixed temperature and rate of rise devices. Other ways to activate a preaction valve are smoke detectors, gas detecting systems and automatic signals from other safety systems.

Alarms are standard accessory equipment on water control valves. They provide an audible signal in the building if the valve operates for any reason. An alarm is also sent out if a problem is discovered with the equipment. The alarms send a signal to central station or a public fire alarm system. Often the signal is sent to both the central station and the public alarm.

Preaction System with a Recycling Feature: A special kind of preaction system is a recycling system for controlling sprinklers. This system shuts off the water when the fire has been put out or the heat drops. If the fire rekindles or the heat rises sharply, water is discharged again. The system continues cycling on and off as long as the fire persists.

Combined Dry Pipe and Preaction Systems: These systems have the basic features of both types of systems. The piping system contains air under pressure. A heat detecting device opens the water control valve and a quick opening device. The system then fills with water and operates as a wet pipe system. If the heat detecting system fails, the system will operate as a standard dry pipe system.

DELUGE SPRINKLER SYSTEMS

A deluge sprinkler system is designed to wet down an entire area in the case of a fire. This system is needed when there is danger of a fire rapidly spreading throughout the building. The deluge system will slow down the spread of the fire. Deluge systems are suitable for hazardous occupancies. This includes buildings in which flammable liquids or other hazardous materials are handled or stored.

The sprinkler heads in the deluge system are open at all times. Under normal conditions there is no water in the piping. The air in the piping is not under pressure. A closed control valve prevents water from flowing into the system. A fire detection device automatically opens the control valve when a fire is identified. A supervisory device signals when the valve is opened. When the valve is opened water flows into the system. The water is then sprayed out all of the sprinkler heads. The water control valve may also be opened manually.

Open and closed sprinkler heads may be used together in a single system. This is usually done where deluge protection is not needed over the entire area.

NON-AUTOMATIC SPRINKLER SYSTEMS

In this type of system all pipes are normally dry. Water is supplied when needed by pumping water into the system through the siamese connection. Some of these systems are supplied by manual operation of a water control valve.

These are several nonautomatic systems: (1) Perforated pipe systems – These have a single line of piping drilled at intervals for water discharge. These systems are usually found in basements or other areas difficult to reach in firefighting operations; (2) Open fixed spray nozzles for transformer vaults or other hazardous areas; (3) Exterior exposure sprinklers (or window sprinklers) use open sprinkler heads to form an external water curtain on the walls of a building; and (4) Foam supply systems are used for the protection of special hazardous occupancies.

GARBAGE COMPACTOR SPRINKLER SYSTEMS

Waste compactors are usually found in tall multiple-dwelling complexes such as apartment buildings. They are used to reduce the trash buildup in a building. They consist of a tall chute that has an opening at each floor. Each opening is used for trash disposal. Occupants of the buildings take their trash and throw it through the opening and down the chute. The trash piles up in the chute. At the bottom of the chute there is a device that regularly crushes the trash into smaller blocks of waste. The blocks of trash are then removed and taken to a garbage dump. The compactor may be located indoors or outdoors.

The buildup of trash in the compactor chute is a fire hazard. Fires have been started in several ways, for example, by a smoldering cigarette thrown into the compactor chute. Sprinkler systems must be installed to put out fires that may start in the compactor chute. Any of the standard water supply sources may be used to supply the compactor sprinkler system. For example, gravity tanks, fire pumps and pressure tanks are all used as water supply sources. Fire doors must be installed in the chute to allow firefighter access to burning trash.

The Certificate of Fitness holder must know the location of all sprinkler heads, control valves, supply lines and compactor rooms. A sketch of the entire compactor sprinkler system should be drawn by the Certificate of Fitness holder. This sketch should be posted in the compactor room in a frame under glass and made available to all representatives of the Fire Department. The Certificate of Fitness holder may be questioned about this sketch by inspectors from the Fire Department during routine inspections. A sign indicating the location of all control valves should be kept in the compactor room. This sign should be displayed with the sketch in the compactor room. All control valves in the sprinkler system must be labeled. The label should show the purpose of the valve and should be attached to the yoke of the valves. All indicating valves in the compactor sprinkler system must be sealed open.

A minimum of six extra sprinkler heads must be available to replace any opened or damaged sprinkler heads. Opened or damaged sprinkler heads must be replaced immediately. A garden hose connected to a water supply must be kept in the compactor room. This hose may be used to put out small fires or smoldering material in the compactor room.

The Certificate of Fitness holder must conduct an inspection of the entire sprinkler system at least once a month. Special attention should be given to the condition of the sprinkler heads in the compactor chute and the compactor room. Any defects or violations must be recorded in a detailed inspection report. All inspections are recorded on a card kept near the main control valve. The Certificate of Fitness holder should sign and date the card each time an inspection is made. If any minor defects in the system are discovered they must be reported to the owner of the building. If repairs are not made within 30 days the Certificate of Fitness Holder must notify the Bureau of Fire Prevention. If any major defects are discovered they must be reported to the local fire company, the owner of the building, and the Bureau of Fire Prevention. Major defects must be repaired immediately.

When a fire is discovered in the compactor the Certificate of Fitness holder should notify the local fire department immediately. He should not attempt to enter the compactor chute to put out the fire.

FIRE PUMPS

Fire pumps can be used as the main water supply source for a sprinkler system. Fire pumps may also be used in combination with gravity tanks and pressure tanks. Fire pumps are designed to discharge the water from a supply source into the fire protection system under pressure. The pressure with which the water is discharged from the pump is called the total head. The total head is usually measured in pounds per square inch (psi). The higher the psi rating of the pump, the greater the pressure of the water that is discharged. Fire pumps must deliver at least 25 psi to the highest line of sprinkler heads in the fire protection system.

The Centrifugal Pump

The centrifugal fire pump is the standard pump used in most fire protection systems. This is the preferred pump because of several features. It is reliable, compact, and requires little maintenance. The centrifugal fire pump can be powered by a variety of drivers. Acceptable drivers include electric motors, internal combustion engines, and steam turbines.

Principle of Operation

The water available to the centrifugal pump must always be under pressure. The centrifugal pump cannot draw water from the supply source. A water tank can be used if the tank uses gravity to supply the pump. In other words, the weight of the water forces the water to flow into the pump. This type of water tank is called a suction tank. An example of a suction tank supplying a centrifugal pump is shown in the picture below.

The water flows from the tank through the supply inlet into the pump. As the water passes to the center of the pump it reaches a rotating impeller. The impeller "grabs" the water on the inlet side of the pump. Then the impeller discharges the water under increased pressure into the fire protection system.

There are several kinds and models of centrifugal pumps. Some centrifugal pumps can discharge water from 25 gpm (gallons per minute) up to 5,000 gpm. Most centrifugal pumps have a single impeller and are therefore commonly called single stage fire pumps.

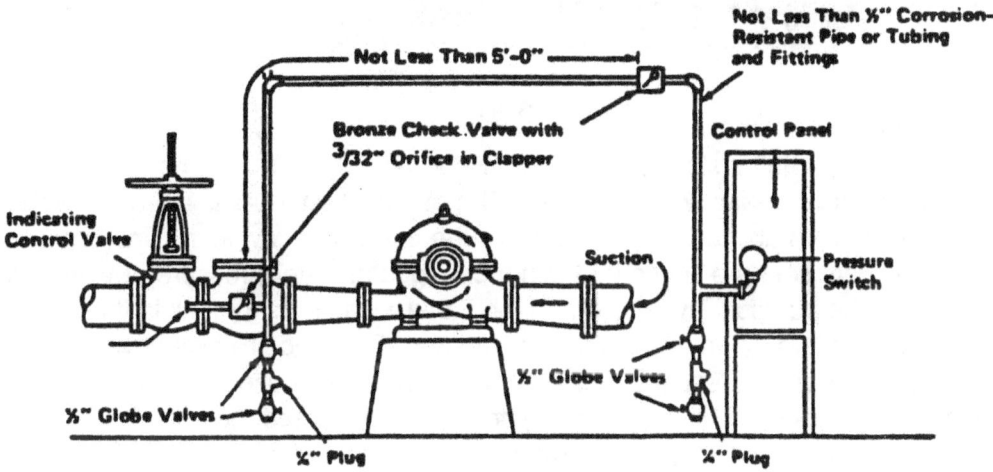

The Vertical Turbine Pump

A vertical turbine pump is really a modified centrifugal pump. The vertical turbine pump is able to draw water from streams, ponds, wells, etc., and does not need the water supply to be under pressure. Instead it draws the water into the pump by suction. The water pressure is increased when it reaches the rotating impellers. Then the water is forcefully discharged into the fire protection system.

The vertical turbine pump is able to draw water from wells. However, it is recommended not to use a well as the main water supply source. A well may dry up without warning. Should the well dry up it would make the fire pump useless. It is better to draw water from the well and to fill a water storage tank. The fire pump should then be attached to the storage tank since it is a more reliable supply source.

It is important to inspect the water intake hose, foot valve, and screens regularly. Mud, gravel, leaves or other materials could cause damage to the pump or obstruct the sprinkler system piping. A vertical fire pump arrangement using a water reservoir is shown in the picture below.

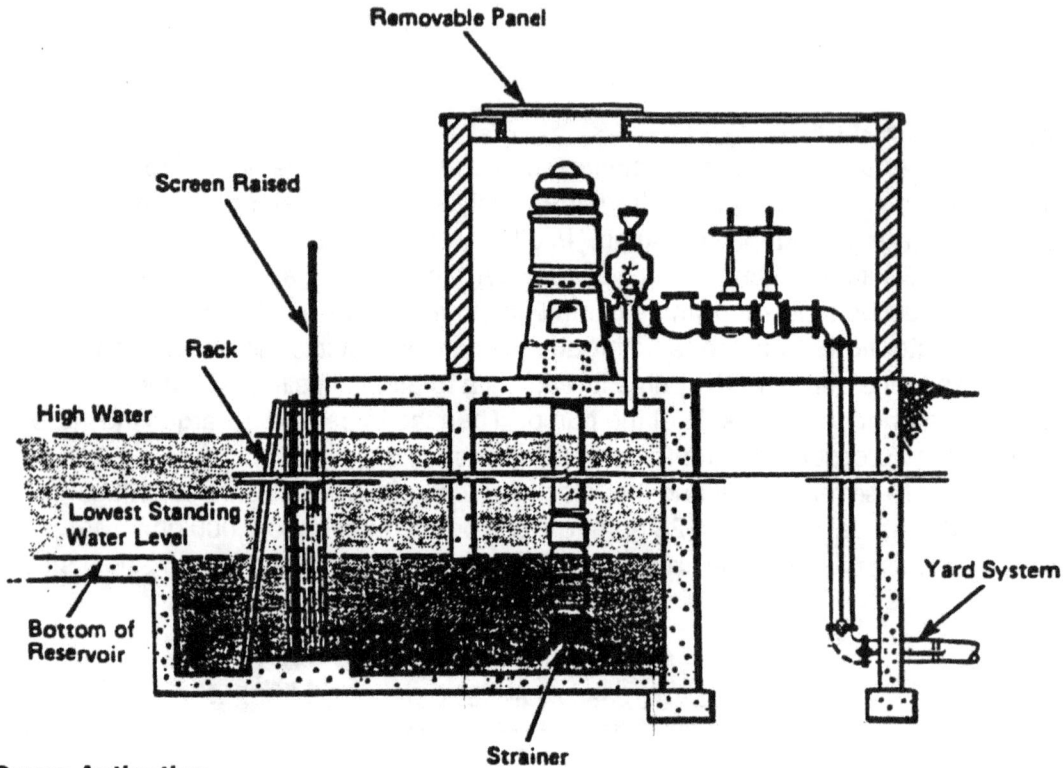

Pump Activation

A fire pump can be started automatically or manually. The pump can be started automatically by a controller, which activates the pump when there is a drop in water pressure. Controllers also activate the pump if there is water flow in the fire protection system. The controllers are set so that minor changes in water pressure or water flow do not activate the pumps. This could happen if there was a minor leak in the system.

The controllers for fire pumps are expensive. They require extensive maintenance and periodic testing. If an electric motor drive is used, a standby power generator is sometimes required. If an engine controller is used the appropriate fuel storage tanks should be filled and checked regularly.

Manually activated pumps are usually used in combination with a gravity tank or a pressure tank. Gravity or pressure tanks operate when there is a pressure drop in the fire protection system. For example, the opening of sprinkler heads will cause the pressure to drop. The operation of the pressure tank and its alarms alert the Certificate of Fitness holder to start the fire pump. Manually operated fire pumps are often found in industrial and manufacturing occupancies that have personnel on the premises at all times.

Sometimes remote push buttons are used to activate the pump. These remote push buttons are designed to start but not to stop the fire pump. Pumps may also have a timer installed that keeps the pump running for a set time after it is started. The timer is designed to reduce wear and tear on the pump and its parts. Excessive starting and stopping will put a lot of wear on the pump.

Pressure Maintenance Pumps (Jockey Pumps)

Pressure maintenance pumps are sometimes referred to as jockey or makeup pumps. They are often found on sprinkler systems. These pumps operate automatically when there is a slight drop in pressure due to leakage in the system. They also come on when there is a pressure surge. The jockey pump restores the pressure in the fire protection system to the desired level. If the drop of pressure in the system is greater than the capacity of the jockey pump, then the fire pump comes on.

Fire Pump Location

The fire pump should be housed in a room that is fire resistant or made of noncombustible material. The pump room should be located as close as possible to the fire protection system. The pump room should always be kept clean and accessible. The fire pump, driver, and controller should be protected against possible interruption of service. The temperature inside the pump room should always be maintained above 40 degrees Fahrenheit. This will prevent freezing of the water in the system. The pump room should only be used for fire protection functions.

Operation and Supervision

When fire pumps are activated by electric automatic controllers, they must be constantly monitored. The electrical power supply should be available at all times in case of an emergency. Supervisory devices are installed on the pumps to provide a signal when there is an electrical power failure. Similar supervisory devices are installed where steam turbines or internal combustion engines are used.

Pump Inspection and Maintenance

Regular inspections and maintenance of the pump should be made by the Certificate of Fitness holder. The pump should be activated each week according to the manufacturer's specifications. This will determine if the pump is working properly. When the pump is in operation a small water leak is desirable and should not be considered a malfunction.

If an automatic controller operates the fire pump, the pump can be started by reducing the water pressure in the system. This can be done by opening the test drain or starting a large water flow from the system. Starting the fire pump this way helps to determine if the automatic controller is working properly. The pump should not be allowed to overheat while the test is made.

The centrifugal pump relies on the water supply for coding and lubrication. The centrifugal pump should never be operated without the pump being supplied with water.

All parts of the pump and the controlling equipment should be visually inspected every week. The inspection should include the condition and reliability of the power supply. If any problems are discovered with the equipment immediate action should be taken to correct the problem.

Fire pumps should be fully tested annually to make sure that the pump, driver, power supply and all other parts are working properly.

Booster Pumps

Booster pumps are sometimes used in sprinkler systems. They are small pumps with limited power. Booster pumps are usually located in the basement of a building. The booster pump is used when the water pressure available at the highest sprinkler head does not quite meet the needs of the sprinkler system. This small pump increases the water pressure in the sprinkler system until it reaches acceptable levels. The booster pump should not be confused with the fire pump or the jockey pump.